THE REAL
DAVID
STOCKMAN

John Greenya and Anne Urban

INTRODUCTION BY
Ralph Nader

St. Martin's Press   New York

Design by Mina Greenstein

Library of Congress Cataloging-in-Publication Data

Greenya, John.
    The real David Stockman.

    On t.p. "real" is italicized.
    1. Stockman, David Alan, 1946–   2. Cabinet
officers—United States—Biography.   3. United States—
Politics and government—1981–   I. Urban, Anne.
II. Title.
E840.8.S68G74   1986   353.0072′22′0924 [B]   86–3905
ISBN 0-312-66470-2

First Edition

10 9 8 7 6 5 4 3 2 1

THE Real David Stockman

To Charles Holmes and Robert Cochran, two departed friends who are sorely missed; and to Ellen Ferber and Joseph C. Goulden, whose longstanding friendship and encouragement are deeply appreciated.

JOHN GREENYA

In memory of
Judy Marie Urban

When the cold rains kept on and killed the spring, it was as though a young person had died for no reason.
—Ernest Hemingway

ANNE URBAN

Acknowledgments

My *special* thanks go to: Bonnie Benner; Anne Burford; Jack Goeken; William Gordon; Stuart Krichevsky; Mary Ellen Lynch; Donna McCarty; Robert Miller; Ralph Nader; Larry Neilsen; Ann P. Payne; Susan Sadtler; Daniel Wander; and of course to my wife Suzanne and our sons, Jim, Bob, and Mike.

—JOHN GREENYA

This book owes much to many, but especially to: Ron Brownstein; Larry Elveru; Sheila Harty; Christopher Herrmann; Kathleen Hughes; George Kateb; Joseph Markley; Ralph Nader; Beverly Orr; Phil Simon; and Hazel T. Sullivan.

—ANNE URBAN

Contents

3 • The Stockman Legacy

Introduction

"Hey wait a minute, not so fast!"

DURING HIS LAST month on the public payroll, in late summer of 1985, David Stockman had more to contemplate than the largest deficit in world history and the doubling of the nation's cumulative national debt during his four-and-a-half-year tenure as Director of the Office of Management and Budget. He was thinking of how he could transform that deficit-generating experience into a personal fortune. Day after day, emissaries from America's leading publishers came to his office or invited him to grand free lunches to pump their proposals and to discuss his terms. Stockman brushed aside suggestions that he use a literary agent; he was used to handling huge sums, and would negotiate directly—and save himself ten percent. (Not all who called were chosen to make a pitch. A certain select few were allowed, as one of them phrased it, "an audience with Stockman.")

On August 1, Harper & Row announced that it would publish *The Triumph of Politics: The Failure of the Reagan Revolution*, and that it would pay Mr. Stockman *at least* $2 million—a record for any sub-Presidential book, and mega times what Dwight Eisenhower received for his memoirs. At about the same time, Stockman announced his acceptance of an offer to become a managing director of Salomon Brothers, the New York investment house. (As Peter Ross Range wrote in *The Washington Post* magazine, "After five months of writing at about $100,000 a week, [Stockman] must report in January for his new duties. . . . He won't be making as much there: only about $20,000 a week.")

Once again, David Stockman, age thirty-eight, rides off into the future, leaving a trail marked by twists and turns, disaffected mentors, and consistent only in its callousness. Once again a major administration figure will produce a self-serving history that will not be subjected to any official review or process of accountability. So it is incumbent upon us as citizens to say to the David Stockmans of this or any other administration so shockingly unmindful of the common good, "Not so fast!" And to say to the ex-czar of the federal budget, that inasmuch as his legacy will be with us for years, public measurement needs to stay current with the consequences of his influence over hundreds of billions of dollars and their human or inhuman manifestations across the country.

The power of the boss at the Office of Management and Budget, backed by the President, is more than a shaping power over the government's purse and its distribution—whether to the weak or the powerful, the rich or the poor, the armaments or the civilian sectors. Under Reagan and Stockman, OMB had literally the policy power of life or death, health or disease, equity or inequity, repair or deterioration, information or ignorance, and open or closed government. When Stockman turned thumbs down on life-saving and disease-preventing standard after standard and clearly signaled to agency heads not even to propose such standards, more than a few Americans paid the ultimate price and many were maimed. Tens of thousands of motorists will be killed or injured in frontal crashes for a decade because Stockman and his allies revoked a 1977 Department of Transportation crash protection standard that was to commence incremental application starting with the large 1982 model year automobiles. It took a unanimous Supreme Court decision declaring such revocation to be unlawful in 1983, and some additional public pressure on the department, to recover and possibly limit the preventable carnage to a decade.

There have been other prices exacted as a result of the Stockman legacy. One is the repeated sacrifice of the expectation that facts and figures matter both for accuracy and government's credibility. As he revealed in the now famous *Atlantic Monthly* interview, Stockman was speaking to Congress and the public with a forked tongue, saying one thing and believing another, knowing that the budgetary dollar assumptions and projections were "cooked" and admitting that supply-side economics was just another phrase for the old "trickle down" philosophy.

Another sacrifice has been the government's historic role as compassionate connector between help and the helpless. Stockman openly denigrated what he termed entitlements for the needy while masking with expedient cowardice his internalized contempt for the vast subsidies awarded the corporatists feeding from over one hundred federal corporate welfare and bailout programs. His operating mode was to lunge after those too unorganized—or just plain too weak—to fight back, but merely to grumble over the waste, fraud, and corruption in the military contracting and public lands leasehold activities. He was never a brave man, but he could rarely resist the temptation to play the bully.

Managing and controlling the impersonal violence of an industrial society, environment, and marketplace has received the bipartisan support of many Congresses in the post-war period. Stockman and the other Reaganites, with impetuous disdain, slowed down or derailed that humanitarian carriage. Using a rigged cost-benefit formula designed to produce a chorus of "noes," dozens of existing, pending, or long-maturing safety standards were scuttled. So extreme were the dogmatic immaturities of Stockman's OMB gang that even Reagan loyalists like Anne Burford of the Environmental Protection Agency and Thorne Auchter of the Occupational Safety and Health Administration sometimes were outraged at the arbitrary and groundless negations by OMB. Stockman nihilistically assaulted every area of consumer, worker, and environmental protection—food, drugs, autos, rail, aviation, drinking water, acid rain, workplace carcinogens, and household product safety alike. Whether his weapon was inadequate budgeting or policy countermand, the effective result was: no-law-and-order for the corporate-bred violence of pollution or product defects. For the Stockmanites, non-regulation and de-regulation were not propositions to be examined, but articles of faith.

It was government by assertion, and, as befits that imperial posture, the OMB under Stockman sunk to new depths in undermining the public's procedural right to know and to participate in open exchange. *Ex parte* contacts with business lobbyists and OMB officials became routine, but the public was neither allowed to know or to rebut. Joan Claybrook, president of Public Citizen, described these OMB obstructions in a February 6, 1986, address before the Consumer Federation of America:

> On the slender reeds of two presidential executive orders of doubtful legality, Ronald Reagan's Office of Management and Budget has attempted to emasculate federal regulation of public health, safety, and

the environment, programs that, as enacted by Congress, embody the national consensus on the proper role of government in these areas. There are three concerns: (1) OMB's usurpation of the regulatory decision making authority that Congress has intentionally and clearly delegated to Cabinet officers and other federal officials; (2) OMB's use of off-the-record contacts and information when it decides whether to approve or quash proposed regulations. These secret contacts with favored lobbyists and campaign contributors rarely find their way into the public record on which agencies and courts depend in their review of regulatory actions; and (3) OMB's restrictions of the collection of information that agencies consider necessary to their mission and that the rest of us—politicians, the press, the public—rely upon to tell us whether the government is doing its job.

Not even the documented need to protect the safety of infants and children escaped the curled lip of Stockman's OMB—which blocked a simple warning label requirement on aspirin and related medicines intended to reduce the incidence of Reyes Syndrome, and held up for eighteen months, until exposed by the press, a government standard for the proper ingredients in infant formula.

The grossest national display of child abuse was OMB's knowing contribution to the increase of hunger in our country. In January of 1986, the respected Physician Task Force on Hunger in America, based at the Harvard University School of Public Health, reported that:

> Between 1982–1985, some fifteen national studies concluded that hunger was again a serious problem. This conclusion was reached by entities as diverse as government agencies, national religious organizations, policy groups and university researchers.
>
> Less than a year ago the Physician Task Force on Hunger in America reported to Congress and the nation that hunger in this country constitutes a national health epidemic. At least 20,000,000 citizens [nearly half of whom are youngsters] suffer from hunger at least some days each month, and evidence points to a worsening situation. Not only is hunger increasing as a problem, but federal food programs designed to feed the hungry have been weakened. . . . We face the paradox, then, that as hunger increases, food stamp coverage is going down.

Even at OMB, it is common knowledge that hunger means higher infant mortality and morbidity, brain damage, and increased vulnerability to disease and environmental toxins, such as lead, during childhood. With the Reagan government spending at record deficit levels, poverty in the United States has increased sharply since 1979.

Notwithstanding the active and damaging roles played by OMB in these urgent areas of human concerns, the media paid far greater attention to the endless tales of supply-siders and OMB's maneuvering between revenues falling beneath its projections, deficits rising above its predictions, and the voodoo economics of Ronald Reagan that George Bush complained about in the 1980 primaries.

Certainly in his relations with Congress, Stockman had dollar signs for horizons and not the detailed, factual content of program substance. He could mouth the slogans of de-regulation and soar into abstract dogma without knowing very much about the meat and poultry inspection services, or even his avowed specialty, the auto safety and fuel efficiency regulatory programs.

In Congress, those tactics did not produce many legislative victories. As Representative Leon Panetta (D-CA) told Anne Urban, Stockman's ineffectiveness in passing legislation was rooted in a "lack of sense of balance in his efforts—he just charged ahead with his ideas. He may have made points with himself and even with the people back home, but he just didn't get anything done." At the time, that was not particularly important to Stockman and his colleagues. They were not trying to run a government; they were trying to attract political support from business, traditional conservatives, and the ever more vocal New Right, and to force the Democrats into disarray. The predominant strategy used by Stockman was not to offer workable alternatives, but to provoke potentially embarrassing votes and present absolutist positions reduced to political slogans.

As *The Real David Stockman* demonstrates, the effort produced some sadly foolish positions. In one Congressional debate, Stockman charged that the Superfund designed to clean up hazardous waste dump sites would make EPA "literally the czar . . . over every hazardous waste site in the entire country . . . even every backyard rubbish pile that has been accumulated anywhere in the country." Did anyone in Congress believe that legislation designed to forestall future Love Canals would result in the regulation of the accumulation of trash bags in America's backyards?

In September 1979, Congressman Stockman proposed to eliminate all entitlement programs that aid "employable adults." Asked where these people would find jobs, Stockman said flatly, "The jobs would appear." His tax preferences rested on similarly shaky wish fulfillment: sharply reduce the tax burden for business and the wealthy, Stockman and the supply-siders argued, and the resultant economic growth would thereby ensure that federal revenues would actually increase. From the Congressional Budget Office to the *National Journal*, a number of independent analyses have concluded that the Reagan Administration program makes the rich richer and the poor poorer.

In office, David Stockman backed away from unsupportable positions only when forced by the evidence and public outrage. On the immense budget deficits engendered by the tax cuts, there can be no argument: the OMB computers continued to give Stockman the same message they had since the opening days of the administration. So, here, he steadily retreated, discarding supply-side dogma and working to sabotage its agenda in favor of reducing the deficit. In this way, in the eyes of the supply-siders, Stockman, who had been such a staunch ally, turned out to be a Trojan horse—to use his own description for supply-side economics. (During his interview with William Greider for the *Atlantic Monthly*, Stockman, in a burst of candor he has regretted ever since, acknowledged that "Kemp–Roth was always a Trojan horse to bring down the top rate. It's kind of hard to sell 'trickle down,' so the supply-side formula was the only way to get tax policy that was really 'trickle down.' ")

On other matters, less subject to quantification and immediate assessment—where the victims are difficult to count and the damage is not always immediately visible, as in the case of long-gestating disease induced by environmental exposure—Stockman stuck to his slogans. The administration stubbornly maintained that its program did not harm the truly needy, though there are few in either party who would agree that Reagan's cuts have not affected the substance of social programs. Even now, the administration still asserts its rhetorical support for clean air and clean water and a safe workplace while working assiduously against governmental efforts to provide those social goods.

For the American people, this is the meaning of Stockman's Trojan horse. He and President Reagan promised relief from government waste and cloaked the edifice of the administration in that noble goal. But at the core of that edifice rests a most unsavory reality. The Reagan–Stockman agenda has been an unabashed attempt to reify a collection of anti-government slogans that discount every government program to help the less fortunate, no matter its worth, and that invariably sides, on matters large and small, with the most powerful in society. Such a program permits neither empirical analysis nor compassion in resolving the problems of America.

Stockman's continued adherence to a position that opposes government social programs and beneficial health and safety regulations arrests any suggestion that he has been tempered by the failed supply-side experiment. Now, outside the Reagan domestic policy councils, Stockman is turning, predictably, into the "Trojan Horse unbound" on the book promotion trail. Nevertheless, in the administration or out of it, Stockman and the aggressive ideologues who share the same views will surely keep advancing their slogans for as long as they can deny the evidence of the suffering caused by their policies.

For years, politicians such as David Stockman and Ronald Reagan have told the nation that taxes for the wealthy could be slashed without losing revenue; that government regulation could be rolled back without endangering lives; that budgets could be cut without harming the needy. As shown so meticulously in this book by John Greenya and Anne Urban, the failure of these programs— the lesson available even to David Stockman at the end of his long odyssey—reaffirms the tragedies of entrenched ideologies so defiantly divorced from reality and human sensitivity.

Unfortunately, the Stockman mentality lives on—in the thinking and performance of his successor, James Miller (his former OMB associate and one of Ronald Reagan's heads of the Federal Trade Commission). After shearing the states of federal revenues and supporting further state revenue reductions (by advocating the end of state and local tax deductibility on federal income tax forms) Miller outdid himself by telling a Congressional committee in February 1986 that regrettable as it might be, "We believe the homeless are not a federal responsibility, but a state and local responsibility." This is more of the same from those wonderful folks who brought you Ed Meese saying, "People go to soup kitchens because the food is free and that's easier than paying for it," and the President himself, who opined that homeless people who sleep on grates do so "by choice."

The authors of this book convey a threefold message:

1. High government officials should not be viewed as "out-of-government-therefore-out-of-mind," because their legacy continues to affect the nation in many ways;

2. These same ex-officials continue to be sought after for expressions of opinion by the national media; and,

3. The public is given no retrospective evaluation of their Washington careers in order to establish and advance standards of public expectation that might have a deterrent effect on those who follow and are tempted toward similar behavior.

Public review of the performances of major governmental appointees will help to pierce the camouflage that official rhetoric drapes over official deeds. This volume contributes to that needed literature through its careful documentation of what David Stockman did—in contrast to what he says he was doing. His many remote victims deserve no less.

—Ralph Nader
February 1986

I
GOING THROUGH CHANGES

1 • Michigan to Harvard

DAVID STOCKMAN is a man of many mentors. William H. Bartz, his maternal grandfather, introduced him to politics at a fundraiser for George Romney, a moderate Republican who was Michigan's governor and an also-ran in the presidential primaries in 1968. Later, Reverend Truman Morrison refined the young David Stockman's study of the philosopher Reinhold Niebuhr, and helped him get into the Harvard Divinity School. Harvard professors Nathan Glazer, Daniel Patrick Moynihan, and James Q. Wilson introduced Stockman to early neo-conservatism. "Liberal" Republican Representative John Anderson gave him his first job in Washington, his first real job of any substance outside the academic world. Once Stockman reached Congress, the popular conservative Jack Kemp took him under his wing, tutoring him in the doctrine of supply-side economics. Finally, it was Ronald Reagan who offered David Stockman the job of his dreams.

With the exception of his grandfather, in time—and by different degrees—David Stockman would turn on all of these mentors and the politics, philosophies, or economic theories they espoused.

The signs were there in the early years, but few knew how to read them until, suddenly, they were confronted with the fact of a 180-degree change. Like Stockman's fellow anti-Vietnam War protestors in the 1960s—who were startled to learn that he had left the Harvard Divinity School without a degree not long after he'd drawn a "safe" number in the draft lottery—the family and staff of former Representative John Anderson were stunned to learn in 1980 that Stockman had played the role of Anderson in order to give candidate Ronald Reagan practice for his upcoming presidential debate. Said one former staff person who had worked closely with Stockman and seen the special relationship between mentor Anderson and mentee Stockman, "When we learned what Dave had done, we were *crushed*." Finally, in the words of Dr. Arthur Laffer, whose supply-side economic theory Stockman rode from the House of Representatives into one of the biggest and most powerful government jobs in the world, and who has since seen Stockman also deny that faith: "Dave was changing from a Marxist to a Baptist every hour on the hour."

Who is David Stockman, and why—in the face of undeniable career success—do so many people still have serious reservations about him?

Born on November 10, 1946, David Stockman lived for a few years in Cape Hood, Texas, until his father, Allen Stockman, moved the family to the Midwest, to Berrien County, Michigan, where his wife Carol's parents had a 150-acre fruit farm. There David Stockman, and later his sister and three brothers, would grow up in the house Grandfather Bartz had built, a comfortable three-story frame house with a stand of birches in front and neatly painted barns and acres of grapes out back.

It was a Norman Rockwellian atmosphere, and a thoroughly Republican one at that. The L-shaped Fourth Congressional District is in the southwest corner of Michigan, across the state from Detroit symbolically as well as geographically, and while it lies close to the borders of Ohio and Indiana, with their similar politics and small-town virtues, it is only a ninety-minute drive from Chicago. But it is not a drive many residents of the Fourth District make with any regularity. Home is truly where the heart is—a lesson Stockman would remember well when he decided to run for Congress.

In addition to the rolling farmland, the district has two major cities, Benton Harbor and St. Joseph (St. Joe), which are next to one another but completely dissimilar. Most of the people in industrial Benton Harbor, which houses an RCA Whirlpool plant, are black, whereas those in largely residential St. Joseph are white and, relatively speaking, prosperous. Basically, the Fourth District is agricultural. Its ethnic makeup (except for a sizable black enclave near the cities of Dowagiac and Cassopolis) is largely German-American, resembling northern Indiana and Ohio rather than the rest of Michigan. Television weather people call the area "Michiana."

It is an intensely conservative and Republican area. As *The Almanac of American Politics* put it in 1978:

> If you want to understand something of the political background of the 4th district, visit the county seat of Hillsdale. Here the courthouse and the local college were built when the Republican Party was young, and the college, in particular, exemplified the things Republicans then stood for. It believed in absolute honesty and was inclined toward temperance; it was one of the first American colleges to admit women, and was strongly opposed to slavery. . . .
>
> Now, when we are three quarters of the way through the twentieth, the political ambiance of Hillsdale is quite different (or perhaps it simply hasn't changed much). This was one of the few colleges where there was virtually no protest against the Vietnam war; hair always remained short and skirts long; temperance is still encouraged. . . . There is little emphasis on women's or blacks' rights. . . .

That sort of Republicanism is typical of the 4th district as well, and of the two congressmen who, between them, represented the district for 42 years. From 1934 to 1962, the 4th elected Clark Hoffman, an irascible opponent of federal expenditures who made even H. R. Gross of Iowa look like a free spending New Dealer. When Hoffman retired, there was a rather decorous Republican primary to replace him, the winner of which was Edward Hutchinson. Within ten years, this opponent of the Civil Rights Act of 1964 became the ranking Republican on the House Judiciary Committee, in which capacity he became familiar to millions of Americans—a plodding, often dull speaker who, with an earnestness that cannot be gainsaid, stayed true to his party and his President. Nothing, until Nixon finally released the June 23rd tape, could convince him Nixon was guilty of anything; then he faded quickly from history. Hutchinson was reelected in 1974, but with only 54%—a very low figure for a Republican in this district; after that showing Hutchinson, past 60 and comfortably well off himself, decided to retire.

The twenty-nine-year-old who succeeded him, David Stockman, was indeed, as *The Almanac* put it, "a very different sort of Republican."

By all accounts, young David Stockman had two very obvious virtues: his ability to work hard and his intelligence. Today, the Stockman family farm has the latest in grape-picking equipment; an automated picker allows two people to harvest the whole crop without outside help. Once picked, most of the grapes are sold to local wineries, a definite growth industry, while the machine is rented out to other farmers—but that was not the case when the children were young. Then, David and his three younger brothers and one sister—Gary, Donnie, Steve, and Linda—had the task of picking the grapes, strawberries, and tomatoes.

As they were close in age, they all competed to see who could work hardest and longest. One good friend said of David, "Even as a child he'd get up at four in the morning to beat his brothers and sister out to the field to harvest his father's grapes. He loved to do all the work by himself." And a high school friend, on hearing that in Washington Stockman normally worked an eighteen-hour day, remarked, "It's probably more like twenty." Another high school peer, Richard Ast, now a reporter in St. Joe, and still a Stockman friend and supporter, says, "Dave got his ideas about when day was done from working on that farm. He was out driving a tractor till twelve when everybody else was quitting at six."

Like nearly everyone else in the area, Stockman's parents have always been staunch Republicans. (Indeed, his maternal grandfather had been the chairman of the county Republican Party, a post David's mother would covet, but not attain, for years.) One local party member noted, with pleasure, "You could run a dog—even a dead dog!—against a Democrat in this district, and as long as it was a *Republican* dog, damned if that dog wouldn't win."

In 1964, as a high school senior, young David Stockman, aping his parents' preferences, organized and ran a group that supported Barry Goldwater for President. Stockman explains, "I was a conservative from a Republican family . . . I thought Goldwater was the greatest thing since sliced bread."

Mabel McKinney, who taught all the Stockman children in what was literally a one-room schoolhouse, remembers Stockman fondly—wearing a hat with tricolored crepe paper streamers on the day "Cookie the Cop" brought an American Legion flag to school. She recalls that Stockman would go home each day, sit on the doorstep, and teach his younger family members the lessons of the day. Pleased to see her former pupil so successful, McKinney adds, "I always said he would be a doctor, lawyer, or minister."

Just as the primary school was small, so was Lakeshore High School, which David Stockman entered in 1960. Its entire enrollment was 450 students. His graduating class was, as one friend described it, "the last great class of squeaky cleans." Clearly, Stockman was among the squeakiest; he was president of the student council (a photo dug up in 1982 by *People* magazine shows him standing in front of the council wearing a suit and tie, replete with white shirt and socks) and quarterback of the Lakeshore Lancers. Reports that David Stockman was a football star are slightly exaggerated. As Rick Ast reports, "None of these people who wrote about Dave being the football star bothered to mention the season was probably the worst in the history of Lakeshore." More telling, perhaps, is the fact that Stockman had to try out three times before he made the basketball team, the point being, as his cousin Ron Both said, "Most kids wouldn't try out again after failing the first time."

"When Dave was a senior, we had a real small football team," recalls his high school teacher and football coach Glenn Arter, "and I'd say, 'Keep your heads up and take your whipping.' Dave wasn't very big for a quarterback. But when he got knocked down, he got right back up again. He never whined."

Ron Both says that David's most notable quality was his ability to work hard: "He'd milk the cows, pick fruit, make hay. He'd play baseball, basketball, football, swim, and work on the farm at the end of the day, and he was never gloomy or serious."

Throughout high school, Stockman was something of a loner, "just not the kind of guy you brought your troubles to," says a friend from those days, Jerry Catinia. "After all," he continues, "farming is a fight for survival, and battling it out with four other kids is a fight for survival. I thought Dave might open up a little more when he got older, but I can't really see that." And another classmate remarked, "I suppose I never thought Dave would go far—at least not in the way he has. I guess I figured he would wind up in a laboratory or something where no one would have to see him or deal with him in public."

Rick Ast, now a reporter for *The Herald-Palladium*, and who grew up on a neighboring farm and was in high school with David, is a strong if not uncritical supporter of Stockman's. He remembers Stockman as being "okay" in sports, and always trying very hard. "He was always very popular. I don't recall him having a steady girl; he dated around." Ast says, somewhat reluctantly, that Stockman may have been arrogant intellectually, "but not personally."

As for his youthful politics, Stockman's first hero was Barry Goldwater. He readily admits that it would have been unusual for him not to admire the conservative Goldwater, given his family's politics. But there were some young people in the St. Joe area who had a slightly different view of Stockman's political leanings. One of those is Virginia Tilley, now a teacher of reading and English at a junior high school in Benton Harbor. Before that she taught at Lakeshore, the same school from which both she and David Stockman graduated. She was four years ahead of him.

Tilley is somewhat unusual in the Fourth District in that she is a convert to the Democratic Party. "I used to be Republican. My parents were Republicans—this is a *very* conservative area—and I worked hard at it, but Richard Nixon was more than I could take." Eventually, Virginia Tilley would take part in demonstrations in opposition to the war in Vietnam and on behalf of civil rights issues in Chicago and elsewhere, activities that were frowned on by her conservative friends and neighbors.

"I grew up in the same neighborhood as the Stockman family, and I thought all of the kids were rather liberal, at least compared to their parents and to the other parents around here. I remember David as being a very likable person, but later on, when he ran for and was in Congress, we had some very heated public arguments. I couldn't understand why he had become so very conservative. I finally concluded it was simple political expediency. I feel that he is basically a good guy, but he just wouldn't stand up for anything. Frankly, I have to say, harsh as it sounds, that he's a prostitute."

Rick Ast, the newspaperman who has been a friend of Stockman's for twenty-five years, disagrees. He feels that Stockman has changed little, basically, and that if he has flip-flopped on an issue (such as his belief in supply-side economics), it was because to do so was "politically expedient."

By the time he was a senior, David Stockman was generally considered a serious—though certainly not too serious—young man with a bright future, at a time and in a place when becoming a professional man or an executive with one of the area companies (such as Whirlpool, Clark Equipment, or LECO, a manufacturer of lab equipment that later relocated) was probably the height of local ambition for young people who were not from farming families.

One might expect that the young David Stockman was the leading light of his high school graduating class, but that was not quite the case. As one of his classmates from the Class of 1964 put it, "There were a lot of bright lights in our class. Dave Stockman was among them, but he was not the brightest." Although not a senior class officer, he was president of the eighteen-member student council, a body that included two other Stockmans, his sister and one of his younger brothers (which gave the family almost 17 percent of the votes).

If he had any goal other than working as a farmer, his close friends did not know it. The townspeople, had they cared to speculate about his politics, would probably have cast him in the same political category as his parents and his maternal grandfather—strongly conservative. But people his own age, such as Rick Ast, would not have agreed. "We took a high school class in economics together," recalls Ast, "and I remember that Dave was beginning to sound quite liberal."

Virginia Tilley's sister June Kabel was in David Stockman's Lakeshore High graduating class. She remembers that he ran with the "right clique," which she did not. "He always said hello to me and was very nice. He was well liked by everyone. But whenever there was any controversy, like students protesting some school policy, he was not in the forefront. Then, when he went to Michigan State and got involved in the Vietnam War protest, I was really surprised to see him in that. He was not the smartest in the class, but, as I said, he was always nice and friendly to me. Later, I thought he changed completely."

Glenn Arter, teacher and coach to Stockman, also remembers Stockman somewhat differently. "I don't recognize the guy with the thin lips and the creased brow. I remember an All-American kid who always had a smile for everyone. His grades were so-so, but that's because he was mixed up in everything—student government, sports, work. He was hard-working and gave everything he had. Dave was a class and team leader."

Arter does not pretend to have been prescient about Stockman's future. "I would not have picked him to be President of the United States. I guess what happened was that while his interests were very general in high school, later on he chose to specialize. He filtered things down, and concentrated that great energy he'd always had. I was positive about him, though I have to say that I didn't agree with the philosophy of what he was at Michigan State."

In the fall of 1964, Stockman left home to enter Michigan State University, located in East Lansing, approximately 110 miles from his family home in Stevensville and not far from the crossroads town of Hollywood. He planned to major in Agriculture, but that would change. (None of the Stockman children became farmers. Linda is an educational consultant; Steve is a lawyer; Donald owns a landscaping business; and Gary, the youngest, is a probation officer.)

Michigan State was an intriguing place in the early to mid-1960s. Anti-war feeling was rising, as the country felt the squeeze of trying to have, according to the phrase of the day, both "guns and butter." Ironically, the architect of that effort was a man who had also spent time in Michigan—as president of the Ford Motor Company—Robert McNamara, the one-time "whiz kid" who provided President Lyndon Johnson with the intellectual justification behind that doomed attempt to afford an ultimately questionable policy. Almost two decades later, some people would see comparisons between Robert McNamara and David Stockman.

Michigan has two state universities, MSU and the University of Michigan, and it is said that from any high school class, the bright ones go to Michigan and the rest go to Michigan State. Why didn't David Stockman, clearly one of the bright ones, follow that pattern?

According to Rick Ast, "That doesn't happen to be true. It really depends on what school [within the university] you're interested in. Dave started out in Agriculture, and the department at Michigan isn't as good. And MSU has a fine Department of History, which he later switched to. Once you're at East Lansing, it's real easy to switch departments."

Although MSU had, in some circles, a reputation as a "sleepy" college where students studied farming and paid little attention to anything else, by the time Stockman arrived, the campus was being politicized by the war in Vietnam. Seventy miles away in Ann Arbor, a group of students were drafting the Port Huron statement, but that same level of anti-war commitment was not present on the MSU campus. The University paper, *The State News*, did run full-page protests against the war, but it also featured such traditional fare as a picture of two undergraduate coeds walking their pet guinea pigs on leashes.

Within a year, Stockman had switched his major from Agriculture to American History, and he'd also begun to take courses in religion. Interestingly, he did not take any economics courses. Years later, he would attempt to make up for that lack by reading widely, if not deeply, in the field, concentrating on popular, nonacademic newspapers and periodicals. To this day, many are dubious about Stockman's ability in that area. Robert Walker, who worked with Stockman in John Anderson's congressional office, recently observed, "He has no formal economic background, and did not acquire, through his reading, a true understanding of economic theory. If it's a question that can come out of a computer, Stockman can give you an answer."

One would have predicted, based on his first three years at Michigan State, a routine senior year for David Stockman. But by 1967 he had evidently undergone a change in his attitude toward the war in Vietnam, which was supported wholeheartedly by almost everyone else in his hometown. In the summer of 1967 Stockman did not come home to pick strawberries, as he'd done during his other two college summers; instead, he worked as the only paid member of MSU's Vietnam Summer project.

According to Michigan State Senator Lynn Jondahl, who hired him for the project, "Stockman's responsibilities were twofold: he coordinated the overall resistance effort and served as the MSU spokesman," which, says Jondahl, "involved going door-to-door, setting up educational coffee houses, setting up public forums—all in the interest of actively encouraging people, especially young men of draft age, to resist the Vietnam War."

A letter dated June 16, 1967, reads:

Dear Mr. _____
This note is to acknowledge your $5.00 contribution to Lansing Viet Nam Summer. We are grateful for your support. In the near future we will bring you up to date on the developing summer plans.
Within a few days we will be soliciting office, telephone, and canvassing help and would appreciate any help you would care to give.

Very truly yours,

David A. Stockman
Secretary, Steering Committee
Lansing Vietnam Summer

Stockman also signed a Students for a Democratic Society (SDS) petition that appeared in the April 12, 1967, *State News*, declaring he would "refuse to fight against the people of Vietnam, refuse to be inducted into the armed forces of the United States, resist the draft and aid and encourage others to do the same." Dwarfed by the large headline proclaiming "WE WON'T GO," the announcement contained the names of thirty-three men and nineteen sympathetic women.

It was primarily the SDS affiliation that earned Stockman the dubious distinction of having his own "Red Squad" file. The squad, an intelligence unit of the Michigan police, gave this description of David Stockman: "dark, long brown hair, but clean and very good looking." Stockman recently gave his own characterization of his "record" and of the (now defunct) Red Squad as "an archaic whiff of another era." And, of his summer as an organizer of anti-war activities, he says it was "pretty much of a bust."

(When he learned of his OMB director's involvement in anti-war activities, President Reagan—who in 1965 had remarked, "It's silly talking about how many years we will have to spend in the jungles of Vietnam when we could pave the whole country and put parking stripes on it and still be home by Christmas"—remained unperturbed. Typically, he turned it into a joke by referring to: "some of my own views when I was quite young: for heaven's sake, I was even a Democrat.")

The "We Won't Go" declaration prompted various responses, one of the angriest from a man who called himself "an ex-US Marine and Haslett graduate student." In his letter, he accused Stockman and the other protestors of preferring to "chase the girlies around the campus of MSU [rather] than stand the chance of being eyeballed through the rifle sights by a Viet Cong in the jungle." In a counter response that was noticeably more controlled than some of his later writings (especially his "Dear Colleague" letters as a U.S. representative), Stockman expressed concern over statements that "accept war as a way of life," and their "sad commentary on the moral vision and sensitivity of American society."

While still at MSU, Stockman also chaired a group called the Peace Coordinating Committee, an offshoot of the University Christian Movement. The committee collected signatures urging "an immediate halt in American bombings of North Vietnam and recognition of the National Liberation Front." The MSU newspaper quoted Stockman as saying, "We don't expect any change in the administration's policy from this action, but rather a change in the minds and political orientation of Americans."

The three men who hired Stockman for Vietnam Summer—Michigan State legislators David Hollister and Lynn Jondahl, and Reverend Truman Morrison—were all impressed by Stockman's knowledge of the war. Hollister remembers Stockman as "well-read; he seemed to know the history of the war," and "although he tended to be abrasive, I respected him for his knowledge of the issues." Neither Jondahl nor Hollister would characterize Stockman as a "radical" in those days, but both seem convinced that, in Hollister's words, "his rhetoric, his way of thinking, established him as a credible liberal. Stockman seemed to have a social conscience then."

(Stockman's social conscience on occasion left something to be desired during his MSU days. Rick Ast recalls that one night, Stockman, who lived in a different dorm, "came to our room twice in the same night. He had a blind date, and stopped by on his way over to the girl's hall, but when he got there, and she came down, she was so ugly that he turned around and was back in our dorm, ten minutes later.")

When Stockman became OMB director, Lynn Jondahl remarked, "I would never have described him as a compassionate student, but I would have hoped that in his present position he would at least have a sense of the effects of his policy on people."

Reverend Truman Morrison was the professor who introduced Stockman to what he has termed a major interest, the writings of the theologian–philosopher–social ethicist Reinhold Niebuhr. (Niebuhr's work has attracted such diverse devotees as Jimmy Carter and George Gilder, the conservative author of *Wealth and Poverty*.) Morrison, who had studied under Niebuhr at the University of Chicago, prodded Stockman's study of the man. But he has since come to feel that "Stockman missed the point."

In 1981, Reverend Morrison told a reporter from *The Washington Post*, "David always was thinking about David a great deal of the time. He is very narcissistic. David has always been intent on his own personal advancement." And a year later, Morrison, who wrote one of Stockman's letters of recommendation to the Harvard Divinity School, told Anne Urban, in explaining his comment that Stockman had missed the point about Niebuhr, "Niebuhr felt that no matter how immoral we are, we are motivated by more than self-interest. . . . I'm very worried about what I'm hearing, frankly. Compassion—that's what I'm looking for from David."

Reverend Morrison should have been worried about Stockman on a different score. He had arranged for a $500 interest-free loan to Stockman from his church, Edgewood United in East Lansing, an amount equal to half of the Harvard Divinity School's tuition at that time. Despite a series of dunning letters from Reverend Morrison's successors at Edgewood United, it took David Stockman thirteen years to repay the loan. At about the same time he finally repaid his obligation, Stockman, then the director of OMB, was on Capitol Hill before the Budget Committee defending the first of his deep cuts.

In reference to his proposed cuts in the college student loan program, Stockman said, "I do not accept the notion that the federal government has the obligation to fund generous grants to anybody that wants to go to college. It seems to me that if people want to go to college bad enough then there is opportunity and responsibility on their part to finance their way through the best they can."

If Reverend Morrison had a reaction to that statement, it was not recorded.

2 • Harvard to Washington

DAVID STOCKMAN spent almost two years at Harvard but left without a degree, in Divinity Studies or anything else. He did, however, pick up several new mentors. He says he left when he did because his interest in academe was supplanted by a fascination with "Boston politics." Others held a different view—that the safety of his high number in the military draft lottery made the "protection" of Divinity School no longer necessary. Whatever the truth, it was the mentors he picked up in Boston who would make his next career move possible.

In 1968, armed with a cum laude degree in History from Michigan, Stockman headed off to the Harvard Divinity School. Although he denies it, many who knew him well from MSU and from home maintain that avoiding the draft took precedence over theological concerns. John Anderson's wife Keke, who would come to know Stockman well several years later when he moved to Washington to work for her husband, says, "Anyone who knows him knows he went to Divinity School to escape the draft. He can't admit it, but I know it to be so."

Eventually, in 1970, Stockman received number 282 out of a possible 365 in the draft lottery. Only those with numbers lower than 216 were drafted that year. Not long after receiving his number, Stockman dropped out of Divinity School.

At Harvard, Stockman was disappointed to find out that "nobody was interested" in Reinhold Niebuhr. Indeed, ten years later he told the *Detroit News* that when he arrived, the Divinity School was "a shambles. There were big campus strikes and radicals tried to burn the ROTC building." The idealistic young man from the Midwest found himself disgusted by what he termed the "shrill absolutism" of the Left, by the "simplistic formulations and idealistic notions that are attractive when you're twenty."

Stockman was well within bounds to react so strongly. Certainly it was one of the most turbulent times Harvard had ever seen. One of his classmates, Michael Taylor, remembers, "It was not at all unusual for a student to jump up in class and shout 'That's a bunch of crap' or something like that at a professor."

In the spring of 1968, the Divinity School was divided by a problem of its own: whether to accept the offer of a campus dorm from the Rockefellers. Combined with the attempt to occupy the ROTC building, the arrest of students, and the suspension of classes, it was a year, as Dean Krister Stendahl wrote in an issue of the Divinity School bulletin devoted entirely to the "crises in the universities," when "moral issues were not only discussed in the classroom but became the very setting in which we teach and live." Of the part Harvard Divinity School students played in the protests, Stendahl wrote: "It is a fact that during these last years seminaries and divinity schools have attracted a substantial number of well-qualified students of a highly radical kind."

For whatever reasons, despite his extensive anti-war activities at Michigan State, Stockman took little if any part in the events at Harvard, and his was not a particularly memorable stay. When contacted about the OMB director, Taylor, who had been one of Stockman's hallmates in his freshman year, asked, "Oh, was that the same Stockman?" Another classmate had only vague memories, recalling him as wearing a tweed suit and reading George Kennan.

Disillusioned with the Divinity School, Stockman began taking courses in public policy and government under the tutelage of two increasingly disaffected liberals, Nathan Glazer and James Q. Wilson. In the spring of 1970, Stockman studied "Issues in Social Policy" with Glazer. According to the syllabus, the course focused on the "common emergent problem" of reconciling equality and liberty. Glazer argued that social programs generally took more away in liberty than they provided in equality, a view Stockman would later reiterate repeatedly, both as a member of the Congress and as head of OMB.

Still, while Stockman studied with him, Glazer's own views had not gelled into the neo-conservative doctrine he espouses today. It was his first year teaching at Harvard, the Great Society was still new, and he had never voted Republican in his life. In a 1982 interview, Glazer said, "I guess the thing that surprised me about Stockman at the time was that he was a Republican. I had thought of him as a sensible liberal. I think of everyone as a Democrat."

His course seems to have had a great influence on Stockman. And, in a 1979 interview with the *Detroit News*, Stockman, then a congressman from Michigan, stated: "It was one of Wilson's courses in organizational theory which totally changed my outlook. I decided that political parties, business enterprises and fraternal organizations—the building blocks of society—are motivated by the preservation instinct, by the need to survive and thrive."

From this realization, Stockman derived his belief that "self-interest is an inherent part of the human condition and what we need to do is harness it, not abolish it." Wilson seemed surprised that Stockman credits him with changing his outlook. "It was a course in organization," he says, "not political theory per se. I wrote a book about it which was essentially the outline of the course. It sold about ten copies."

His time at Harvard provided another experience that contributed to Stockman's "totally changed" outlook: his experience as a live-in babysitter in the home of Daniel Patrick Moynihan, then a part-time Harvard professor and a part-time domestic policy adviser to President Nixon. Like Glazer, Moynihan was another disaffected Democrat. Stockman claims, "I was looking for a way out of the left, and here was a respectable, impressive, alternative, anti-left ideology."

One member of the Moynihan household, however, has come away less than impressed by the lessons Stockman purports to have learned there. Liz, the senator's wife, expressed "deep disappointment with Dave," and regretted that he had not "learned the lessons that were fought out night after night over the dishes."

Stockman made another contact while at Harvard that would prove valuable in getting him to Washington. That contact was *Washington Post* political columnist David Broder, who, as a fellow at the Kennedy Institute of Politics in 1969, taught a seminar. One of his students was David Stockman, and one of his guest lecturers was Representative John Anderson of Illinois, a moderate Republican.

Broder, who recalls that he was "vaguely aware that Stockman was looking for a job in Washington," later heard from Anderson about a staff vacancy on the House Republican Conference, of which he was the chairman. As it turned out, both Broder and Moynihan recommended Stockman, who then left the Harvard Divinity School, without a degree, after a stay of only two years.

Washington, D.C., in the late 1960s and early 1970s was a city filled with causes and confrontations. Protests against the war were still being staged, and one might have expected that Stockman, given his anti-war work and credentials only a few years earlier, would have taken part. But he did not. In fact, a high school friend from St. Joseph recalled that when he and another mutual friend arrived in Washington for an anti-war protest, Stockman wanted no part of it and walked away from them.

His all-consuming interest was work. Having shed his liberal skin, he was readopting Republicanism at a rapid pace.

According to the congressional "Yellow Book," the House Republican Conference "formulates party rules and floor strategy, selects party leadership, votes on committee assignment recommendations . . . and studies positions for the party to take on major legislation." Stockman began with an annual salary of $7,000, not particularly good or bad for the time but certainly adequate for someone living, as Stockman did, in small rental apartments or group houses with other single people. At the beginning his duties were fairly mundane, answering letters and doing research.

Mundane or not, Stockman took the job very seriously. A former co-worker remarked, "Many was the time I would come in and find him asleep in a chair somewhere after working on one project or another all night." A former girlfriend has a vivid memory of David Stockman at this time:

> At one point I confronted him and said I really didn't feel as if we'd gotten to know one another any better in the past few months. I'll never forget what he said, something like, "I guess you're right. I guess I like issues more than I like people."
>
> All he did was work. He worked ninety-nine hours a week, ninety-nine hours a *day!* I liked him—I was a real knee jerk liberal then, and he would tell me that we weren't really so far apart politically; it was just that he was a "fiscal conservative"—but after a while it just got to be so boring. He didn't have a car and he lived on Capitol Hill, so we always walked to restaurants on Capitol Hill, and then afterwards, if I wouldn't let him come back to my apartment, he'd go back to the office and work. Sometimes, he'd go back to the office anyway. As I remember, the only thing he did for recreation was listen to rock music.

His favorite group? The Grateful Dead. And a male colleague, when asked if Stockman was the kind of guy you would go out for a beer with after work, recalled, "I wouldn't even *suggest* it. I'd rather have a beer with a tree stump."

Eighteen months after he'd given Stockman the job, John Anderson, who must have been pleased with his performance, elevated him to executive director of the House Republican Conference.

While heading up the conference staff, Stockman was responsible for initiating the Republican *Legislative Digest*, a publication used to brief members on pending bills, much like its counterpart put out by the Democratic Study Group. One former staffer says of the *Digest*, "It was a project we had been talking about for years. Stockman was the first one to really make an effort to do anything about it." (Another ex-colleague remarked, "Stockman may not be the brightest guy in the world, but what he lacks in brainpower he makes up for in his willingness to work hard and really plow through a project.")

Michael MacLeod, who also worked for John Anderson, and who succeeded Stockman as executive director of the House Republican Conference, says that Stockman "had no interest in the day-to-day, only in supplying the intellectual gasoline to John Anderson's engine."

As executive director, Stockman focused on health and energy issues—two areas in which he later exerted himself as a congressman. "He was responsible for these massive in-depth analyses on some of the dryest topics known to man," said one Republican House aide, laughing. In those analyses, and in his general manner of speaking, it appeared that Stockman's time in Washington was leaving its mark. "The major thrust of my writing," he explained in 1979 to the *Detroit News,* in reference to the point of his many articles and papers, "has been the fact that we have proliferated the number of social programs to an enormous degree in the last ten years." He was learning Washingtonspeak. He was also learning Washington's ways.

To this day, Stockman's relationship with Anderson remains unclear. Anderson consistently refuses all requests to be interviewed about David Stockman,[1] although he offered the names and numbers of three of his former staff members who'd worked for him at the same time, saying, "They could be more objective about David Stockman than I could."

One of the three mentioned by Anderson is Mike MacLeod, who worked for Anderson through his third party race for the presidency and today is a political analyst with the fund-raising firm of Craver, Mathews, Smith & Co. MacLeod says, with no prodding whatso-ever, "There was more than just a mentor–mentee relationship between John Anderson and Dave Stockman; it was definitely a father–son kind of thing. That's why David's 'turning' hurt Anderson so much."

Robert Walker, another person whose name was supplied by John Anderson, and who also talks of the closeness that developed between Stockman and his mentor, went to work for Anderson half-days in 1971 while a student at American University. He met Stockman then, and has been observing him ever since. "My first impression was that he was always very studious, dedicated, and worked *very* hard. He was an extraordinarily hard worker, worked long hours—definitely a workaholic. At that time he seemed pretty much in tune with John Anderson politically." As for Stockman the person, Walker says, "Dave was never much of a socializer, but it would be wrong to suggest that he never had his light moments."

---

1. When approached by Anne Urban in 1982, Anderson's reason for refusing to talk about Stockman, as given by his wife Keke, was that he was considering writing a book about his last terms in Congress and his bid for the presidency. While that book remains as yet unwritten, John Anderson continues to say no to requests that he talk about David Stockman. Mrs. Anderson told John Greenya repeatedly, "We will have no comment about David Stockman."

Walker left Anderson's staff to go to law school, later returning in 1976 to work on the *Legislative Digest*, which by then was being run by MacLeod. At that time Stockman was running for Congress. He had changed markedly, according to Walker. "I think," he says slowly and carefully:

> that there were a couple of reasons why, ultimately, John Anderson felt such a keen sense of betrayal. First of all, Anderson felt that ever since David went back to Michigan, he had been shaping his views to fit the constituency, as seen by the "pork barrel" article he wrote in *Public Interest*. It was clear by the time he got to Congress that he had undergone a major metamorphosis. One can't fault David Stockman for having a genuine change of heart, but John Anderson—who won't criticize Stockman because it would appear to others like sour grapes—felt that Stockman's change was one of expediency rather than conviction.
>
> The other thing that hurt so much was not just that Stockman played John Anderson as practice for Ronald Reagan's debate with Anderson, but that he *volunteered* to play him. Clearly, Stockman wanted to ingratiate himself with the man he hoped would be the next President—and don't forget that Stockman had already come out, early, for John Connally, but when it was clear that he didn't have a chance, he switched to Reagan.
>
> David's political ambition got the best of him and overrode his sense of judgment to the point where he said, in effect, "I'm more than willing to stab my old boss in the back to get ahead."

Another point that clearly rankles Anderson and those who worked for him was that David Stockman had claimed that his real job on the House Republican Conference was "to keep Anderson a Republican," that the congressman's party peers feared he was getting too liberal and that they wanted to oust him from this key Republican post for that reason. To some who know both men and were around at the time in question, to allow this misimpression amounts to little more than raw opportunism on Stockman's part. Indeed, they suggest that it was Stockman who was responsible for the "greening" of the liberal John Anderson. Bob Anderson, another aide who also worked with the two of them at the time, once told a reporter, "I don't share Dave's view of the past. . . . If you look back at Dave's views then, he was mainly a Keynesian. I don't think Anderson ever envisioned Dave's role as keeping him fiscally conservative."

According to another Anderson aide of that era:

> It would not be fair to say that Stockman set Anderson's priorities or influenced them. John Anderson set his own priorities. He may have been grateful to Dave for providing him with analytical tools that he could use in support of his own ideas. It's important to remember that John Anderson never thought of himself as a mainstream Republican, but that he honestly felt that his views, on such issues as civil rights, for example, were healthier for the future of the party, and that if the party didn't adopt them that would limit its future. That hasn't turned out to be the case in the short run, but it still may well turn out to be true. In any event, John Anderson must have felt back then that David Stockman was going to help him in selling a new vision of the Republican Party. But—and while I'm guessing at Anderson's reaction, I'm sure it's very close to the truth—when David Stockman signed on with Ronald Reagan, John Anderson would have thought that it was the grossest of political sellouts.

This former aide remembers Stockman at the beginning of his apprenticeship to Anderson as being "very bright, very aggressive, very hardworking, all of which are talents that could also be viewed as weaknesses, depending on where you were coming from. It's one thing to be intellectually arrogant with your peers and colleagues but quite another to be the same way with members of Congress."

As for Stockman's work habits, this same former aide recalls:

> Even then he was always playing with numbers and reports into the night. He was very single-minded, certainly not the kind of a guy who would come up to you after a long day and say, "Let's go get a beer." So, after a while you think of him as a guy who would rather be working, and when the rest of you go out, you don't bother to ask him because you know he'll say no.
>
> In many ways, though, Dave and John Anderson were alike in that they had this parallel sort of academic, studious strain. Anderson himself was not the kind of guy who would have drinks with the other members at the end of the day. So what would have hurt John Anderson so much in the end is that Stockman went over to Ronald Reagan, a man whose agenda was so contrary to Anderson's own plans and dreams for the Republican Party.

To those aides who were around at the time, the personal relationship between Stockman and Anderson seemed clearly to be that of father and son. Richard Bohr, a friend of Stockman's from Harvard who had dinner with both Stockman and Anderson, has said, "Anderson was very, very proud of Stockman. It certainly was more than an employer–employee relationship." In fact, during the four years that Stockman worked for the conference, John Anderson hired two of Stockman's brothers, stayed at the Stockman family home when he was in Michigan, and opened his own home in Washington to Stockman.

It should be noted that John Anderson has a history of bringing along bright ambitious young men and grooming them for better jobs, both on and off the Hill. One of them is Paul Henry, today a Republican congressman from Michigan's Fifth District, which includes Ann Arbor, and part of which abuts David Stockman's old district. Henry, who has been in the Congress since 1984, had been on Anderson's congressional office staff, as opposed to the House Republican Conference, but worked with and knew Stockman at the time, though his contact with him was limited because, "It was a position of transition. I was on my way back to Duke to finish my Ph.D. at the time." While Representative Henry is much kinder to Stockman than are some of his former Anderson-mates, he declined to comment on or answer questions about why John Anderson won't talk about David Stockman, except to say he would not be surprised if there were "a lot of hurt and feelings of betrayal lingering after the presidential election."

According to Paul Henry, Stockman was extremely able and bright, and if he viewed his job on the conference as calling for him to moderate Anderson's liberal-leaning views, then that was fine because it was both necessary and a service to Anderson and the Republican Party. As for Stockman's own early political views, Henry clearly remembers him as more neo-conservative than liberal. "After all," he says, "he was recommended for the job by Patrick Moynihan." Henry continued, "It was the job of all of us with the conference in those days to get John Anderson to temper his comments. . . . It should be remembered that there has been a shift in the political thinking of both David Stockman *and* John Anderson."

A man who agrees with Representative Henry's views on the need to keep John Anderson from sounding too liberal is John Bibby, now a professor of political science at the University of Wisconsin at Milwaukee, who was the first permanent director of the House

Republican Conference, and who helped interview Stockman for the job. Of his memory of that interview, Dr. Bibby says, "It was obvious that he was very bright, but I guess the thing that surprised me in that summer of 1970 was that he was a liberal Republican, or at least moderate to liberal. He turned out to be more of a conservative as a member of Congress, which pleased me."

Another thing that pleased Bibby was to learn of the job young Dave Stockman did in 1972 when he prepared "an analysis of what the McGovern budget would do"—apparently the first recorded instance of Stockman's interest in budgetary matters—"so I was not surprised later on that he turned out to be a budget virtuoso." And Bibby too believes that John Anderson needed to be reined in from time to time.

Some observers have attributed the eventual Stockman–Anderson parting of the ways to Stockman's offending Anderson by impersonating him in the warm-up debate with Ronald Reagan. Indeed, Anderson told a close supporter of his presidential campaign that he considered Stockman's action a "personal betrayal." But since then John Anderson has had nothing to say on the record about his former aide.

Stockman has not been similarly reticent. Asked about his former employer by a reporter at the Republican National Convention in 1980, Stockman had little that was flattering to say. He said he considered Anderson's switch from pro- to anti-nuclear power "totally opportunistic," and he dismissed Anderson as a "tool of the corporations," out for his own gain. (Interestingly, these would be the same charges leveled against David Stockman just a few years later by people who were then his ideological kinfolk: Arthur Laffer, Robert Novak, and Jude Wanniski, all of whom now feel that Stockman has sold out to the traditionalist wing of the Republican Party.)

There are other reasons why Anderson may well have felt betrayed by Stockman long before he learned, secondhand, of Stockman's "role-playing" in 1980. For one, even though he may have had growing doubts about his mentee's political, philosophical, and social leanings, he kept Stockman on the payroll in 1976 while the young man was gearing up to run for the seat held by Anderson's Republican House colleague, Edward Hutchinson. Some even suggest that, in effect, Stockman was doing little if any work for Anderson at the time.

What, then, was David Stockman like during his first incarnation in the nation's Capitol? By all accounts, bright as can be, and also by all accounts, a certified workaholic. Barely sociable, in the memory of those who worked with him, he was nonetheless pleasant. Obviously, considering the mentors he had already attracted, he could be ingratiating when he chose to be. Most of all, though, he kept things and himself to himself.

In 1971, Stockman was robbed of a gold watch and almost $100 while near his home in the Capitol Hill area. A year or so later, one of Stockman's roommates, who'd left the house and driven off on a date, realized he had left his wallet at home. He went back, double-parked, and was running toward the house when he was stopped by a gunman who demanded his wallet. When the young man tried to explain that he didn't have his wallet, that that was why he had come back home, the gunman shot and killed him.

With one exception, no one interviewed about David Stockman's early life in Washington had heard of either of those incidents from Stockman himself.

---

3 • The Re-Making of a Conservative

STOCKMAN'S BEST remembered work for the House Republican Conference was analytical, usually consisting of detailed examination of dry documents and pages of figures and charts that even other interested parties would not undertake. Once the work was done, others—especially Republican members of Congress— were only too happy to use the fruits of the young workaholic's efforts. One such Stockman product was his 1972 analysis of George McGovern's budget proposals. That turned out to be a big favorite with Republican incumbents who wanted to be able to explain to their constituents why the McGovern plan was really nothing more than—to borrow a phrase that was not yet in vogue— "voodoo economics."

As much as he enjoyed the work, though apparently not the contact with or service to the significant number of Republican members whom he considered his intellectual inferiors, David Stockman was developing an irresistible urge to run for office himself. About his initial impulse to run he told the *Detroit News*, "After a couple of years as director of the Republican Conference I came to the conclusion that I ought to run as soon as I had the opportunity. Like a lot of other people, I thought I was as capable as many of the members I saw ambling around the halls of Congress. So I started to plot how to get myself in a position to do that."

Edward Hutchinson stood in Stockman's way. An attorney from Adrian, Hutchinson had been the area's congressman since 1962 and fully intended to return to his seat in 1976. Hutchinson's only close general election had come in 1964, when Lyndon Johnson swept the state and even managed to carry the staunchly Republican district with 55.9 percent of the vote. Seventeen years later, the district had not forgotten Johnson's victory. "You can still stir up a lot of trouble in some of the local places around here by reminding people that somebody had to vote for Johnson," said one resident. But even with Johnson's success in 1964, the Democratic Party was unable to mount a serious challenge to Hutchinson, who won by a comfortable 8.6 percent of the votes cast. Looking at its nearly unbroken record of selecting Republican representatives, Stockman must have realized that if he won the primary, he was as good as elected.

That, however, presented Stockman with an unusual set of problems. In the Fourth District, getting to Washington was less a matter of appealing to a broad public than proving fealty to the faithful. Many Republicans were not entirely convinced of Stockman's merits. It didn't take all that long a memory to recall Vietnam Summer; many people, including a number of people his own age, felt that the David Stockman they'd known in the late 1960s had been "quite a liberal when he left here."

In a 1979 interview, Bunny Hoover, a Berrien County Republican Party activist, told a reporter, "When Dave first came on the scene [in 1976], I was skeptical. . . . I said, 'Prove you're really a conservative.' He has." With Bunny Hoover's admonition to "prove" he was a conservative ringing in his ears, Stockman had a lot of convincing to do.

Fortunately for Stockman, there weren't very many doubting Democrats in the Fourth District. As for the Republicans, having seen their own Mr. Hutchinson turn in a less than sterling performance on television during the House Judiciary Committee Hearings, they were less inclined to quarrel over the genuineness of Stockman's return to the conservative fold than they were to ask, "Can he beat Ed?"

What's more, Stockman was sounding more like his old conservative neighbors every day. As Virginia Tilley, a former neighbor who is four years older than Stockman, points out, "Dave was not anti-civil rights as a youth, but he certainly was as an adult. I teach in a deprived area, and I believe that the increase in child abuse is a result of the policies of David Stockman and people like him who say, 'They [the poor blacks] brought it on themselves. Benton Harbor deserves what it gets.' "

It is important to understand the area Stockman was seeking to represent. Hillsdale College, which sits in the district, is a good place to visit to learn the ways of the area. Founded in 1844, the college has long been a friendly haven for conservative thinkers. A recent booklet published by Hillsdale features articles written by George Gilder, the author of *Wealth and Poverty*, and Paul Craig Roberts, a founding supply-sider who left his position in the Reagan Treasury Department to take the William Simon Chair at Georgetown University. The back cover of this publication—"Champions of Freedom"—describes Hillsdale as a place which "holds that the traditional values of Western civilization, especially including the free society of responsible individuals, are worthy of defense. In maintaining these values, the college has remained independent throughout its 137 years, neither soliciting nor accepting government funding for its operations."

The college admissions pamphlet offers this assurance: "Hillsdale College proudly adheres to the non-discriminatory policy regarding race, religion, sex or national or ethnic origin that it has maintained since long before governments found it necessary to regulate such matters." (Of the fifteen photographs in the booklet depicting students, not one is black or Asian.)

Comfortable in his seat and blessed with a supportive constituency, Ed Hutchinson would probably still be in Congress if not for two events: his performance as a senior ranking Republican on the

House Judiciary Committee during the Watergate hearings; and, soon after those hearings, Dave Stockman's well-timed, well-planned, and very well-financed arrival home.

When asked in 1972 what he felt was Hutchinson's greatest accomplishment, F. A. Jones, then chairman of the Barrien County Republican Party, replied, "His rise in seniority on the Judiciary Committee to a powerful position, but his general record is very good." But Hutchinson's "rise" was, as is often the case in Congress, more a testament to his longevity than to his competence.

Under the glare of national publicity surrounding the Watergate hearings, Hutchinson wilted. One of the few, if not the only, notable contribution Hutchinson made to the proceedings was his insistence that Nixon should not be removed from office "for every little impeachable offense." A House Ways and Means aide remembers Hutchinson during the hearings as "the one who was going to doze off at every minute. Came in with his breakfast on his tie, that sort of thing."

The hearings came as a revelation of sorts to Michigan's Fourth District. Chester Byrns, a circuit court judge who would eventually adopt Stockman politically, says of Hutchinson, "Nobody realized what a nonentity he was until the Watergate investigation. . . . He didn't know what to do. That came as a dreadful shock to people around here." Stockman's assessment of Hutchinson's role was pithier: "Simply put, he missed the brass ring."

Few public figures have proved as adept at grabbing the brass ring as David Stockman. Resigning from his position as conference director in early 1975, Stockman returned to southwest Michigan to explore the possibilities of running for Congress. The aspiring candidate brought along Dave Gerson, a former staffer destined to serve as Stockman's advance man. Known to many simply as "The Ger," Gerson had been an intern in the House Republican Conference under Stockman and would later serve as his top aide at OMB. (One observer described Gerson as "the closest thing to a David Stockman clone one can imagine.") More importantly, Stockman brought back an inch-thick sheaf of papers outlining his strategy for winning the nomination and the general election. Given a copy of Stockman's "game plan," marked "strictly [sic] confidential," on the occasion of their first meeting, Fred Mathews, a politically active optometrist from Dowagiac, thought the young Stockman was certainly "not an idle dreamer."

Mathews met Stockman through State Senator Charles Zollar, whom the young candidate had sought out for help. In 1972, Zollar had opposed Hutchinson in the Republican primary—Hutchinson's first challenge since 1962. Although Zollar was locally popular, Hutchinson defeated him almost two to one. But the defeat left Zollar even more convinced that Hutchinson was vulnerable. Not entirely sold on Stockman as a candidate who could beat Hutchinson, Zollar referred Stockman to Fred Mathews for a second opinion.

Mathews had been toying with the idea of running against Hutchinson for nearly a decade. Swept up in a plan to reestablish a local community college, he had decided against challenging Hutchinson in 1976. Mathews had not lost interest in orchestrating a challenge, however, and the arrival of Stockman presented such a possibility.

The two men had lunch, and Mathews was impressed enough to give Stockman his first $1,000 campaign contribution and agree to help raise more. After eating, Mathews took Stockman on a walking tour of downtown Dowagiac to introduce him to other local barons—shopkeepers and restaurant owners who were also members of the Chamber of Commerce and the Dowagiac Jaycee's chapter. It was in one such shop that Stockman met Jack Strayer.

Strayer was working in a local clothing store to earn some extra money on his first break from graduate school. As Mathews and the owner talked, Strayer told Stockman that he thought it would be a good idea for him to take over the seat when Hutchinson retired. Stockman became "irate" over this well-meant observation and insisted that he intended to beat Hutchinson.

Despite this sour start, Stockman and Strayer have maintained a close, albeit stormy, friendship. Following their uneasy introduction, the two arranged to have dinner in nearby Niles, Strayer's hometown. Although Niles does not offer much in the way of elegant dining, the two managed to run up a $35 bill. Strayer insists, "That was a lot for 1975, especially in Niles." Somehow Strayer, the young graduate student, wound up paying the tab—an occurrence that still puzzles him.

The bond appears to have been cemented when Strayer recognized a passage that Stockman quoted from Reinhold Niebuhr's *Moral Man and Immoral Society.* Strayer dropped out of graduate school shortly thereafter to work on Stockman's campaign and eventually left his Niles sweetheart to join Stockman as an aide in Washington.

Since Stockman had not lived in the area for most of the previous decade, he counted on people like Fred Mathews, Chester Byrns, and John Globensky, a St. Joseph tax attorney, to circulate his name among the local VIPs in the district. Local power was concentrated in the upper echelons of the Whirlpool Corporation and the Heath Company, both located in Stockman's hometown of St. Joseph. Byrns recalls one meeting he arranged with a dozen business leaders in order to drum up support for Stockman: "They were skeptical. Dave was wearing his hair long in those days, sort of a Prince Valiant haircut, and that didn't help. He was very hesitant because he knew who these people were. Lord, how he studied them. He had a nervous habit of stroking his mouth when he talked. And he gave very long answers to questions." Although Stockman seemed short on social graces, Byrns observed that he "fascinated these people because he was a walking computer. He was using facts and figures that these business leaders could look up . . . they were impressed."

In a roundabout way, Irving Kristol got the Stockman campaign off the ground. A noted neo-conservative, Kristol is known as a persuasive recruiter of young academics and politicians. Ben Wattenberg, a former liberal turned staunch neo-conservative, was one such recruit. Wattenberg told *The New York Times,* "He gets this guy a job on that magazine, that guy to write this article, this guy to teach in that university. He's a great 'mentioner' of the right people to the right people. He's at the center, where the neoboys'· network interconnects."

In the spring of 1975, Stockman's article on the "Social Pork Barrel" appeared in the neo-conservative journal *The Public Interest.* Nathan Glazer, by then a co-editor of the magazine with Kristol, recalls asking in reference to the Stockman piece, "But isn't this obvious? Hasn't this been written before?" Despite his initial misgivings, the article was printed and, according to Glazer, commanded a "favorable response" from the magazine's subscribers.

It also commanded favorable responses from two influential Washington journalists, David Broder and Meg Greenfield, both of

The Washington Post. Although these two columns would be seen by few voters in Michigan's Fourth district, they would be helpful in making Stockman appear less a typical voice of a narrow, very conservative constituency, and more of a "big picture" thinker, especially four years later when the new Reagan Administration was looking around for people who viewed the world as they did.

Broder wrote of Stockman's article in his own column:

> This tendency [Congress's "pork barrel" approach to federal spending] in lawmakers of both parties is brilliantly dissected in an article by David A. Stockman in the Spring issue of the magazine, *The Public Interest.* Stockman is on leave as executive director of the House Republican Conference and is a fellow of Harvard's John F. Kennedy Institute of Politics.
>
> Stockman's is not a partisan critique. Quite the contrary, his analysis demonstrates the high degree of sham in much of the rhetoric that always surrounds domestic budget debates in the Congress.

That appeared in May of 1975. The following September, Greenfield added her impressions, among them, "In a brilliant article . . . David Stockman coined the term 'social pork-barreling' to describe the way in which Congress has enlarged programs for the poor or for special hardship cases into billion dollar subsidies for the middle class."

No less a personage than the "great mentioner" Irving Kristol then praised the Stockman article in a *Wall Street Journal* column. That piece was subsequently mentioned by a newspaper editor in Michigan's Fourth District, who added his own praises to Kristol's. Back home, Judge Byrns admitted, a *Wall Street Journal* mention is "like getting into the Bible . . ." (After the election, Stockman would joke, "That article is how I got to Congress.")

Stockman's *Public Interest* article describes the legacy of the Great Society as "a grab bag of gap-ridden programs" that "increasingly looks like a great social pork barrel." Without discussing the possibility that such programs as Head Start, Family Planning, Emergency Food and Medical Services, and Upward Bound were popular because they were effective and/or tried to meet a legitimate social need, Stockman vented his clear disapproval of them—despite the fact that many of his fellow Republicans now supported them—saying that these Republicans had discovered another "opportunity to prime the social spending pump." He dismissed the programs as being "largely welfare- or service-oriented." (Just how short a step it would be from denigrating these programs to creating an atmosphere within OMB that made them "expendable" would become all too apparent within a few years.)

Three years later, in the spring of 1978, Stockman, now a congressman himself, took on the knotty problem of welfare reform. In an article for the *Journal*, a publication of the Institute for Socio-Economic Studies, he quoted from Jude Wanninski's new book, *The Way the World Works*: "As a general rule of the economic model, the only way a government can increase production is by making work more attractive than non-work."

Like much of Stockman's writing, the facts in the *Journal* article are but the takeoff point for some very sharply worded and highly opinionated statements:

> Faced with these astoundingly high marginal tax rates, the welfare recipient has come forth with an outpouring of creative effort and ingenuity that matches or even surpasses the kaleidoscope of tax-sheltered investments devised by the wealthy. . . . in short, high marginal tax rates are the analytical key to understanding the whole range of problems associated with the welfare issue. . . . The irony in all this is immense. We offer strong financial incentives to welfare recipients to shelter a few hundred dollars in earnings from tax by concealing them. Then we pay welfare workers $15,000 a year to ferret out fraud and bring it to the attention of $30,000-per-year prosecuting attorneys. This can never be a winning proposition.

To some, the irony was in Stockman's own conclusion: Introduce a negative withholding system, thereby removing the disincentive to seek work on the part of able-bodied welfare recipients. And he added another note that might well have more appeal to employers than to unskilled employees: "Because the negative withholding system would attach to the workers and not to the family unit, it would encourage more than one family member to enter the labor market. It would actually be to the advantage of the family to have two workers with nominal wages of $3.00 per hour instead of one worker earning $6.00 per hour." (But three years later, this form of "pragmatic compassion"—or what a former OMB aide would term, in late 1985, "compassion in the *macro* sense"—would be less and less evident.)

John Anderson, who would become thoroughly disenchanted

with his former aide, told a close supporter in 1982 that Stockman's shift was due more to his "opportunism" than to his self-described "intellectual maturity." According to Keke Anderson, the initial wedge that led to strained relations between Anderson and Stockman was that "John began to sense that there was just too much drive and not enough human aspects there."

Others concur with Anderson's assessment. Faced with the task of "proving" he was a conservative to the powers-that-be back home in the Fourth District, Stockman jumped in with both feet. Fred Mathews, however, still thinks of Stockman's initial decision to run as a conservative as being "pragmatic," that at the time Stockman was "still questioning, still looking for his ideas."

"I'm reluctant to argue that he was simply an opportunist," said Robert Anderson, one of Stockman's former professors at Michigan State. "But I suppose I am a little cynical about Stockman's commitment." And a close friend believes that the choice of which ideology Stockman will choose to embrace is simply a matter of "believing whatever comes along and is useful . . . who knows what he may be selling ten years down the road? Underneath it all is a tremendous lack of commitment."

Even Rick Ast remarks of Stockman's break with John Anderson and his organization, "I heard he just dropped them after he'd gotten what he could from them."

Whatever compassion David Stockman may have been exposed to in the employ of John Anderson had all but disappeared by 1979 when he told the *Detroit News:* "As you mature intellectually, you begin to realize that some of the simplistic formulations and idealistic notions that are attractive to you when you're twenty don't seem very realistic when you're thirty. At twenty it sounds great to say that self-interest is the most destructive force in society and that capitalism needs to be abolished. Now I believe that self-interest is an inherent part of the human condition and what we need to do is harness it, not abolish it."

4 • "If Elected, I Shall . . ."

WITH THE AID of his "inner circle" of powerful supporters, Stockman launched a sophisticated and modern effort, unlike any the sleepy, rural Fourth District had ever seen. It began with the distribution of biographical sheets on Stockman announcing that the twenty-eight-year-old candidate was "actively exploring" the possibility of running. The sheets carried a photo of Stockman without two of his trademarks, gray hair and aviator glasses. In addition to touting Stockman's past political experience, the leaflet proclaimed that the young candidate had won "numerous state and national awards in the 4H Club program," a wise thing to include when running for office in a district that was 67 percent rural. Conspicuous by its absence was any mention of his membership in the Students for a Democratic Society or the Peace Coordinating Committee.

A single sheet of information distributed at the time bore Stockman's name at the upper left and was divided into three paragraphs: WASHINGTON EXPERIENCE, NATIONAL RECOGNITION, and EDUCATION. It appeared to be quite straightforward, in keeping with the candidate's MSU–Harvard–Washington background; but like most pieces of campaign literature, it gilded the lily somewhat.

"Stockman," it said, in an almost impersonal tone, "has been increasingly recognized as one of the nation's leading experts on the runaway Federal social spending programs . . . [and] is also regarded as an authority on the Congressional process. . . . He had also been frequently asked to speak before groups such as the American Management Association, the National Association of Manufacturers and other trade associations to brief businessmen on how to make their views count in the legislative process."

The section on EDUCATION read:

> Stockman graduated cum laude from Michigan State University in 1968 with a major in History. That fall he entered Harvard Divinity

School to pursue graduate studies in social ethics and later, political science and government. He interrupted his graduate studies in 1970 to take a position in Washington as a Congressional staff aide.

Stockman recently returned to Harvard as a Fellow of the University's prestigious Institute of Politics. He was one of ten individuals selected for this Fellowship in a nationwide competition among those holding key governmental, journalistic and other public affairs positions. He spent part of the 1974–75 academic year at Harvard fulfilling the program's teaching and writing responsibilities.

(Whoever wrote the handout sheet had a skillful touch; not too many people would have chosen the word "interrupted" to describe the period after Stockman left Harvard for Washington.)

On February 2, 1976, David Stockman formally gave notice of his candidacy from under the roof of a Holiday Inn down the road from his Michigan home. He then proceeded to "blitz" the district by visiting the heart of each of its seven counties by helicopter. That, and the less than enthusiastic response from his supporters, gave the incumbent a glimpse of the future. Two days later, word came from Washington that Ed Hutchinson intended to retire.

Spending $163,733—about $100,000 more than Hutchinson had ever found it necessary to use—Stockman gave the district a crash course in modern campaigning. With the aid of old voting lists, the candidate concentrated his efforts on the 20 percent of Republicans who had voted in the last primary and were likely to cast another primary vote.

One way Stockman reached these voters was the "coffee," held at the home of local housewives and designed to raise both money and contacts. Generally held at ten or eleven on a weekday morning, these coffees formed the backbone of the campaign. In one local newspaper report, five are cited on the same day, with an appearance by Stockman at each. Jack Strayer, who had a hand in planning many of these get-togethers, recalls that they were generally successful. But there were a few "real bombs," like the time Strayer's aunt arranged a coffee meeting and nobody showed up "except for Dave with about fifteen local press people in tow."

Lee Boothby, a Berrien Spring attorney, promised to be Stockman's stiffest primary opposition. Blessed with the endorsement of Hutchinson, Boothby, according to a local paper, "counted on an ultraconservative core as his base strength." Although he had run against Hutchinson in the 1962 Republican face-off, Boothby was now promoted to the "carbon-copy" of his former foe. His promoters did their work too well. The Fourth District, along with the rest of the country, was restless and ready for a change in 1976. In a conservative area like southwestern Michigan such a change might not be as pronounced as in other parts of the country, but there did seem to be a desire to move from the "old guard" brand of conservatism to a fresher, more vigorous face. Boothby seemed to have both feet stuck in the past. In addition to Boothby, Stockman faced two lesser opponents in his race for the Republican endorsement: David Fraser, an out-of-work salesman, and Helen Tauke, a Benton Harbor substitute teacher.

Against these home-grown opponents, Stockman stressed his Washington experience—an anomaly in a year when many candidates, including Jimmy Carter, were running at least in part as outsiders. It was an effective ploy. Local editorial writers in the area picked up on Stockman's main selling point. Wrote the Niles *Daily Star* six days before the primary:

> As for Stockman's absence from the district, his years since 1970 in the Congressional pressure cooker will be much more valuable to the people of this area. He won't have to spend time learning the Congressional ropes. It is an advantage the district will come to appreciate as other new faces in the house struggle to find their way around next January.

The Lenawee *Daily Telegram* added what it perceived as yet another beguiling feature of David Stockman's: "At 29, Stockman is also young enough that he could have a very distinguished career in the House of Representatives and also might make an attractive U.S. Senate candidate in a decade or so."

In the months before the August 3 Republican face-off, Stockman found time to take on all the conservative shibboleths: welfare, legal services, federal spending, and government regulations. Three days after he announced his candidacy, a headline in *The Herald-Palladium* intoned, STOCKMAN: WELFARE SYSTEM "DESTROYING OUR SOCIETY." The article quotes Stockman as saying the welfare system makes it "foolish for a family to work and pull its own weight. . . . [it] is the most urgent problem facing the nation." In this same speech to a local Lions Club, Stockman insisted that "huge state-to-state variations in payment levels" had transformed Michigan into a "social magnet" for welfare families, and called for a standard nationwide benefit level in order to "protect our border from the present burdensome influx of recipients." (When confronted by a statement similar to this during a 1982 Senate hearing on the Reagan Administration's proposal to shift more of the welfare burden back to the states—the so-called New Federalism—Stockman shifted uneasily and replied, "I would suggest one's views of things change as evidence and facts present themselves and conditions change.")

On July 20, two weeks before the primary, the "Lenawee Scene" section of the *Daily Telegram* ("covering all of Lenawee County with complete saturation") quoted Stockman's message to a group of clergymen: "Self-restraint and self-reliance have long been essential attributes of the American people. But the easy availability of handouts and free federal money are inflaming appetites and encouraging us to expect more than we can afford." According to the *Telegram*, Stockman warned that failure to curb this giveaway system "will not only mean financial catastrophe but also moral ruination."

As the August 3 primary approached, all seemed to bode well for Stockman, until one week before the primary, when Fred Mathews received a late night call from an acquaintance in the Boothby camp. Mathews was informed that the Boothby campaign was releasing a story that would "destroy" Stockman with "something from his past." When Mathews pressed his source for details, the caller hung up. Rounding up what Mathews refers to as the "inner circle" of campaign workers, the group huddled around Mathews's backyard pool to discuss the impending blow. After a fruitless attempt to determine the story, the group tracked down Stockman at an eleventh-hour fundraiser. Over the telephone, Mathews asked him, "Dave, is there anything in your past, anything that you aren't telling us about? Anything you haven't even told your mother?" Stockman paused, then insisted that he was at a complete loss. After a while the disheartened group split up and headed home.

The next day Stockman's involvement in the SDS anti-war movement was splashed on the pages of a number of local papers. But the release fizzled. Rising to the occasion, Stockman subdued the ghost of his radical past by minimizing his former activities. Satisfied that their prodigal son had seen the light, the Fourth District took him to their hearts and forgave him by favoring him almost two to one over Boothby—28,832 to 13,590.

The general election presented itself as something of a formality. In the interim, Stockman bloomed—sporting an ever-increasing number of conservative petals. Lynn Jondahl recalls a confrontation with Stockman when the two were speaking at a Boy's State gathering, a group of high school senior leaders from across the state. Stockman made his speech and sat down next to Jondahl, who says, "He looked very confident and self-satisfied. . . . Oh, he said things like, 'Why should Michigan have to pay for roads in New York City?' " Recalls Jondahl, "It struck me as a very parochial view of the world. I chided him at the time as his speech was very much the Republican, Chamber of Commerce sort of thing, but he just gave me some line about how he was older now and more realistic—joking, half joking." Jondahl remembers Stockman as anxious to assuage his self-doubts while head of the Republican Conference by assuring Jondahl that "Anderson's a liberal." Those self-doubts faded quickly once Stockman began his campaign in earnest.

Some of Stockman's campaign promises now seem almost humorous. A campaign leaflet headed "The American Heritage: Keeping Faith With Those Who Built It," maintains that "Medicare coverage is inadequate" and strongly favors an "annual limit of $500.00 on out of pocket expenses for health care bills." While in Congress, Stockman would help draft the "National Healthcare Reform Act of 1980," which provided catastrophic coverage "after a member of the Plan has spent no more than $2,900 in one year." The pamphlet firmly states: "Dave Stockman believes that the Social Security should be reformed to provide ironclad guarantees for those who paid taxes during their working careers." In 1981, Stockman would lead the administration's ill-fated efforts to slash Social Security benefits. And although Stockman's early tenure at OMB is perhaps best summarized in his famous call-to-arms—"I don't believe that there is any entitlement, any basic right to legal services or any other kind of services"—his campaign literature proclaims that "the nation owes those people who built our heritage the decent retirement income to which they are entitled."

Stockman was an unenthusiastic campaigner. "I don't dislike campaigning," he once admitted, "but if I had the choice between reading a five-hundred-page report on auto industry regulations and a day of campaigning, I'd take the former." A former staffer recalls that Stockman frequently spoke of his constituents as "the great unwashed." Often impatient with his area's residents, he proudly asked a *Detroit News* reporter after an encounter with a Fourth District schoolteacher in 1979, "Did you see how I got the subject off the teacher's school and onto the Department of Education? I never miss an opportunity to focus on the big picture." This desire to always "focus on the big picture" frequently baffled members of the Fourth. Ort Middough, a resident of the town of Paw Paw, expressed a frustration no doubt common to members of Congress who have heard Stockman testify. According to Middough, "I never threw a question at him that he didn't have an answer to. Only trouble is, I'm never sure I'm smart enough to know if he's telling the truth."

The voters may have encountered problems understanding him, but they had little trouble electing him. In November 1976, Stockman captured 61 percent of the vote to Democrat Richard Daugherty's 39 percent. At the tender age of twenty-nine, David Stockman's plotting had paid off.

"Of the twenty-four newly elected Republican congressmen in 1976, only two failed to appear on the Capitol steps for the traditional freshman photo," recalled Mickey Edwards (R-OK), who was also a '76 rookie. One of the absentees was undoubtedly ill. Of the other, Edwards joked, "Missing that picture set the tone for Dave's tenure in Congress. He was probably too busy working on an alternative budget proposal, writing one of his infamous 'Dear Colleague' letters, or poring over some car safety regulations."

Perhaps he simply didn't care to be photographed with the others, seeing as he already had a relatively low opinion of the average member. As one writer observed, "Humility was not Dave Stockman's strong suit when he arrived in early 1977. At the orientation session for new GOP freshmen, everyone introduced himself, usually with a bit of personal biography. When it was Stockman's turn, he got up and said, 'My name is Dave Stockman. I have a great deal of experience on Capitol Hill. My staff and I will be glad to help any of you freshmen get adjusted.' "

Prior to his election, Stockman had filled out the *Congressional Quarterly's* "1976 Candidate Questionnaire," listing his occupation as "resigned as Ex. Director U.S. Rep. Conf." He said he was a United Methodist, and that his ethnic background was German. He listed membership in only three organizations, Michigan State Alumni, Kiwanis, and J-C's [sic]. And the only "Party posts, campaigns managed or other political work not listed above" that he cited were "State Convention Delegate 1974, 1975, 1976." Given the skimpiness of Stockman's political experience, one would have to say that his time spent with John Anderson certainly paid dividends.

Being a freshman in Congress is often described as "the lowliest position on earth." Newcomers like Stockman had to face all the trials of a rookie—lousy office space, little choice in committee assignments, and a number of elders who viewed freshman representatives as something akin to pledge boys in a college fraternity.

Freshman Dave Stockman was not alone. As election years go, 1976 brought in a large group of congressional rookies. Ultimately, fifty-one members of the 94th Congress (1974–75) retired, died, or sought higher office, leaving a record number of seats vacant. If anything, arriving in 1976 made Stockman's prospects even less auspicious. "In 1976, being a Republican freshman was the lowest spot in the congressional hierarchy," as Representative Mickey Edwards put it. On the national front, the situation looked dreary for the Republicans. Not since Lyndon Johnson left office in January 1969 had one party controlled both Congress and the White House. Democrats ran well on the theme of "Putting trust back into the federal government"—a reminder of the presidency and party that brought America Watergate. An astonishing 36 percent of those senators seeking reelection (9 of 25) were defeated, while in the Democratic-controlled House the turnover was a mere 4 percent (13 of 381).

Of the nine incumbents defeated in the Senate, seven were ousted by challengers who ran campaigns on the post-Watergate theme of restoring integrity to government. An eighth won by casting himself as an outsider. It was only in the Daniel Patrick Moynihan challenge to James Buckley (R-NY) that a genuine ideological split dominated the debate. In all, the Democrats picked up ten seats in the House, giving them a two-to-one margin.

The presidential race was not much more stimulating. Jimmy Carter confessed to having lust in his heart. Gerald Ford maintained that the Soviet Union did not dominate Poland. As the election drew near, George McGovern admitted he had never seen an "emptier campaign." In Nevada, voters acknowledged that the American public did not have much from which to choose; given the option of voting "none of the above" on Election Day, 3,000 of the 175,000 voters in the state cast their presidential ballots accordingly.

A CBS national news survey of voters leaving the polls in 1976 listed ten reasons why they cast their ballots as they did and asked them to check as many as three. Of those who voted for Carter, the leading replies were:

Restoring trust to government	49%
Job guarantees	29%
Controlling inflation	23%
Watergate and the pardon	20%

When Carter voters were asked what they disliked about Ford, a full 47 percent checked "the Nixon pardon" and another 37 percent felt "he has too many ties to big business." Watergate and its aftermath had left a sour taste in the mouths of many of those who voted for Ford as well. Among Republicans who opted for Ford, 19 percent disapproved of the Nixon pardon, as did 31 percent of the Independents. With Watergate looming over it, the Republican Party was moribund.

But 1976 offered one bright spot for Stockman and like-minded politicians. Well-funded conservative groups were proliferating. In 1976, the organized Right donated over $4 million to candidates. "At least we're all playing football now," gloated Paul Weyrich of the conservative Committee for a Free Congress, "whereas before we weren't using the same rules or in the same league."

Stockman arrived in Washington for his first term with two staffers in tow: Dave Gerson, who would be his legislative assistant, and Jack Strayer, his personal secretary. After contacting his former Harvard professor, Nathan Glazer, in search of someone with an energy background, Stockman also hired Fred Khedouri. Fresh out of the University of Chicago, Khedouri had spent a summer working for Ralph Nader and eventually would marry one of his co-workers in the Nader office, Glazer's daughter Sarah.

Stockman's staff was a hard-working group, "clubby," with some aspects of a secret society. Strayer remembers Stockman as "always looking for the cold facts—memos had to be written in his own little language—one-word sentences, that sort of thing." It reached the point where the "whole staff could do nonverbal communications."

Prior to his election, Stockman had assured the Fourth District that, if sent to Washington, "I intend to seek appointment to the House Appropriations Committee and grasp the problem at the roots." Before he could take hold of the nation's worries, however, Stockman had a more immediate problem: getting onto the Appropriations Committee. He never solved it. Despite four years of personal lobbying, Stockman never made the Appropriations or Budget Committee. His forays on the budget were made as a guerrilla, from the outside.

He did manage a seat on Interstate and Foreign Commerce (the name was changed to Energy and Commerce in 1981), a committee that grabbed national headlines in the 1979–80 energy shortage. Other assignments were less notable. Library and House Administration was not a prize. The Population Committee rarely met.

Entering what was a political no-man's-land for Republicans, David Stockman remained undaunted. Throughout his years as a congressman, Leon Panetta (D-CA) recalls, "Stockman was a thinker, but he had a big problem relating to people and getting his ideas across." During the 1976 campaign, Stockman described the House as a "cosy club of careerists." According to Panetta, Stockman exhibited a "basic antagonism toward the legislative process" during his political tenure on the Hill. "He wound up being a loner in the process who was saying to hell with the rest of you," remembers Panetta, adding, "It's almost as if in his position at OMB he [was] coming back to defy the process—coming back to get us good." One of Panetta's colleagues agrees. "There was an ever-present smirk on his face. He always gave off the sense that I am the smartest kid on the block as if to say, 'I know what I'm doing and you don't.' "

As a politician, Stockman displayed a "get tough" attitude that bordered on hostility. When asked what kind of reaction he expected from Michigan's Republican Governor Milliken to the 1980 budget proposals, Stockman replied icily, "He has to face the fact that the picnic is over. . . . There must be some painful cutbacks. I don't intend to tell the governor what these should be. That's his business, but the days of the federal handout are over."

Stockman developed little rapport with state officials in Michigan, alienating a number of them with his heavy-handed tactics. Jumping into a fray over the choice of a state Republican chairman, Stockman managed to leave "a lot of people cooled off to him," according to a Michigan source active in state politics. Ultimately, Stockman won this battle. But he then proceeded to bully those who had sided with him by insisting state Republicans become more organized, more "computer-run," as another person who was angered by Stockman's ceaseless prodding says. Upon learning of Stockman's appointment to OMB, one state Republican official expressed his dismay: "it's not so much a concern about ideology as it is the piranha factor."

Nor did Stockman seem particularly interested in Michigan's state legislators. State Representative David Hollister, a friend from Stockman's Michigan State days, wrote to Stockman on at least two occasions and never received replies. "Other congressmen from both sides of the aisle would come down to Lansing and get a feel for what was going on there," says Hollister, "but never Dave Stockman, not Stockman."

Stockman had perhaps even less use for his peers on Capitol Hill. In 1977, he told U.S. News and World Report:

> If you could go to the floor and suddenly freeze everything and give a little third grade test on the issues, you'd be appalled by how much people don't know about what they're voting on.
>
> Just to give you an example: I went to the floor recently to vote on an amendment and had to come in on the Democratic side. I asked a number of Democrats what the issue was and they said, "This is an amendment to cut off funds for women and children." So I went to the Republican side and asked, and someone told me it was an amendment "to stop the giveaway to foreign devils." That's about the level of discourse that goes on. . . .

Obviously, Stockman took himself more seriously as a self-styled "man with a mission." In a 1978 newsletter, he told his constituents, "I'm not about to turn into another cog in the bureaucratic machine." As a congressman, Stockman spewed forth a regular stream of articles and position papers. While other congressmen may leave a stray newsletter or a few pamphlets tossed on an end table for visitors, Stockman's office boasted an entire "David Stockman speaks out on . . ." bookshelf that housed a myriad of written opinions on a number of subjects. Pieces for The Washington Post, The Journal of Socio-Economic Studies, and Congress Today, a Republican National Committee publication, figured prominently in this display area. Over the years, Stockman attacked the gasoline rationing plan proposed by Carter as the "bureaucratic hoax of the decade" and scorned what he called the "senseless stampede to synfuels." A December 1978 letter from Stockman to Carter's Agriculture Secretary Robert Bergland began: "This is to express my unabated outrage at the Department of Agriculture's recently announced intention to prop up the price of Idaho potatoes." Stockman continued: "After you spread the taxpayers' and consumer's gravy on the Russets, where will you strike next: Broccoli? Turnips? Peppermint?"

Stockman's sarcasm bordered on the vitriolic. "It is about time that the Department stop playing nursemaid to the proliferating array of cry-baby commodity groups in this country. . . . Your recent unjustified bail-out amounts to a full-scale charge to the rear. Indeed, your Department's supine capitulation in this potato caper makes the best argument yet for congressional enactment of a 'cold turkey' policy for American agriculture." Clearly angered by the tone, as well as the content, of Stockman's letter, Bergland shot back, "Dear Congressman Stockman: This is in further reply to to your juvenile letter of December 28 . . . ."

The conservative *Detroit News* would praise Stockman several years later, saying, "His special intellectual gifts are never more effectively employed than when they are pricking the illusions of reflexive liberals." The observation is keen. While Congressman Stockman shone when tearing down proposals, his attempts at constructing policies were considerably less effective.

In a 1979 interview, Stockman admitted he was not much of a horse trader or head-counter. "I'm more interested in ideas than votes because we can't make rational policy in a country this complex unless we're guided by ideas. Time and time again we get into trouble because we're guided by pure expedience and political pragmatism. Congress simply drives me crazy that way."

5 • Manchild in the House

STOCKMAN-STYLE Republicans were soon driving the Democrats crazy. The out-of-power strategy of Republicans such as Stockman was to force themselves to prominence as perpetual naysayers. Stockman had little use for compromise; more often than not his proposals were defeated by wide margins on the floor of the House. But he and his colleagues provoked polarizing debates and forced Democrats into votes that could be attacked by New Right groups in the election.

Stockman had a single ideological star. A self-described "fanatical champion of economic growth," he claimed in a newspaper interview that such growth was "the only way that those who came from the part of the spectrum that I did—middle to lower—are going to have an opportunity to better themselves." His "commitment to economic growth wasn't *one* of his ideas," an aide to the House Energy Committee says wryly, "it was his *only* idea." Marching forward with his single-minded notion, he "occasionally brushed against the shifting sands of reason."

Stockman assumed a post position on the right, leading the charge against social programs and governmental intervention in the economy. Before he attended his first hearing of the Energy and Commerce Committee, the *Congressional Quarterly* described him as "most likely among Republicans to vote for regulation." Stockman would make the *CQ* eat those words.

Stockman aimed numerous shots at the efforts of various regulatory agencies. His most frequent sparring partners were the Environmental Protection Agency (EPA), Occupational Safety and Health Administration (OSHA), and the National Highway Traffic Safety Administration (NHTSA), all of which were in regular conflict with the auto companies, the industrial mainstay of his state. In 1979, he led a fight to overrule a 1977 NHTSA order requiring passive restraints (airbags and automatic safety belts) on all cars by 1984. The proposal was strategically well-timed. The week before, Stockman had ruffled feathers back home by leading a fight against the $1.5 billion Chrysler loan guarantee. Claiming in a March 1979 speech that "Transportation Secretary Adams is an economic illiterate," Stockman fumed, "We don't need cheerleaders like Mr. Adams or Joan Claybrook [NHTSA administrator] who don't know a damn thing about the auto industry. . . ." A local paper quoted Stockman as saying, "The real issue is not safety, but consumer 'freedom of choice' versus bureaucratically imposed collectivism."

Fighting the establishment of a Consumer Protection Agency in 1977, Stockman laid out his views on the government's role succinctly: "we already have a mechanism to remove undesirable products from the market. We usually call it 'free enterprise' or the 'free market economy.' People simply will not buy products if they are bad or uneconomical." Stockman insisted, "Let me make up my own mind about what is good for me and what I can afford."

Yet in 1978, even as strident a deregulator as David Stockman seemed to realize that the free market economy was not the answer to every American malaise. Tucked into the back of the *Congressional Record* are Stockman's views that "some form of mandatory efficiency program" is needed to "bring about the shift to more efficient appliances." Stockman admitted that "there is some reason to doubt that market forces alone" will prod this shift, citing the following reasons:

- Given the choice, consumers will generally choose a "cheaper, less efficient" product over a more energy efficient one.

- Higher electric prices alone will not encourage consumers to switch to more energy-efficient appliances, because consumers suffer from a "lack of information that would enable [them] to judge," as well as a "widespread lack of understanding of the little information that is available."

- Appliances in many residences are purchased not by the user but by the builder, "who will continue to seek appliances with the lowest initial cost without regard to increasing electric rates."

With these three reasons, Stockman exposed the hollowness of the arguments he had advanced a year earlier. Insisting that government should "let me make up my own mind about what is good for me and what I can afford" sounds reasonable. But, as Stockman pointed out, individuals may not always be equipped to decide what is best because they have only inadequate information. Individuals, moreover, are incapable of purging their air or water of dangerous chemicals; they can only do so by joining together through a government of laws to require that polluters clean up after themselves.

Ultimately, the remarks were but a blip in Stockman's record of opposing regulation. The young congressman repeatedly rejected the idea of government responsibility in promoting community welfare and protecting public health. Instead, he focused solely on the cost to private interests of government action designed to protect the larger public.

The Superfund, which provided money to clean up abandoned hazardous waste dump sites, was a favorite Stockman target. In September 1980, Stockman labeled the bill "an open-ended enabling statute that makes EPA literally the czar over every hazardous waste site in the entire country, and that includes every landfill, every waste site, every junkyard, every leaching pile, every industrial lagoon on the back of an industrial property, every municipal dump, even every backyard rubbish pile that has been accumulated anywhere in the country." Stockman supported this charge on the House floor by giving a list of chemicals that would constitute "hazardous wastes" under the bill. "Certainly the list of chemicals that the gentleman [Stockman] has read here today suggest that any legislative proposal could be held up to ridicule," replied Representative Edward Madigan (R-IL), "but we are not talking here about a single bottle of rubbing alcohol or a small two-ounce package of rat killer that somebody is going to rub behind a refrigerator. We are talking about hundreds of fifty-five-gallon drums of these chemicals that are leaking into the underground water supplies in the United States of America. Certainly people use those chemicals, but they do not mix them in large quantities in their drinking water."

That same month, Stockman fired off a virulent "Dear Colleague" letter. Claiming (with his usual overstatement) that the House was being "stampeded into action," Stockman proposed to rewrite the bill. Observing that the proposal had been three years in the making, Representative Albert Gore (D-TN) noted wryly, "I would not call that a stampede." Stockman's amendment was defeated on a voice vote. Still, Stockman was infuriated. Asked in October 1980 what he personally regretted most during his time in the 96th Congress, he cited the Superfund, explaining, "They railroaded it. If I had been more attentive, I could have stopped it." Once at OMB, he would slash funding for the program.

As a member of the Energy Committee, Stockman exerted himself strenuously on energy-related issues. One of his fellow committee members explained, "When it came to the free market, he was a religious, firm believer. But the free market doesn't entirely take care of energy. I think that after a while everyone would be forced to say there were deficiencies in that approach. Dave Stockman would never admit those deficiencies." Throughout the energy shortages in the late 1970s, Stockman had a single solution: decontrol the price of oil and gas. He vigorously opposed Carter's standby gas rationing plan in another "Dear Colleague" letter, this one six pages long, in which he said: ". . . By artificially creating $100 billion worth of 'funny money' the plan will transform the gasoline market into a giant Monopoly game in which the swift, smart and sophisticated will wind up with Park Place and Boardwalk, while the average motorist will be lucky to come out with the B & O or Baltic Avenue." Members of the committee were greeted by deaf ears when they argued repeatedly that Stockman's approach—decontrol—would simply ration gasoline by price rather than coupons.

Nor would Stockman accept the notion that there was any reason to conserve energy. In 1979, he told the *Detroit News*, "The energy situation in this world simply isn't that dire. In my view there are many centuries of fossil fuel left." According to Stockman, "the myth of energy crisis" was the work of "self-serving politicians seeking to gain control over energy production." Statements such as that led one House member to remark that "Stockman had a terrible tendency to go in for the rhetorical overkill." Speaking against a proposal for a six-month moratorium on licensing new nuclear reactors proposed in the wake of the Three Mile Island accident of March 1979, Stockman reached a peak of verbal frenzy, declaring: "It's an effort to legitimize and give congressional sanction to all the half-baked and unsubstantiated conclusions being shamelessly propagated by the windmill and woodstove people."

A particularly ironic subsidy present in the Fiscal Year (FY) 1982 budget prepared by Stockman were funds for the Tennessee Clinch

River Breeder Reactor, a plutonium-producing nuclear reactor that has long been the subject of bitter debate in Congress. As a congressman, Stockman had waged a furious crusade against the project—whose costs have skyrocketed even as its projected date of completion recedes into the future. Insisting that the reactor was a tremendous waste of taxpayer's money, Stockman warned, "Today it is the nuclear power lobby looking for a large uneconomic subsidy. Tomorrow it will be the solar power gang, then the windmill freaks and so on in a never-ending stream of outstretched palms." When asked how the program had escaped his weighty ax in his position as head of OMB, Stockman found another exit: "I would suggest to you that I am not running this government singlehandedly."

But, to be sure, Stockman found occasion to break from his ideology—most notably by conducting his own pork barreling. Although Stockman credited his *Public Interest* piece on the social pork barrel for putting him in Congress, he was perfectly willing to engage in a little of it himself to stay there. In December 1980, while Stockman was still a congressman, one of his aides worked to obtain a multi-million-dollar federal grant for Agri Power, Inc., a firm seeking to build an alcohol distillery in Stockman's district. On another occasion Stockman urged the Economic Development Agency (EDA) to approve a $226,000 grant for an industrial plant in the Fourth District, writing that this was "the type of program EDA should be funding." Soon thereafter he voted to abolish the EDA. An aide to Stockman was quoted as saying that "He [Stockman] tried to do his share to get a piece of the pie for his district" once the program was in place. (To some extent, Stockman went further in "doing his share" than his colleagues by keeping a computer alert system on the lookout for available grants and loans. "I went around and cut all the ribbons and they never knew I voted against the damn programs," Stockman would later tell Greider in the *Atlantic Monthly*.)

No other action has made clear not only Stockman's contempt for the political process but for the voters who elected him. Stockman's efforts to corner "a piece of the pie" for his district were not unusual; efforts to direct Uncle Sugar's largesse to the folks back home are common on Capitol Hill. But such actions seem profoundly cynical from a man who airily postured as being above his congressional colleagues, who assured his voters that he would not "turn into another cog in the bureaucratic machine." The search for subsidies that would translate into a ribbon to cut back home makes even Stockman's reflexive opposition to government activity appear but another appurtenance, to be discarded when it was politically expedient.

"Freshmen are to be seen and not heard"—so goes an unwritten congressional rule. Mark Green relates the experience of the late Carl Hayden's first speech on the House floor in 1913: "He had kept quiet for many months until a matter unimportant to the House but very important to his native Arizona came up. Hayden spoke to the chamber for only a minute and returned to his seat next to a more senior member, who turned to him and angrily said, 'Just had to talk, didn't you?' "

Obviously, David Stockman felt no such qualms. Not only his hard-line positions but his style made him visible from his earliest days in Congress. His frequent articles, rhetorical flourishes, and single-minded intensity in the committees were complemented by a vocal presence on the House floor. The latter effort started modestly. Two weeks after his term began, Stockman inserted a "tribute to Elmer Adams," a retiring Decatur, Michigan, township clerk, into the *Congressional Record*. In February, he rose on behalf of a constitutional amendment to set one term in both the Senate and House at four years and put a twelve-year cap on the period one could serve in either. As a first-year congressman, Stockman still had a possible eleven years to serve under the proposal. Others would not—in the Senate the average term in 1975 was already eleven years. In speaking on behalf of this bill, Stockman claimed, "With offices being vacated in an orderly, reliable fashion, many more people would have the opportunity which the Founding Fathers envisioned: to trade private life for public service and yet never be so far from private life that common woes and aspirations are not forgotten."

Nor was Stockman ever shy about airing his views on a wide range of topics at committee hearings. His lengthy "Dear Colleague" letters were used by some members, such as Mickey Edwards, as position papers. Others sent them straight to the trash. They remain legendary today, especially the anti-Superfund letter of September 15, 1980:

RE: SUPERFUND OR EPA POWER GRAB?

Dear Colleague:

When you vote on H.R. 7020—the chemical superfund proposal—
please set aside the "agit-prop" issued by EPA's mis-education division,
and recall the following basics:

Abandoned Sites Only

H.R. 7020 has nothing to do with current and future waste production or midnight dumping and other improper disposal of hazardous
waste. Every pound of the estimated 34.4 million metric tons of
hazardous industrial waste will soon be tightly regulated under a cradle-
to-grave control system established by the Resource Recovery and
Conservation Act. Penalties for violation are severe. That's why the
stock market value of high technology disposal companies like Waste
Management, Inc., and SCA has skyrocketed and midnight dumpers
are on the run.

Superfund is concerned only with *abandoned* and *inactive* sites—
with the unfinished business left by inadequate disposal standards and
practices in the past.

The Documented Problem Is Limited

Thus far, only 400–800 abandoned dump-sites that may pose threats
to public health or safety have been reliably identified. The 30,000 to
50,000 estimate tossed out by the EPA is rank speculation. It was based
on a contractor's tally of hurried, unstandardized, arm-chair guesses
made by EPA regional offices, some of which even included ordinary
municipal landfills containing rusting refrigerators and rotting garbage.
The study was termed "little better than a guesstimate" by The Eckhardt
subcommittee.

Tailor Made for the States

This particular pollution problem is tailor made for state rather than
Federal action. Unlike air, water and current hazardous waste pollution, abandoned dump sites *don't travel across state lines*. In fact, EPA
estimates that 41 states will assume responsibility for [clean-up]. Given
these conditions, I am proposing something quite novel in the environmental field: let the states investigate, inventory and clean-up their own
abandoned dumps! The Federal role would be limited to providing no
strings financial aid ($500 million over five years) and technical assist-
ance.

LET'S GET OFF THE SUPER BUREAUCRACY KICK

Prior to 1970, this solution would have appeared quite sensible. But for ten years we've been in an environmental time-warp. EPA and its minions in the press and the professional environmental lobbies have assumed an absolute monopoly right to flood the American economy with regulations, litigation and compliance costs that are out of proportion to any environmental problem—real and imagined—that has reached the Congressional calendar.

It's time to get off this super bureaucracy kick—unless you really believe that the present drastic deterioration of our economy, productivity, international competitiveness, and living standards will soon miraculously fade away.

It won't happen so long as we keep writing blank checks that authorize hot-shot junior lawyers and zealots ensconced in the EPA to bleed American industry of scarce funds needed for investment, modernization and job-creation. Like every other major environmental enabling act of the past decade, H.R. 7020 has absolutely no definitions of the waste sites being regulated, no cost-benefit limitation on the monitoring and clean-up expenditures being incurred, and ample authorization for punitive litigation, taxes, and penalties against every "deep pocket" business it can haul into court. The only saving note is that after Chrysler, Ford, U.S. Steel, Firestone, White Motors, etc., there aren't many deep pockets left to prosecute. In subsequent letters I intend to itemize the horrors for small business, local governments, non-chemical business firms and the national economy and job creation which lie buried in this bill. But for now let me just remind you of two things the committee report and proponents have not bothered to mention.

1. *This bill was written at 2:00 A.M. in the morning in a smoke filled room by a handful* of lobbyists, subcommittee members and staff. The full Commerce Committee membership did not even have a print until 10:00 A.M. the next morning—at which point it was gaveled through under a gag rule by the end of the day. As such, it consists of a series of sloppy compromises grafted onto an EPA proposed empire expansion—Superfund—for which absolutely no solid case has been made.

2. *Not a pittance of evidence for a dominant Federal role.* As written, every decision to define, identify, monitor, clean-up abandoned sites or sue for cost recovery will be made by EPA bureaucrats pursuant to five different rule making exercises required by the

bill. Yet this pre-emptive extension of Federal power was not based on even a shred of evidence that state environmental officials are so morally benighted or technically inept that they could not handle the abandoned site problem on their own, given modest financial help. . . .

Rather than unleash another multi-thousand bureaucratic army, new taxes on business, new powers to litigate and punish, and a new multibillion drain on our faltering national economy, I would urge that you consider a policy more in conformity with the economic exigencies of the present hour. Let's help the states protect their own citizens and water supplies from threats posed by a modest number of abandoned industrial dump sites. My substitute is designed to do just that in a simple and effective manner. . . .

At a September 1979 hearing on welfare, Stockman offered a proposal to "provide no entitlements whatsoever to employable adults," meaning everyone except "the aged, blind, disabled and mothers with infants." When asked by Representative James C. Corman (D-CA) where jobs would be found for these "employable adults," Stockman gracefully sidestepped the question—a talent he would perfect at OMB—by simply repeating that his proposal would "get people to go out in the market and take jobs and they will be made available." Pressed further as to precisely where these jobs would materialize, he merely insisted, "The jobs would appear."

This ideological fervor and rigidity was to characterize Stockman throughout his congressional career—and later as head of OMB. One Senate Energy Committee aide commented, "Stockman represents a radical break with American tradition. He is the embodiment of an era of theology, not philosophy." During the welfare debate, Stockman had no precise answer as to where his jobs would appear—his confidence that they will be available stems more from his faith than from any secular explanation.

In Congress, Stockman stood at the head of a "new breed" of conservatives who often had as little use for traditional Republican conservatism as they had for the Great Society. "It is easy to see where Stockman and his ilk have their roots," observed one aide who worked with Stockman while he was on the Hill. "They advocate the same sort of abrupt breaks with policy that the radicals of the sixties advocated. In a significant sense they are the brothers and sisters of the anti-war movement."

Indeed, Stockman raised more than a few old guard Republican eyebrows with his 1979 welfare hearing suggestions that "we get very radical here, that we throw out the traditional concept. . . ." "Those welfare proposals really shocked some of the people around here," recalls one staffer who remembers the hearings. Perhaps even more shocking was Stockman's willingness to "throw out" the old concepts for new ones premised only on the vague prospect of jobs appearing.

Stockman's last appearance before a House committee while a congressman was a fitting one. In March 1980, Stockman, with Representative Phil Gramm (D-TX), offered a proposal to balance the budget by cutting $24.6 billion from federal spending. The two had met in 1978 when Gramm, then a conservative Democrat, first took his seat on the Energy and Commerce Committee. "The first day we were in the committee," remembers Gramm, "of course I didn't know Dave Stockman from Joe Doe. We had a hearing and Stockman asked a question which struck home. I thought, 'Here's somebody on the other side who's awake.' So after the thing, I started to go over and introduce myself just as he was coming over to meet me. At that point we started working together on all sorts of things."

The Gramm–Stockman proposal called for a cut of $200 million in government-sponsored science research. Stockman admitted the proposal would be a "problem for the think tanks, for the academics and for the social science fixers . . . [who should] find some other watering trough for their efforts." Mass transit programs and fixed rail systems were cast aside as a "snare and a delusion" by Stockman. In outlining the $25 billion plus in cuts, Stockman said, "In the Justice function, very quickly, we would abolish the Legal Services Corporation." According to Stockman, the "only loss would be that a few thousand law school students would have to find a real job." And in a conclusion that must have snapped many House Budget members into wide-eyed clarity, Stockman divulged that had he been offering this proposal as a "one-man document," he would have proposed $50 billion rather than $25 billion in cuts.

Stockman would later tell a local reporter, "I was quite active in the whole budget battle in 1980. We didn't achieve high success." Indeed, Gramm–Stockman was largely ignored.

Also discounted was another proposal enthusiastically supported by Stockman, the Kemp–Roth tax bill to cut marginal tax rates by 10 percent across the board for three years. Stockman met regularly with the supply-side "cabal" that included Jack Kemp, Jude Wanniski, and Arthur Laffer, among others.

Against all odds, the Kemp–Roth tax bill made it to the floor on August 10, 1978. Stockman spoke at length in support of the bill, claiming it would cause "no credit imbalance, no pressure on the Fed to pump up the money supply, and no additional inflation." The bill was soundly defeated.

Though his efforts were, for the most part, unrewarded, the Fourth District enthusiastically returned Stockman to Washington in 1978 and in 1980. Stockman admitted he was lucky to have the Fourth District, as "their sentiments are almost completely compatible with my views." Nor was Stockman facing formidable competition. In a *Washington Post* article, he described his opponents thus far as a "cocktail waitress on leave" and a man who drove around the district with "seven kids inside the car, a canoe on top and an unemployment check in his pocket." Winning elections, Stockman observed, "is often purely a matter of default."

Money also made a difference: a month before the November 1978 election, Stockman had spent $28,783. His opponent, a Benton Harbor Democrat, expended $622. The bulk of Stockman's funds came in large bills, not the fives and tens of small-town contributions.

In his 1980 campaign, Stockman's two largest donors were the Automobile and Truck Dealers Election Committee ($4,000) and the Southwest Michigan Board of Realtors ($3,000). Eyebrows arched when Stockman accepted a $2,000 contribution from the American Medical Association (AMA) and then two months later came out vehemently against the Hospital Cost Containment Act that the AMA had indefatigably opposed. His Federal Election Statement for the last six weeks of 1980 was found to contain two reporting errors. When contacted about the second by a local Michigan reporter, Dave Gerson replied simply, "They [the FEC] are morons."

Business groups supported Stockman's efforts through other means. Stockman collected over $13,000 for eighteen speeches he gave in 1979. (He turned over almost $4,500 to charities, since the House limit on honoraria was set at $8,743 that year.) Stockman's highest fees were paid by the American Petroleum Institute ($2,000), while the National Automobile Dealers Association, the American Imported Auto Dealers, and the American Automobile Association paid out $1,000 each.

It might be helpful to learn how some of David Stockman's House colleagues viewed their fellow member, toward the end of his four-year stint. As a prerequisite in discussing Stockman, it is best to choose observers who have a proper vantage point, are also quite intelligent, and possess a keen understanding of how the House works. One who qualifies on all counts is Bob Eckhardt, a Democratic congressman from Houston who had served fourteen years when he was defeated in 1980. Now practicing law in Washington, Eckhardt, a complex man who enjoys quoting Shakespeare and drawing political cartoons almost as much as he does talking about politics and politicians, served on the House Energy and Commerce Committee with David Stockman. Says Eckhardt, choosing his words with care:

> He [Stockman] was an *able* person on the Commerce Committee, but not a natural leader. I remember he would always read, in a monotone, when "speaking" on the House floor and nobody listened to him. But he was heavily relied on by the Republicans for policy direction, though not for leadership on the floor, mainly because of his youth and his lack of seniority.
>
> He was always frank and open and easy to discuss things with because you knew where he stood. As a person, I rather liked David Stockman. He did have a definite political philosophy, and was outspoken; and while the differences between liberals and conservatives may be sharp in some areas, he was not one of those conservatives who built up barriers. He was less effective than some other conservatives who weren't so rigid as he was; nonetheless, he didn't *bristle* just because you disagreed with him ideologically.

Eckhardt recalls a notable physical difference between Stockman and other young Republican members: "You got the idea of a whiz kid, which he tried to promote, with those big glasses, and also he wore his hair long, unlike the other Republican members, who usually looked like little bank clerks."

As to the question of whether or not David Stockman could have become a power in the House of Representatives had he stayed longer, Eckhardt feels that he may well have acted "as a great influence on Republican members because he was willing to work as a top staffer would work. But even though he had all the facts and figures in his head, he didn't have the talent of a Wilbur Mills, for example, who could stand up there at the front mike and answer questions off the cuff."

Was Eckhardt surprised when Stockman was named budget director? "Yes. I had always thought he was very competent, but without that which moves one to great success and high place in politics." As for his policies in that job: "He has one limiting factor, and that is that he lacks in humaneness. I don't see any bitterness or cruelty there, but he can't put himself in the position of the underdog in society. He is concerned a great deal with detail, which isn't to say that he doesn't have a mind that can encompass principle, but that he is *not* a man of good judgment. David Stockman has no meanness, but he looks at things in general terms, and his way of thinking is that a sacrifice of much hurt [to individuals] would be made up by a rise in the general good."

As for Stockman's role in the Reagan Administration, Eckhardt is much kinder to him than to the others:

I think he was *combatting* the deviousness of those other Reaganites who were opposed to him. So much of the Reagan White House is demagogery; they say one thing and mean another. It's like the couplet from Wyatt, "For faire to speake and so to mean; such sweet accord is seldom seen." I don't know if he spoke "faire," but at least he meant what he said. He thought he could speak and have his views affect the administration, but the administration was not used to saying what it meant.

I always thought of David Stockman as a lesser Alexander Hamilton. He is capable of saying the things Hamilton did that indicated distrust in humanity in general, in the citizenry as individuals. I don't think he has a very high opinion of the intelligence of the common man. Also, there's a touch of arrogance in Stockman, as there certainly was in Hamilton and which was his undoing. [When asked, "Whose undoing?" Eckhardt smiled, and said, "Just leave it nicely ambiguous."]

I find it intriguing to compare Stockman and Hamilton. For example, Stockman's detailed knowledge of the budget process can be compared to the work of Hamilton, who framed the banking system. And Hamilton had great influence on George Washington and on John Adams, and then he fell out with Adams—to whom, I might add, he felt himself to be intellectually superior, as David Stockman probably did with Ronald Reagan and certainly did with Ronald Reagan's staff people.

Another former Democratic House member had a similar recollection of Congressman David Stockman, saying, "My first impression was one of tremendous energy and perception in addressing issues. He did his homework, and we worked together on some tough issues such as the legislative veto and the cost benefit stuff, but I always felt there was a sharp edge there. And I mean sharp in the sense of a mild perjorative. I didn't get the feeling that he had a great deal of tolerance for people who weren't his intellectual equals."

Unlike Eckhardt, this man found Stockman very doctrinaire:

I felt he had a whole scheme of political ideologies that brooked no opposition. We *could* work together, but that was because they were issues in which we had a common interest. Otherwise, I don't think there would have been much give. I always had the impression that David would rather lose one hundred percent on the issues than win by fifty percent.

I had the idea that David Stockman was a cold person. He didn't understand the consequences of these issues on people. It wasn't that he knew and didn't care, but a combination of his not believing the naysayers and really not feeling the impact of these policies.

By 1980, Stockman had established himself as a leading exponent of both supply-side economics and neo-conservatism. In the early months of the year, he began talking like a man whose time had finally come. Describing himself as "outgunned, outmanned and outvoted" during his first two terms, Stockman now proclaimed, "The Democrats are disintegrating, there's no discipline in the ranks." As the Democrats drifted from their ideological moorings under Carter's increasingly Republican bent of government, Stockman gloated. "We smell blood," he told *The Wall Street Journal*.

Meanwhile, the Republican Party, swelled by business campaign contributions, was beginning to march to a more cohesive tune, centered on implacable resistance to government regulation, an increasingly bellicose military and foreign policy, and demands for sharp budget cuts. In such diverse events as the defeat of the proposed Consumer Protection Agency, the congressional emasculation of the Federal Trade Commission, the failure of Carter's proposed urban policy, and the shelving of the SALT II Treaty, the congressional realignment sought by conservatives and business groups could be seen. Rather than attacking the fundamental themes propounded by Stockman and like-minded Republicans—that government was the problem, not the solution to a host of ills—many Democratic officeholders, led by President Carter himself, grew defensive and sought to accommodate the growing cry. But the Democrats could never go as far as Stockman or Reagan in rejecting government's role and still hold on to any of their traditional constituents (or indeed, any of their ideals). As a result, they were trapped in an uneasy middle ground, increasingly vulnerable prey for sharp barbs of the ever more vocal far right of the Republican party, and left without a clear, motivating identity of their own.

Stockman was doing his part to prod along the disintegration of the Democrats. In March 1979, he organized a fund to support candidates aligned with his conservative philosophy. In a solicitation letter for his "Free Enterprise Fund," Stockman said contributions would be used to help "break the liberal stranglehold on Michigan." Stockman's political action committee (PAC) managed to raise $20,500 in its first year, which was turned over to Republican candidates in neighboring Michigan states.

Convinced that Stockman was one of the "five top contenders for the presidency" in 1980, Fred Mathews wanted to run Stockman in an exploratory bid in Iowa—though Stockman would not reach the eligible age for the presidency, thirty-five, until November 10, 1981, more than a year after the election. But Stockman had other ideas. He discussed with Mathews the possibility of running Jack Kemp. When Mathews asked him why he wanted Kemp for President, Stockman replied, "That way I could be director of OMB."

None of these proposals materialized and Stockman threw his support behind Richard Nixon's Secretary of the Treasury, John Connally. Jude Wanniski recalls, "Stockman was vehement in his belief that Ronald Reagan would not win the nomination . . . he argued that what we needed was a real tough guy like Connally." When Connally's campaign crashed, Stockman quickly bailed out. He told a Michigan reporter that his support for Connally was a "misjudgment on my part," and said he was "fully comfortable with Ronald Reagan in terms of his views and his basic policies." In retrospect, Jude Wanniski notes, "Stockman was the last to sign onto the Reagan team. He was always a Connally man because he believed that Reagan was too soft-hearted to throw widows and orphans into the streets."

Along with Jack Kemp, William Roth, Bob Dole, and John Tower, Stockman played a major role in the writing of the Republican Party platform. Stockman focused on the energy plank, which called for government to turn energy policy over to the oil industry by relaxing or lifting regulations, and Stockman was later viewed as a likely Energy Secretary after Reagan was elected.

Stockman was a good party man. Even while running his own congressional campaign, he found time to stump for Reagan's energy policy. At a Harvard Institute of Politics forum in the fall of 1980, he maintained, "Our problem isn't lack of energy resources, rather it's a surplus of regulatory controls and bureaucratic impediments." Shortly after the Republican Convention he wrote an article entitled "Our Grand New Platform." In his piece, Stockman argued that the platform's refusal to support the Equal Rights Amendment (ERA) and its rejection of the *Roe* v. *Wade* decision (which had legalized abortions) was the Republican repudiation of the "incessant social engineering pursued by the nation's liberals. . . ." For the first time since 1936 the Republican Party refused to endorse the Equal Rights Amendment, but Stockman said, "It would be inappropriate to become stalemated in the debate over whether or not to ratify it. The important thing is to make it a reality in everyday life." Indeed, Stockman held that the platform had something for everyone: "a fair amount of sound traditional economic philosophy as well as some innovative things."

As the campaign drew to a close, ardent supply-siders feared their influence over Reagan was waning. Wanniski spotted a traditionalist in every corner waiting to woo the California governor over to the "old Calvinist view of the world where everyone has to suffer." As the September 21 Anderson–Reagan debate approached, Wanniski came up with the idea of having Stockman stand in for Anderson, his old employer, in a trial run for Reagan. He called Kemp, who in turn contacted an agreeable Reagan. Early in September, Stockman first met Reagan for a practice session.

Having mastered not only Anderson's positions but his mannerisms and speech patterns as well, Stockman so impressed Reagan in three mock debates that he was invited to impersonate Carter.

Later, when Stockman was asked who won, he replied, "I think Mr. Reagan did—ultimately, but I hit him pretty hard along the way. They even began to doubt my loyalty." Of the Carter mock debate, he said, "It was probably the toughest thing I've ever done. I had to have a crash course, a total immersion, in order to give his [Carter's] position on every issue imaginable."

It was this decision on Stockman's part that so bothered John Anderson and the others on his staff with whom Stockman had worked, and which caused Mike MacLeod to remark, "When we learned what he had done, we were *crushed.*"

Six days after Reagan's victory, the *Detroit News* was asking, "Will the Administration Pick From Us?" Many thought Stockman would be offered the Energy Secretary post, a position he did not want. Jack Strayer recalls, "Stockman was desperate for OMB." But the anxious congressman minimized the rumors: "I see what's being written in the papers but I really don't see any drastic changes in the works. I think I can do more good right where I am."

Wanniski had written an article in the summer of 1980 recommending cabinet heads for a Reagan government. "I wrote this piece and wound up suggesting William Agee [head of the Bendix Corporation], for OMB," says Wanniski, "and that suggestion came from none other than David Stockman." When it came time to choose Cabinet members, though, Agee was ruled out due to well-publicized rumors about his personal relationship with then Bendix Vice-President Mary Cunningham (whom he later married).

Prospects for installing supply-siders into top cabinet posts looked grim. The supply-siders pushed to have New York financier Lewis Lehrman named Treasury Secretary. But according to Arthur Laffer, Lehrman was "too radical for the [Milton] Friedmanites." New York financier and former Merrill Lynch head man Donald Regan got the job instead. Anxious for some representation, the supply-siders decided to lobby for Stockman as OMB director. "I talked to Stockman every day right up until the time he was appointed, trying to figure out ways we could make sure he got the OMB slot," says Wanniski.

A widely publicized memo sent to Reagan by Stockman and Kemp shortly after the election improved Stockman's visibility within the President-elect's inner circle. In the "Dunkirk Memo"— actually written by Stockman and based on an earlier, unnoticed paper by Lehrman—the President was urged to "declare a national

economic emergency soon after inauguration."[2] The two representatives suggested Reagan should tell Congress "that the economic,
financial, budget, energy and regulatory conditions he inherited are
far worse than anyone had imagined." In short, Reagan must grab
the "golden opportunity" for "permanent conservative policy revision."

Describing the federal government as a "coast-to-coast soupline"
in the twenty-three-page memo, Stockman and Kemp outlined
deep and sweeping cuts for the budget. This outline would become
the game plan for Stockman's work as head of OMB. Before a year
had passed, however, Kemp would shy away from the proposals and
come out against further budget cuts.

Although Reagan did not declare an economic emergency, as the
memo urged, and it was Kemp, not Stockman, who was invited to
the White House to discuss the paper and economic policy in
general, Stockman hung on to the hope that he would be named
OMB director. Kemp had little interest in the post and continued to
lobby on Stockman's behalf, as did the rest of the supply-siders, or
the "wild men," as Wanniski calls them.

A few days before Stockman received official word, he opened up
the morning's *Washington Post* and saw his name as that paper's
prediction for the OMB job. With him at the time was Jack Strayer,
who thinks "he might have cried—he was that happy. He wanted
that job more than anything."

On Thanksgiving Day, Reagan called to offer Stockman the
budget post. Joking about the mock debates that had pitted the two
men against one another and subsequent whispering that Stockman
had beaten Reagan, the President said, "I've been looking for a way
to get even. I think I'll send you to OMB." And so, weeks before his
confirmation hearings were even held, Stockman "hit the ground
running" and set about the task of making sweeping changes in the
federal budget.

---

2. The full text of the memo is reprinted as Appendix A.

II

REAL POWER: GETTING AND LOSING IT

6 • Young Man With an Axe

"I HAVE NOT filed a formal statement this morning because I have submitted thirty or forty pages to the committee in response to a wide series of questions, both on substantive policy issues as well as management and organizational issues regarding OMB. But I do wish to make a few comments before we begin the questioning this morning."

It was January 8, 1981, and David Stockman, *sans* prepared text, was appearing before the Senate Committee of Government Affairs for his confirmation hearing as OMB director. Text or no text, he managed to ad-lib a few hundred well-chosen—and increasingly self-confident—words before the questioning began. It was a proud moment for David A. Stockman:

> Mr. Chairman, for the past eleven years, I have devoted myself to the study of important and difficult issues of public policy with which OMB must contend, and I have done so from the end of Pennsylvania Avenue that ultimately disposes these issues—the Congress of the United States.
>
> Mr. Chairman, I started at the bottom as a Congressional intern eleven years ago. I developed professional skills in policy analysis as a legislative assistant in the House. I gained management and leadership experience as executive director of the House Republican Conference, a post in which I served for four years. More importantly, during the past four years as your colleague I have learned some invaluable lessons about the pervasive tensions between good and desirable public policies on the one hand, and the necessities for accommodation and compromise on the other.
>
> And I believe this experience that I have in the Congress is unique among the many distinguished public servants who have served at OMB and its predecessor agency, the Bureau of the Budget.
>
> It has convinced me that the budget process, and the process of economic policy formulation in the broader sense, must always be a

cooperative endeavor between the executive and legislative branches. The cost to the Nation of a breakdown in that relationship can be severe and sometimes irreparable.

I think it is especially true at this difficult time in the history of our Nation. The basic performance level of our economy has deteriorated very badly these recent months and years. In 1970, I would venture to suggest that there was probably not one in a thousand economists who believed that we could experience nearly eight percent unemployment, vast idle industrial capacity, twenty-one percent interest rates, unprecedented growth rates in the money supply, and rising double-digit inflation all at the same time.

But that is the unfortunate state of affairs today. Nor was there one budget expert in a thousand who believed that Congress could make a good faith effort to pass a balanced budget, subsequently pass a reconciliation bill last fall, enact relatively tight appropriations bills, and still end up seven months later with outlays that are now estimated to be $45 billion above the forecast of last June, with revenues that are now estimated to be $15 billion below the forecast of last June. We do not have the first balanced budget in fifteen years, as we had expected, but instead face one of the largest deficits in the history of the Federal Government.

That, too, is the fact of life that we face today.

In my view, Mr. Chairman, these facts are sobering. They define the dimension and magnitude of the task facing our President-elect as he seeks to formulate new economic, tax, budget, and regulatory policies designed to stop this deterioration. And they define my prospective challenge at OMB and yours here in the Senate of the United States.

In conclusion, Mr. Chairman, while I am a sober realist about the problem that we face, I am an optimist about the solution because I know that the members of this committee and the Congress as a whole are determined to find a workable solution. If members of this committee and of the Senate choose to confirm me, I can assure you as an ex-colleague, that I will remain a strong, steady, and accessible ally as together we seek to resolve the economic difficulties which afflict our Nation today. . . .

One has to wonder what the senators thought of a two-term member of the House of Representatives referring to them as "ex-colleagues." In the special language of Capitol Hill, it is one thing for a senator, flush with noblesse oblige, to call a congressman "colleague" (as several did to David Stockman) but quite another for the congressman to presume to use the term.

For the most part, the questioning was not what anyone would call "tough," but there were some pointed queries. Senator William Cohen of Maine, who mentioned that he and Stockman had been acquaintances since their days at the John F. Kennedy Institute of Politics at Harvard, quizzed Stockman about an article written by Howard Samuels, a former Under Secretary of Commerce. Said the senator, "Inflation in short is a social and political problem that cannot be solved by monetarist tinkering or a package of business tax breaks, according to Mr. Samuels."

Stockman responded:

> . . . I read that article very carefully and I have to say that I disagree with it about ninety-eight percent. I think it sounds rather persuasive or rather interesting on the surface, until you realize the whole article is a tautology. It says basically that inflation equals high costs, and that it is only a matter of whose costs you don't like. I don't think that unions are causing inflation. I don't think that wage costs are causing inflation. If we get into that kind of an analysis, it becomes merely an arbitrary kind of political gamesmanship. . . .
>
> I don't think we are going to break the inflation spiral. I think it would be totally fruitless. I think it would be an absolute waste of time to go chasing some of these costs through an activist Government program depending on who has got the most muscle in Congress or elsewhere.

Not willing to give up on Mr. Samuels's argument, Senator Cohen persisted: "What he [Samuels] was suggesting was not simply allowing an untargeted reduction in corporate taxes without some incentive to reinvest. . . . Do you totally rule that out as a policy you would advocate?"

David Stockman's reply might as well have been drafted by the Chamber of Commerce: "I guess I would say that I don't think we need any legal assurance that funds that are retained by the business sector after a tax cut will be reinvested. They will be sooner or later in one way or another. . . . They don't go into a mattress." So much for prognostication.

The toughest questioner was Ohio Democrat John Glenn, who wasted no time in coming to the point. "Mr. Stockman, you have been very critical of the entitlements programs and the way they grow. We are all concerned about this. Can you give us a list or give us your priorities in cutting back on entitlements? Which ones would you cut first?"

Stockman replied:

> . . . I can state for you today my general approach, my general philosophy on the matter, and that is to say that I believe that in some general or theoretical sense that entitlements are very good things, for those groups in our society who have a very clear case for public support, for public benefits due to reasons that are beyond their capacity to control in the kind of society and economy that we live in today.
>
> But having stated that principle, my further point is that these entitlements have to be defined carefully. I am afraid that in the case of food stamps, social security, and many others over the years, we have added elaborations, new categories and new elements of eligibility in a way that has not been very thoughtful, in a way that has not been entirely justifiable. That is the kind of review we need, not of the program, but of the universe of people it covers. . . .

That did not quite satisfy Senator Glenn. "I would hope that you could give us a better rundown of where you would see your top priorities." Reading to the witness, Glenn reminded Stockman that he had once written that "Welfare as we know it should be abolished for all but the non-working—the aged, blind and disabled whose eligibility can be ascertained by reference to physical characteristics."

"That is a rather harsh cutoff," said Glenn. "Do you still subscribe to that?"

Stockman pointed out that the line in question had been written in reference to the AFDC program specifically, and then added, as if it somehow softened what he had written, "That wasn't any policy that I have ever introduced in a bill or anything else."

Next, Glenn asked Stockman what he had meant when he wrote of "a coast-to-coast soupline," and this time the witness said, "I guess I should say, first, that sometimes my metaphors may not be quite as exact as they should be." Later, after more prodding from the Ohio Democrat, this time regarding his views on reindustrialization, Stockman commented, to general laughter, "Let me say . . . if I do manage to get confirmed for this job, I think I am going to stop writing."

In answer to a question from Senator David Pryor of Arkansas, Stockman cited his disapproval of yet another idea that he would later support, in the form of Gramm–Rudman–Hollings, a balanced budget amendment:

The effect, then, would be to throw into the courts in one way or another the responsibility for defining expenditures, and the responsibility would not simply stop with definition. It would sooner or later have to move to substantive considerations and decisions as well, and in the process the Congress would have alienated one of the central and essential powers that were granted by the Constitution; namely, the power to raise and spend money for the public interests of this country.

So I don't think it is a very workable solution in the operational sense, but I certainly understand the motivation, the objective behind it, and I just happen to have enough confidence in the capacity of the members of this Congress and in the more regular procedures that we created, the budget process, and so forth, to solve the problem that that proposal has generated without creating an enormous new set of problems in the process.

In the second round of questions, Senator Thomas Eagleton of Missouri reminded Stockman that he had, as a congressman, said on the House floor, "deficits themselves are neither good or bad. They promote neither inflation nor employment. They cause neither recession nor expansion. In fact, they are absolute economic eunuchs until they join hands with other policies and other economic facts." Why, asked the senator, having said that, had Stockman just testified that budget deficits were the *only* cause of inflation? Stockman responded, "I don't think I said that." He went on to add that "the ultimate cause of all inflation is excessive money creation."

Senator Glenn was even sharper in his requestioning of Stockman. Of course, he had no way of knowing that a quote he read from an interview with Stockman in *The Village Voice* had a distinct note of foreshadowing in it. "Reindustrialization policy," the OMB director-designate had said in 1980, "is just a game for hyping the political control over the forces of the economy and for preserving the weakest assets in the economy."

"How do you square that with what you just told me?" asked Senator Glenn.

Stockman: I think I agree with that statement.

Glenn: You just told me you were for reindustrialization. Now you are saying it is a hyping of "political control over the forces of the economy and preserving the weakest assets in the economy," and that is the only purpose of it.

Stockman: The context was reindustrialization policy employing some mechanism like a reconstruction finance corporation.

Glenn: That wasn't mentioned in this interview.

Stockman: That was the context in which it was stated. They didn't necessarily reprint everything I said. But what I was saying is that if you do create a Central Government program to reindustrialize and you create something like a reconstruction finance corporation, that political muscle will determine how capital is allocated. I don't think that is a good solution.

Glenn: *The Village Voice* has drastically misrepresented your views here.

Stockman: That could be the case. It has happened to me before. I am sure it has probably happened to you and others on the committee on occasion.

After another exchange that failed to satisfy him, Senator Glenn said, in apparent frustration, "I am having a difficult time getting a good answer, as to how we are going to reindustrialize, and where the money is going to come from. You said a while ago as general economic conditions improved we should let business retain more profits to invest as they see fit. I agree with that. However, that is long term. What do you do now about the steel industry . . . about the auto industry? Unless we find some way of getting some capital back into these industries, they may never recover. How are we going to take care of that during your four years in office?"

Stockman's very general answer was another piece of evidence to support the thesis that he was far better at taking apart—and destroying—someone else's program than he was at building one of his own.

Toward the end of the hearing, in response to a question from Maine's Senator Cohen about his opposition to tax credits for conservation, Stockman expanded on his answer, saying, "I don't think energy is a social policy issue. I think maybe stable homes might be. I think maybe private schools might be. I think maybe preserving ethnic neighborhoods might be. But I don't think energy is. It is an economic issue."

Senator Cohen took a broader and more humane view, and in

explaining it, he put his finger on what so many people see as Stockman's greatest failing—his inability to see the people behind the lines on the pages of his budget documents:

> Heating of homes creates a certain social problem. . . . You indicated that you did not want to raise any economic philosophy to a status of a theology. I agree with you wholeheartedly. But it occurred to me as I was listening to your statements about the need for deregulation, about the free market system, I tried to bring it back to a practical application.
>
> I talked to my father this morning. He turned seventy-two and is still working in his little bakery shop. In Bangor, Maine, it is thirty-five below zero. Maine happens to be a very poor state economically. We have perhaps the lowest per capita income of any state, under six thousand dollars a year. Now we have had temperatures at thirty-five below zero for the past week. We have people who can't heat their homes.
>
> Assuming we permit immediate deregulation, assuming the price of oil climbs five or ten cents per gallon, or higher, what do I tell the people of the State of Maine who can't pay their oil bills and those deliverers who can't deliver the oil? It creates social as well as economic problems. So you don't have an absolute clear economic philosophy. You have to consider the social consequences and implications of that economic philosophy.

Stockman, of course, had an answer for the senator's mild lecture. But the point of Senator Cohen's lecture, as the events of the next five years would make clear again and again, was very well taken.

Stockman exhibited such zeal and grabbed so many headlines in the first few months of the Reagan Administration that budget cutting often appeared to be not merely the major but the *only* issue in Washington. He got off to a remarkably quick start on the budget during the transition, ferreting into the details of departmental programs before most cabinet members had decided on the quickest way to commute to the office. Stockman also had the advantage of a clear head start, having drawn up a "counter budget" in March of 1980 with conservative Representative Phil Gramm, who became a key ally in the 1982 budget battle. Armed with these advantages, Stockman acted swiftly, leaving most cabinet appointees with little time to repudiate massive cuts in their programs.

Of all the President's men, David Stockman emerged as the most responsible for the selling of Reaganomics. His role in the budget battle was that not only that of star but also of main producer and director. The quintessential power broker, with his fingers on all levers of government, Stockman drew to himself—many would say usurped—from the agencies and Congress, the power of control over the federal budget. His budget efforts drew some fiery condemnations, both for the substance of the cuts he proposed and for the legislative techniques he used to move them into law. As star of the budget spectacle, Stockman "brought the House down," according to Representative Pat Schroeder (D-CO)—"down to the level of trained seals."

As budget director, Stockman vaulted to national prominence. In one year, he went from being a junior—though vocal—representative in a minority party to the top of the Washington power structure, a regular guest on network television and before congressional committees, and a familiar face on the covers of national magazines.

At the time of Stockman's appointment in November 1980, the bulk of cabinet positions had not yet been filled. Of those who had been appointed, a majority were taking a deep breath before jumping into the grueling months ahead. Few had much background in the programs they were to run; only a handful, such as Caspar Weinberger at Defense, Richard Schweiker at Health and Human Services, and Alexander Haig at State, had significant Washington experience. While most of Washington was slowly gearing up for the change of power, Stockman launched into a flurry of activity. Still in his Longworth Building congressional office, Stockman began poring over the 613-page budget proposed by Carter line by line, item by item, looking for cuts beyond the $25 billion he and Phil Gramm had presented to the Budget Committee a few months before. It was a Herculean task, immediately raised to the level of legend by sympathetic Washington columnists. Commenting on this line-by-line review of the budget (which for most people would hold about as much charm as reading through the Manhattan telephone directory), *Time* magazine's Hugh Sidey could hardly contain himself: "With the help of a handful of aides, he analyzed every significant governmental issue." (In his book *Greed Is Not Enough*, Robert Lekachman rejoined, "Oh, wow, as Charles Reich used to say.")

The success of Stockman's efforts rested on the support of his boss, Ronald Reagan. In a September 1980 speech, the presidential candidate had told the American people, "One of the most critical elements of my economic program is the control of government spending. Waste, extravagance, abuse and outright fraud in federal agencies and programs must be stopped. Billions of the taxpayers' dollars are wasted every year throughout hundreds of federal programs. . . ."

Reagan may have convinced the voters that budget reductions could be enacted painlessly, but in Washington few officials were convinced. Chairman of the Senate Budget Committee Pete Domenici (R-NM) took a hard line in early January of 1981: "You never heard Pete Domenici make the argument that you could have significant defense increases and multiyear tax cuts simply by eliminating waste and fraud." Stockman knew this too, in private at least. He would later tell William Greider, "The idea is to try and get beyond the waste, fraud and mismanagement modality and begin to confront the real dimensions of budget reduction." But at the time of the budget hearings, the administration's budget campaign continued to rest on assuring the public that while "waste" was being eliminated, the truly needy were being cared for.

Throughout his campaign, Reagan's commitment to a balanced budget was emphatic. For the ills of the economy, he insisted, "The cure is a balanced budget." When Stockman met with the President in January, he used the frightening possibility of twelve-digit deficits as leverage to convince Reagan to seek deep budget cuts from the Hill.

Fearful that cabinet heads would become more resistant to cuts as time passed and they grew aware of their programs, Stockman raced to assemble his package of reductions. In the past, career employees at OMB had made budget recommendations that, if approved, were sent ever higher in the OMB ranks. Under Stockman, however, decisions were made first and then filtered down. It came to be called "top down management." "My impression," remarked one former OMB official, "based on conversations with some of the career people over there, is that Stockman is using his professional staff as gophers. They enjoy the new prestige OMB has. But Stockman decides on a cut and then tells them to go out and justify it." "We have become more producers of fast information rather than more thoughtful analysis and review," complained one OMB reviewer. "Things were frantic around OMB after we threw out the Carter budget," says another OMB professional; "in some cases we made decisions based on anything proposed from above, rather than getting additional information and doing a check ourselves."

Presidential approval for specific reductions came after meetings with Stockman, Reagan, and the cabinet chief whose programs were affected. The heavy-handedness displayed by Stockman in those meetings foreshadowed his tactics in dealing with the House. At least one cabinet member got word of Stockman's plans and schemes. An employee in Stockman's office at the time remembers taking a call from a high-ranking official who explained half jokingly, "I just wanted to call and find out if I've still got a department to head." Unaware of the proposals to be decided upon that day, cabinet members were ushered into these sessions and handed papers outlining and justifying the cuts to be considered. Given the circumstances, nearly anyone would be hard-pressed to repudiate Stockman's axe — let alone someone like Energy Secretary James Edwards. Add to this what Stockman described as "the group line"—that line being simply "cut, cut, cut"—and you are bound to make a gaggle of cabinet heads, as Stockman told Bill Greider, "resentful very fast." Despite bruised feelings, when push came to shove, Stockman usually got the cuts he wanted in the early months.

When these private consultations did not yield the desired results, Stockman often made his aims public. Stockman outraged Edwards and his staff by pushing too hard and too loudly for an immediate decontrol of oil prices early in 1981. "That little gray-haired ideologue punched our clock good," steamed one Edwards aide. "He made points with the political types in the White House and left us to clear up the mess under the hot lights." Secretary of State Alexander Haig showed little patience with this tactic. Early on, Stockman and Haig became embroiled in a public dispute over a leaked OMB memo that proposed to halve foreign aid, a dispute that sent Stockman scurrying to make amends with the State Department.

Edwards did not always lose. In a dispute over the signing of a synfuels contract, Reagan overrode Stockman's objections. Opposing the plant on the grounds that the free market, not the federal government, ought to develop synfuel technology, at one point Stockman produced a photograph of an oil shale project built by

Gulf and Amoco—displaying it as proof the projects did not need government aid. Edwards looked confused, conferred with his aides, and later sent President Reagan a letter explaining that Gulf and Amoco had applied for government subsidies for the project. Of the photograph, Edwards said, "It was rather misleading in a way." Of the incident, "I'd like to believe that Dave Stockman was sincerely trying to help me . . . I'd like to believe he was."

Throughout, Stockman was not only looking for cuts but for a way to make the economy work. Reagan's new OMB director told *The Wall Street Journal* in December 1980, "At OMB my job will be to produce growth through economic policy." What Stockman wound up doing, according to his detractors, was trying to produce growth through rosy economic assumptions about how the economy would perform. To supply-siders, optimistic economic assumptions were a prerequisite for putting the economy in the mood to grow. Predictably, the tactic backfired—no matter how optimistic the assumptions in the OMB computer, the economy would tell its own story.

When Stockman was first appointed, he ran the Reagan economic program through test runs using both Congressional Budget Office and Carter assumptions. The results that issued forth from the computers were, as Stockman would tell Greider, "absolutely shocking."

Although shaken, Stockman would assure Greider he had been using "conventional estimates" of the economy's behavior and intended to find purveyors of less conventional predictions. Treasury Secretary Donald Regan and OMB's chief economist Lawrence Kudlow joined in Stockman's search. "We're going to avoid forecasts," announced Regan. "The figures from which most traditional forecasters work are just not meaningful."

It was not an easy search. The most satisfactory model the group could find was one developed by John Rutledge of the Claremont Economics Institute in California. The model Rutledge peddled differed from most in that it assumed that unusually large changes in the economy would take place as a result of changes in public expectations.

Still, the Rutledge model was not enough to make Reaganomics come out right. Retaining (even enlarging) the Rutledge effect of public expectations, Stockman along with others, including conservative economist Alan Greenspan, took matters into their own hands. What they came up with was not a formal model (which can take years to develop), but a general outlook, a scenario of the way the world should work under the Reagan economic plan.

It was not a matter of Stockman sneaking back into his office in the middle of the night to tamper with HAL at OMB, as his critics have charged. It was a matter of the administration adopting economic assumptions that few economists would buy. "It would be wonderful, if the Reagan program would work," said Otto Eckstein, a conventional economist. "If it doesn't, we've got only one economy to sacrifice."

Others were less sarcastic in their assessment, but no less negative. "Stockman is not competent as an economist," exclaimed one former OMB official. "He doesn't understand the parameters of these things. For instance, he claims that if we cut taxes, people will work longer. Most economists believe that would have an effect, but it won't be nearly as large as they claim. Stockman chooses to believe it will have a great effect. And if he would look at the studies, he would see that he is wrong—it's sort of like theology, but believing just won't make it so." (A January 20, 1982, Commerce report would show that despite the Reagan Administration tax cuts, the average work week was down by one hour.) A House budget aide put matters more bluntly: "Either Stockman is a nut or he's a liar. Maybe he's both. This simply won't pan out."

Although the administration's economic assumptions received less attention than the budget cuts sent up to the Hill, they did produce some gasps of astonishment. Representative J. J. Pickle (D-TX) dubbed the predictions "jelly bean talk," and speculated that the highest ranking woman in the Reagan force was "Rosy Scenario." Representative Thomas Downey (D-NY) attacked the numbers as "threadbare evidence" leading to "hallucinogenic visions." And Chairman of the House Budget Committee James R. Jones pointed out that "the administration assumes simultaneous increases in growth and drops in inflation and interest rates which have never occurred in our history." Even Senator Mark Andrews (R-ND) called Stockman on his numbers: "You and I served together in the House and I remember we had the old GIGO rule on computers, and we laughed about it: garbage in, garbage out. Well, if we put in the wrong figures, and base assumptions and changes on wrong figures, we are going to come up with some wrong answers."

While the tradition of the OMB director providing the President with "neutral competence" had been eroding throughout the previous two decades, Stockman smashed the notion to bits. He emerged as a clear advocate of particular assumptions and a particular program down to the last gritty detail. Stockman's role as super-peddler of Reaganomics drew this critique from House Budget Chairman Jones, who had served under Johnson: ". . . a president's intentions are only as good as the advice he gets. And, if the President is not getting credible advice, he is going to have erroneous perceptions that have to be corrected later."

Though obscure, the importance of these figures cannot be overstated. Small changes in the projected rates of unemployment, interest, and inflation could cause billions of dollars of changes in projected federal expenditures, revenues, and deficits. By juggling the numbers, the administration was originally able to mask the unprecedented deficits that, if known at the outset, surely would have hardened congressional resistance to the President's equally unprecedented tax cut. "The whole budget debate was really over economic assumptions. Those assumptions drive the size of the budget. They were the only way the administration's circle could be squared," insists a House budget aide. "You have this crazy situation on the floor where Jones uses fairly realistic estimates and comes up with a budget of $714 billion. Gramm responds by slamming his fist on the desk, 'What difference does it make?' The point is the assumptions didn't change anything. What people ought to look at in the budget is how much we cut services. That's the only relevant factor."

Regularly, the glowing forecast would conflict with the economic reality of 1981. In an appearance before the House Appropriations Committee early that year, Stockman said, "I have suggested our program, if fully effective, will create more than two million new jobs a year over the next several years." Stockman had the right numbers but in the wrong direction. Nearly two million people *lost* their jobs over the course of 1981. In February 1982, Chairman of the Appropriations Committee Jamie Whitten (D-MS) read Stockman's two million statement back to him and announced, "We are going to have to interrupt today because we are going to have to pass a bill providing $2.3 billion for unemployment compensation."

On May 22, 1980, a position paper entitled, "The Giamo Balanced Budget: A Trojan Horse By Any Other Name," had been inserted into the *Congressional Record*. It dubbed the Robert Giamo (D-CT) budget a

> fabulous political fiction—a legislative hoax worthy of Orson Welles' 1930's radio broadcast on the landing of the Martians.
>
> The Giamo "balanced budget" was the proverbial house of cards, a series of constructs based on forecasts of outlays, revenues and economic conditions that had started to tumble even before it was adopted.

The author of the article was David Stockman. Just a year later, the same words could be used to describe his own program.

Armed with the President's broad approval for $40 billion in domestic cuts, Stockman concentrated on little else. For Stockman, budget cutting became an obsession—an obsession that worried the very supply siders who had pressed so hard to have him appointed. Deep budget cuts were not part of the supply-side agenda. Instead, they felt social spending would shrink naturally as the economy grew through the effects of their tax cuts. More importantly, they feared Stockman's devotion to budget slashing was distracting attention on the Hill and in the media from the tax reductions they sought. Ardent supply-sider Jude Wanniski had his first serious misgivings about the OMB director soon after Stockman's appointment upon spying Stockman and economist Alan Greenspan sitting in a corner at the New York Harvard Club contemplating drastic budget cuts. According to Wanniski, " 'A hundred million here, a million there in cuts,' that's how they were talking. So I walked over and picked up some peanuts from a bowl and began to drop them in, one by one. 'Peanuts,' I said, 'here's a hundred million worth of orphans you'll drive into the snow.' "

Says Wanniski, "Those cuts were all part of Stockman's Calvinist view of the world. He says, 'You're all sinners, especially you, the poor, so put on your hairshirts and suffer.' " Wanniski's disgust with Stockman's view of the world prompted him, according to sources, to call Stockman to his face "Jimmy Carter's budget director."

At the start of February, Stockman sent advance copies of his black books outlining his cuts to Republican leadership on the Hill, copies that were quickly obtained by the press. Barraged with cries of "balancing the budget on the backs of the poor," Stockman countered by insisting he had maintained an adequate social safety net for those at, near, or below poverty levels. Yet, as conservative columnists Rowland Evans and Robert Novak announced, "No matter how much talk there was of a 'safety net' for the poor, the principal social thrust of Reagan's revolutionary budget was a shrinking of welfare aid."

Formally releasing the budget one month later, President Reagan justified the cuts by saying, "I'm committed to stopping the spending juggernaut. If more cuts are needed to keep within our spending ceilings, I will not hesitate to propose them." Although the President never went so far as to announce an "economic emergency" as Stockman and Kemp did in their "Economic Dunkirk Memo," he did make a future without Reaganomics look bleak.

Within a week of Reagan's speech, the administration had succeeded in mobilizing attention on its economic plan—most specifically on the budget cuts. The actual cuts, rumors about the cuts, those marginally associated with the cuts, and the chief cutter himself, David Stockman, dominated newspaper headlines, magazine covers, and gossip during congressional lunches. In the course of stumping for his program, Stockman appeared regularly as a guest on political talk shows. Less than two weeks after Reagan's speech, on ABC's "Issues and Answers," Stockman revealed his justification for drastic budget cuts: "The idea that's been established over the last ten years, that almost every service that someone might need in life ought to be provided, financed by government as a matter of basic right, is wrong. We challenge that. We reject that notion."

This stark belittling of social welfare policy earned Stockman *The New York Times*'s "Quote of the Day." It also sent spokesmen at the White House scurrying to soften the hard edge of the budget director's statement. In the same interview, Stockman made it clear who was going to bear the brunt of his challenge when he declared, "I just don't accept the assumption that the Federal Government has a responsibility to supplement the income of the working poor." In short, while President Johnson had declared a "war on poverty," David Stockman was now prepared to fight a war on the poor.

An analysis of the OMB director's proposed cuts demonstrated his dedication to that purpose. The Democratic Study Group reported in early April 1981 that 75 percent of Stockman's slashes were directed at the poor. Numerous later studies by such non-partisan groups as the Congressional Budget Office and the Urban Institute would confirm these conclusions. One former welfare official in the Nixon years, Thomas Joe of the University of Chicago's Center for the Study of Social Policy, reported that Stockman's reductions would more than halve the incomes of many of those at or below the poverty line of $8,410 for a family of four, to less than $4,200 a year.

In a February 1982 hearing, an exasperated Senator Eagleton told Stockman, "When one starts with the premise that virtually everything the Federal Government does is evil, the capacity for subtle distinctions vanishes pretty quickly." Indeed, Stockman insisted with clockwork regularity that the federal government retreat, most especially in the area of social welfare policy. Stockman drew upon the views set forth in neo-conservative journals like *The Public Interest* and *Commentary*—ideas set forth by newly disaffected liberals who viewed the Great Society with alarm, even terror. By the mid-1970s, Edward Banfield, writing for *Commentary*, had an explanation of the Great Society for his readers: "As Americans become more and more affluent, schooled and leisured they discover (and also invent) more and more 'social problems' which (they fondly suppose) can be solved." In essence, Banfield told his readers that they were too rich, too smart, and too lazy for their own good. Charles Frankel, also in *Commentary*, reduced arguments for social policy to cultural pettiness: "Not being able to go to Harvard, though undoubtedly a misfortune in the eyes of the Lord, is still not an acute hardship." And Franklin Hunt, another *Commentary* contributor and a New York lawyer, viewed public interest lawyers as the most dangerous of the "do gooders." He called it "sobering to think what we may be in for from governments with a duty to correct the defects in society discovered by lawyers with teen-age ideas of injustice."

George Gilder, author of *Wealth and Poverty*, added to these disclaimers of social policy by elevating unfettered capitalism to near-religious status. Any "interference" with the "invisible hand" of the marketplace (read any welfare policy), he asserted, actually harmed the poor by causing them to rely on government. It was an idea that Stockman, along with much of Reagan's administration, heartily embraced. (A few months after Reagan assumed office, the following joke became standard fare at Washington political gatherings. Question: How many Reagan officials does it take to change a lightbulb? Answer: None. They sit in the dark and wait for the invisible hand.) Stockman grandiosely called Gilder's book, "Promethean in its insight."

In fact, this argument was only a refinement of the anti-government bromides Reagan had been dispensing for decades. As OMB director, Stockman perfected one of Ronald Reagan's old habits: the art of pitting the taxpayer against the non-taxpayer, with the latter being portrayed as continually out to cheat and defraud the system. Candidate Reagan's account of the *mythical* "Chicago Welfare Queen" was criticized by Ralph Nader's Center for the Study of Responsive Law:

> During one speech she had twelve different names, thirty social security numbers, collected veterans benefits from four dead and nonexistent husbands, because, naturally she's an unwed mother on AFDC. Another time she had eighty names, thirty addresses and phone numbers, but still only four dead husbands—her annual take was $150,000. In fact, the woman was convicted long ago for using four aliases to fraudulently collect $8,000 in benefits.

Some members of Congress railed at what Representative Bill Hefner (D-NC) called Stockman's use of "code words." Addressing Stockman at a February 17, 1982, hearing, Hefner charged:

> You would think there is three hundred billion dollars [in waste, fraud, and abuse] in the food stamp program. I was in the Holiday Inn having breakfast and a lady said, "I want to talk to you about something." I said, "I'm not very busy, have a seat." She said, "I want you to support the President. I am sick of seeing them people go to the grocery store and get groceries and getting beer with food stamps and get in a new Cadillac or Oldsmobile and driving off."
>
> I submit that if there are that many people getting food stamps and driving off in Oldsmobiles, GM wouldn't be in the position they are today. Don't use code words.

Yet, while members of the administration lectured that helping the poor was really hurting the poor, under pressure they admitted that if assistance became truly necessary, they would prefer that the private sector, not the government, do the assisting. Thus were born Reagan's exhortations to reinvigorate the "spirit of volunteerism" in America. Reagan's cries fell a little flat. He had already whipped the ire of the taxpayer into a frenzy. Helping the poor was out of vogue.

Even where the "spirit of volunteerism" and charitable institutions still exist, they are in fact hopelessly inadequate; an October 1981 *Washington Post* story describes sixty to one hundred men lining up each day to receive an average of 60 cents from an area church. And the mayor of one Florida city, in the hopes of discouraging people from picking through garbage cans in search of food, suggested dousing garbage with kerosene to stave off the human "vermin."

Indeed, there were a number of items left in the budget that made it look as if Stockman was going after "weak clients" rather than "weak claims." Stockman's critics pointed to the myriad of business subsidies left untouched as the administration attacked social welfare policy. A particularly ironic subsidy was funds for the Tennessee Clinch River Breeder Reactor—also known on the Hill as the "Howard Baker Protection Special." As a congressman, Stockman had maintained that the reactor was a waste of money.

When asked whether a five percent cut in aid would be difficult for a family at poverty level, Stockman replied, "I don't know." And in a particularly fiery exchange with Stockman concerning the decision (later revoked) to eliminate the FTC's antitrust authority, Representative Benjamin Rosenthal (D-NY) quoted a *Legal Times* article that stated, "The decision was made on the basis of a two-page memo after less than a minute's deliberation by the OMB director, David Stockman." In reply, Stockman insisted this was untrue and in fact claimed he had been "deliberating on it for about ten years," and further maintained that his ruminations on the subject had begun "at a very early age." Yet, childhood fantasies of budget cutting aside, Stockman later admitted to Greider, "We were doing the whole of the budget-cutting exercise so frenetically . . . trying to cut housing programs here and rural electric there, and we were doing it so fast that we didn't know where we were winding up for sure."

7 • On Top of the Job, the Budget, and the World

DAVID STOCKMAN devoted an unprecedented amount of time and energy to his program throughout the winter and spring of 1981. Those around the OMB director noted he seemed to thrive on working sixteen hour days, seven days a week. Representative Richard Gephardt (D-MO) took time out of a hearing on Social Security to remark, "Dave, your hair is getting less gray than it was when you were in Congress. I don't know whether that means you are enjoying your work or whether you are using Grecian Formula."

On a typical day, Stockman rose at 5:00 A.M. and donned a suit bought at Britches of Georgetown, a conservative white shirt, and a sincere red tie. (In early June 1982, the press would gleefully report that the manager of the federal budget had bounced an $800 clothing check.) At six-thirty a limousine would be waiting outside the Towers in northwest Washington, the luxury condominium building from which Stockman would shortly emerge. Formerly the home of George Meany and Jimmy Hoffa, among others, the building offers a nail manicurist, tight security, and $10,000 a year underground parking. One of Stockman's neighbors across the street commented, "He comes out of his fancy apartment building, gets into a fancy car, drives to a fancy office—all you need to do is take one look and you know the man is immune to about ninety percent of the world's population."

The waiting limo shuttled Stockman to the Old Executive Office Building (again tight security) alongside the White House. Here, too, one can feel slightly out of touch with reality. As *The New York Times* recently wrote of the building:

> Crowned by a steep mansard roof and graced by elaborate pavilions, the OEOB has 553 rooms and is a stunning melange of 14-foot ceilings and

awninged windows, of thousands of decorative columns and bronze staircase balusters. It was designed by Alfred B. Mullett, a Government architect gifted with a traveler's eye and an appreciation for the New Louvre in Paris that led him to adapt the Second Empire style of French architecture to the fresh appetites of post–Centennial America.

Throughout most of February and a good deal of March, Stockman was delivering testimony and taking questions on the Hill almost daily; on more than one occasion he crammed in spots before as many as three committees in a single day.

The OMB director was the top draw of the season. Teen-age interns with pocket cameras, business lobbyists with briefcases in tow, and Hill staff with yellow legal pads appeared to wait in line an hour before Stockman was scheduled to testify. All hoped for a closeup of Washington's newest star. An entourage of eight to ten cameramen with sound crews invariably accompanied his appearances on the Hill. From February to March of 1981, Stockman graced the committee rooms on at least twenty different occasions. All told, the OMB director probably spent more time on the Hill during the year than his last three predecessors combined.

When one considers the $750 billion-plus budget he was trying to control, he scuttled to the Hill for any number of seemingly minuscule items—from defending $100 million cuts in housing to soothing a pouting Delbert Latta (R-OH), who felt that as a Republican his name ought to precede Phil Gramm's in naming the budget resolution.

Sitting bolt upright, with his ankles tucked back beneath his chair, Stockman fielded innumerable questions on his proposals. His facts were not always as accurate as his sincere presentation would lead his listeners to believe. Discussing his proposed cutbacks in college loans, Stockman explained, "In the 1960s we didn't have Pell Grants. . . . Yet tens of millions of college students from lower, middle and upper income families alike found their way through college." Of that statement, Jane Bryant Quinn of *The Washington Post* remarked wryly, "Moving as he does in all-college circles, Stockman may not realize how charmed those circles used to be. In 1965 only 5.5 million people in the entire nation were in college. Among 18 to 21 year olds, 39 percent were undergraduates." Nor was Representative Pete Stark (D-CA) overly impressed with Stockman. He recalled that when Stockman was first elected to Congress, his secretary approached Stark, a former bank president, looking for help. "She said part of her job was to balance Stockman's checkbook, that he knew nothing about investments or insurance or how to balance his book," remembers Stark. "So, I sent my secretary to Trover's and ordered a copy of *Sylvia Porter's Money Book*. And that's the basis on which she taught David how to manage his money."

Behind all of Stockman's arguments, insists one House staff member, "was a shoddy syllogism which amounted to sheer sophistry. When you get right down to it, Stockman was simply repeating over and over, 'Budget cuts are good. These are budget cuts. Therefore these are good.' " Pressured to make sweeping changes in a few weeks, many representatives and senators threw up their hands in despair at these hearings, disgusted by both the time limits on their questions and the inadequate information they were receiving from Stockman. Comments by Representative Mary Rose Oakar (D-OH) in the course of a hearing on subsidized housing typified these frustrations: "If I can't ask of him [Stockman] a question because he doesn't have another hour to stay, then how are those people who can't pay for lobbying, those people who don't have the money to pay for these active lobbyists, how are their voices going to be heard?" Likewise in a Budget hearing, Senator Howard Metzenbaum (D-OH) protested, "Mr. Chairman, I do not mind him [Stockman] speaking, but I am on limited time, I do not want to hear this political speech, because this is a political speech."

All in all, it was almost impossible to press a point with the budget director. Representative Thomas Downey (D-NY) cut Stockman short at one hearing: "If I don't interrupt you, you will use my whole five minutes in a marvelous lecture." As Representative Pat Schroeder observed, "You have five minutes to question. Your first question takes thirty seconds. As a former congressman, Stockman knows better than anyone that all you need do to slip out of that question is filibuster for four and a half minutes. It's a built-in guarantee that you can worm your way out of anything."

Stockman rarely argued for additional funds for any program or agency. In a hypocritical twist, however, the budget cutter appeared before a House Appropriations subcommittee in May 1981 asking for an extra $4.1 million for OMB, raising his budget to $38.1 million. When Stockman claimed that his agency had taken on increased responsibilities, Representative Edward Roybal (D-CA) remarked pointedly, "That's what they all tell us—they have increased responsibilities." Representative Sidney Yates (D-IL) observed, "I can recognize the burden . . . but I think every other agency can make the same argument." Asked how he could justify hiking the budget of his own agency while he slashed all the others, Stockman conceded at one point, "It's not easy to explain." Ultimately, the committee denied the request.

After his arduous efforts, Stockman perceived by the end of March an encouraging swell of congressional members supporting "the group line" of "cut, cut, cut." Senator J. James Exon (D-NE) had one explanation for that swell: "The appearance of key administration officials on all the major talk shows and the press releases and propaganda that is being put out around this Nation indicate that unless we have the courage to go along with something that you [Stockman] have created . . . we are somehow un-American."

When not appearing before committees, Stockman could often be spotted roaming the halls of Congress, armed with his "black books," seeking support for his reductions.

While Council of Economic Advisors Chairman Murray Weidenbaum made famous the words "Don't just stand there, undo something," David Stockman might have taken as his own slogan "Don't just stand there, undo everything." Regulatory agencies were especially hard hit in Stockman's black books; indeed, in that area Stockman's axe consistently drew blood. A radical deregulator in his congressional days, Stockman's zeal to undo everything became even more pronounced at OMB.

The November 1980 "Dunkirk Memo," written by Stockman and endorsed by Kemp, contains a boldface heading, TICKING REGULATORY TIME BOMB. According to Stockman, that bomb was due to explode within the "next eighteen-to-forty months," unless "swift, comprehensive and far-reaching regulatory policy corrections [were] undertaken immediately." The RCRA (Resource Conservation and Recovery Act) was dismissed as a "monument to mindless excess." Carbon monoxide emissions standards were "unnecessary." Using industry figures, Stockman toted up the cost of such measures as airbags and OSHA noise regulations as $10 to $20 billion—this while, according to Stockman, providing "modest to nonexistent social benefits."

"David Stockman has a hell of a lot more compassion for Hooker Chemical or GM than he does for Lois Gibbs [the Love Canal citizen-activist] or the fifty thousand people who go through wind-shields every year," fumed a House Energy aide. The *National Journal* hardly knew how to describe Stockman's painting of the regulatory landscape, settling on a tongue-in-cheek "somewhat apocalyptic."

When he had opposed auto emissions standards as a congress-man, Stockman dubbed the measures the "hundred-billion-dollar Cough Remedy." Of sulfur emissions that have played havoc with American and Canadian waters in the form of acid rain, Stockman commented on the House floor, "I keep reading these stories that there are a hundred and seventy dead lakes in New York. . . . Well, how much are the fish worth in these lakes that account for four percent of the lake area in New York? And does it make sense to spend billions of dollars controlling emissions from Ohio or elsewhere if you're talking about a very marginal volume of dollar value . . .?" Ontario Minister of Environment Keith Norton responded angrily, "There are the dollars in lost business in our tourism and outdoor recreation industry; the costs of damage to manmade structures; the potential loss of crops and trees; and, if our worst fears are borne out, the impact on human health."

But Stockman took the same simplistic view of regulatory matters in his position as OMB director. Appearing on the Hill, Stockman justified a cut of $14 million from the $41 million budget of the Consumer Product Safety Commission (CPSC) by saying the agency was "groping for a definable and defensible mission. . . . As established the agency was to ferret out hazardous products and to correct the situation. That being largely accomplished, the agency has a diminished need for resources." (A November 11, 1981, article in *The Washington Post* reported the results of a survey done on regulatory agencies. Of the 53 percent of those interviewed who understood the charge of CPSC, a full 41 percent, up from 36 in August 1979, said the agency was not doing enough, while 12 percent felt it did too much.)

In early April, Stockman's perceptions were borne out: in an impressive 88–10 vote, the Senate endorsed the bulk of the cuts he sought. Following the passage of these cuts, a series of amendments seeking to restore funds to selected social programs were voted down. The Democrats looked to be in disarray. Surprisingly, the greatest challenge to the Republican Administration's drive to squelch social welfare spending came from one of their own—John Chafee of Rhode Island. Chafee's amendment to restore $973 million to inner-city programs was so feared by the White House and by Chafee's fellow Republicans that Vice President Bush hurried up to the Hill to cast a tie-breaking vote if necessary. Bush need not have made the trip; the amendment failed by 40 to 59.

The Senate did find room in its heart to restore partial funding for one program, however: the Export-Import (EXIM) Bank, which provided generous subsidies to such Fortune 500 companies as Boeing and Westinghouse. Stockman had initially targeted the Bank—frequently dubbed "Boeing's Bank"—for large cuts. In criticizing the program, he argued that it served a small group of well-to-do corporations. The proposed cuts in the bank's funding were held up as "proof" that the Reagan Administration was practicing a policy of "evenhandedness" by cutting subsidies to business as well as the poor.

But once again it was "weak clients" and not "weak claims" that ultimately took a beating. In a hearing on housing, Representative Charles Schumer (D-NY) joked, "Someone came over to me and said the slogan of the new administration is 'What's mine is mine; what's yours is subject to cost-benefit analysis.' " That proved true in EXIM's case. The bank's budget was saved in the legislative branch with scarcely a peep of protest from the executive office; the head of the bank, William Draper, even received a letter of hearty endorsement from the bank's ostensible foe, David Stockman. On the Senate side, the fight to put $250 million back into the bank was led by Republican Nancy Kassebaum of Kansas—a state in which Boeing is a major employer.

In the House, Republicans recommended even heftier increases in EXIM's budget than the Senate had. When the recommendation came to the floor in May, however, the Democrats eliminated the hikes. The House accepted—at least for the time being—the sentiments of Representative David Obey (D-WI), who maintained, "There is no reason for us not to ask Boeing, GE, and other privileged characters in our society to share the load."

But overnight Boeing, GE, and the International Association of Machinists lobbied to reinstate the cuts. The following day the House caved in to this heavy push—a move that required over seventy members to change their votes overnight. Having dismissed the Senate restoration of funds as a matter that "did open a little breach that is troublesome," Stockman did not bother to comment on the House actions.

These were but skirmishes. For Stockman, the real battle in the House would be on an overall budget package to be voted up or down with a single vote. Under the Congressional Budget and Impoundment Act of 1974, both the Congressional Budget Office (CBO) and the Budget committees were established. The budget act also contained a provision known as "reconciliation," which could be used to make congressional committees live up to the individual spending targets set at the start of the budget process. Used once under Carter, reconciliation had resulted in some modest $8 billion in savings—a mere fraction of the cuts Stockman was looking for.

Stockman was eager to use reconciliation in a way that led House Rules Chairman Richard Bolling (D-MO) to fume, "I don't think the White House understands the democratic process, much less the legislative process, much less the function of the House." Stockman sought to write the broad objectives of the Reagan economic plan into stone at the start of the budget process. And he managed to convince Congress to do so. The result was a drastic contraction of congressional prerogative. Representative James L. Oberstar (D-MN) saw folly in a situation in which "the budget process . . . started out as a means for Congress, the legislative branch, to seize control of the budget and the appropriating process but instead it has wound up seizing control of us."

It was not easy; the administration launched an all-out effort to ensure a win at the budget battle. Throughout March and April, wavering conservative Democrats were offered presidential cuff-links, tickets for the executive box at the Kennedy Center, and passes to White House lunches. Representative Carroll Hubbard, Jr. (D-KY), a conservative Democrat, remarked, "I realized how big the lobbying effort was when I got a phone call from the President [in early March] and he talked for so long that I had to say, 'I know how busy you are and must get off the phone.' Even my brother in Louisville doesn't talk that much."

Reagan also made a well-timed television appearance urging constituents to call their representatives and demand support for the Republican package of cuts. "Reagan got on the box and sold the people a sham," observed one House staff aide. "I don't for a minute believe that [the representatives] ever believed the program would work. What it boiled down to were wholly unrealistic economic assumptions on the Republican side, but they succeeded in demagoguing the hell out of the whole debate." The pressure on Congress was twofold: acceptance not only of the Stockman spending levels but also of the assumptions behind those levels. Allen Schick, a Washington budget specialist, observed, "I think this is the first time the White House has made acceptance of economic assumptions part of the test of loyalty."

Though the numbers Reagan used in his presentation were questionable, the results were not. Pat Schroeder received "a couple of hundred calls. At first I tried to explain that it was the Democratic assumptions which made us look like we were spending more because our assumptions were more realistic—pretty soon I just gave up." The following day, May 16, sixty-seven Democrats joined the Republicans in accepting the Stockman program of general cuts—Gramm–Latta I—as a guide to making their specific cuts. Fifteen House committees and, across the way, fourteen Senate committees faced a June 12 deadline to report Fiscal Year 1982 cuts of about $36 billion to their respective budget committees.

Events were accelerating. "It's much more complicated than we all thought," admitted House Interior and Insular Affairs Chairman Morris K. Udall (D-AZ). Competing economic assumptions made comparison between rival budgets difficult. Stockman kept down the prospect of future deficits through a "magic asterisk," which the CBO estimated to represent $60 billion in unspecified future cuts. But amidst the chaos, the work rushed forward.

"Overall," commented Leon Panetta, head of the Democratic Task Force on Reconciliation, "most of the committees took their task very much to heart. I thought some of them would say 'go to hell,' but they did a good job of coming up with savings." Ohio Representative Ralph Regula, ranking Republican on the Budget Committee, agreed. "The indications are that most of the committees are coming up with real cuts. . . . They're seriously trying to reach the targets." To be sure, there were some exceptions—the Post Office and Civil Service Committee submitted a proposal that would shut down ten thousand post offices across the country, and another committee proposed to reduce aid to schools bordering military bases—submissions that were dubbed part of the "Washington Monument Syndrome," that is, suggesting cuts that were as politically unfeasible as closing the Washington Monument. The only committee that truly balked at the instructions was, ironically, Stockman's old assignment, Energy and Commerce. Unable to come up with a bipartisan proposal, Chairman John Dingell simply sent over the Democratic plan.

Representative Richard Ottinger (D-NY) attempted to explain the Energy Committee deadlock: "The Republican Administration wouldn't budge. They wanted us to rubber stamp their program." At one point, as he told Anne Urban, Ottinger arranged a "breakfast with [Fred] Khedouri," Stockman's energy liaison. "Khedouri said yes, I said no, I said yes, Khedouri said no, I don't think we could have agreed on whether or not the sun was shining."

Despite these problems, by most accounts the administration won between 75 and 85 percent of the cuts it had asked for. Still the White House was unsatisfied, largely by the House's rejection of most of the block grant proposals that would have consolidated dozens of federal programs, cut their funding 25 percent, and sent them back to the states to oversee. Reagan's deputy press secretary Larry Speakes quoted the President as saying, "I feel more strongly about block grants than almost anything in the package." Stockman, who had warned the House against "creative accounting" and "dishonest scorekeeping," accused Congress of trying to "bust the budget." At a press conference in which he denounced the cuts as "phony," Stockman predicted, "It [the final budget battle] is going to seem less like a family reunion and more like a divorce court in terms of the sound and the fury." Democrats, who had succeeded in cutting $37.7 billion when they had been asked to cut only $35.1 billion, were outraged, claiming the administration would not be happy unless they personally "dotted every *i* and crossed every *t*."

Stockman was prepared to back down on next to nothing. "At the peak of power the arrogance was a little scary," commented Leon Panetta. Shortly before the final vote on the budget bill occurred, Stockman, Panetta, House Budget Chairman James Jones, and the White House's chief lobbyist Max Friedersdorf all met in Panetta's office. "Stockman started in with this political pitch saying we had to cut more," recalls Panetta. "I said, 'You can't come in here at the last minute through the back door and unload a bandwagon of new cuts on us. That's not the way the process is supposed to operate.' "

Budget Chair Jim Jones came in with a similar critique of Stockman's modus operandi. "At the eleventh hour, after all the committees had done their work in the orderly legislative process, the director of OMB, Mr. Stockman, came forward and said, 'That is not enough. That is not the way I want it. I want more.' "

Conservative Democrats who had supported the White House in the first round were also angry over the attacks on the committee reductions. "Many of us are senior members of those committees and had a major voice in making those cuts," explained Representative Bo Ginn (D-GA). "We told Mr. Gramm that we were tired of being manipulated by the White House."

If they were tired then, they would be exhausted by the time David Stockman was through with them. While the House had been working frantically to put together their package of cuts, Stockman had been working closely with a few House members on another package, "Son of Gramm–Latta." In a June 25 effort conceived and spearheaded by Stockman, the House voted 214 to 208 to allow "Son of Gramm–Latta" to be voted up or down in a single vote. This procedural vote offered House members the advantage of not being forced to go on record as voting against specific social programs. Although Stockman claimed it would avoid the "pork barreling" that had transpired in committee rooms, the Reagan Administration found it expedient to do a little pork barreling of its own by offering "sweeteners" in the form of support for expensive sugar subsidies and promises of restored Conrail funding to wavering members of the House. When asked about the "deal" he had received for his vote, Representative John Breaux (D-LA) replied, "I can't be bought. But I can be rented. . . . This was a great trade."

"Everything is clear, we are in an utter state of confusion," despaired Representative Fernand St. Germain (D-RI) on the morning of June 25. Although members of the House were expected to vote on a closed rule for Gramm–Latta II, copies of that approximately 850-page bill were nowhere in sight. When House Budget Chair Jones requested the Republican legislation, Representative Delbert Latta (R-OH) responded angrily, "May I say to the gentleman that all he [Jones] would have to do is walk about thirty-five steps up there and get the document, and then he could walk back and sit down and read the document. He could spend the evening reading it." One of Latta's fellow Ohioans took issue with the co-sponsor of the amendment. Representative John Seiberling pointed out that, "He [Latta] knows full well that that is not the copy that has been sent to the printer, which is what he is going to offer tomorrow. I happen to have seen that copy just before it went to the printer; it was not a copy, it was a stack of paper this high, and it was all marked up in handwritten annotations dealing with substantive law as well as with money."

Representative David Obey (D-WI) was incensed by the procedure the House was being asked to embrace. "We represent," he said, "each of us, on an average, about five hundred thousand people. We, in a sense, are their representatives in a legal case. Many of us are not lawyers but we are making law. I submit that any lawyer who would sign a contract on behalf of his client without reading the fine print ought to be subject to disbarment."

Reagan threw himself into the effort to allow the single vote on the budget package by calling dozens of legislators. A steady stream of Republicans aided the White House effort by making short speeches, allowing the President additional lobbying time. Following a bevy of speeches by Republicans, Speaker Tip O'Neill asked how many more members wished to speak and was answered with an impressive show of hands. "The President will have time to make some more phone calls," O'Neill observed. Taking the cue, John Rousselot (R-CA) stood up and announced, "I just wanted to tell you the President is on the phone."

In the caucus rooms, House Minority Leader Bob Michel and Stockman delivered rousing speeches to win over wavering Republicans. If speeches failed, favors generally did the trick. "They're making deals like crazy in the cloakroom," said James Jones. "It's like a tobacco auction back there." When questioned about the heavy lobbying efforts, Stockman insisted there were "no deals made," but simply some "adjustments and considerations."

While propping up the price of sugar presents no cost to the government, consumers would stand to lose billions. When later asked whether the White House was opposed to the supports, Stockman told William Greider, "They don't care over in the White House. They want to win."

On the same night, June 25, the Senate passed their package of cuts by a vote of 80 to 15.

With the House rules vote won, "Son of Gramm–Latta" appeared the following day. The *Washington Star* described the bill as "1,000 pages of scrawled unindexed legislation," resulting from a "chaotic 24-hour rush." Some House members did not receive copies of the bill at all; others were presented with it still warm from the printer two hours before floor action convened. Everyone who managed to wrangle a copy was faced with "unnumbered pages and long-hand insertions of last minute changes," observed the *Star*. Representative Barber B. Conable, Jr. (R-NY), who had supported Gramm-Latta I, expressed his discomfiture: "I have to be concerned about procedures that force us to make a decision in this environment."

At least on June 26, debate on the House floor seemed modeled after a low-grade comedy, so ludicrous was the situation. At the start of the debate on Gramm–Latta II, Representative Peter Peyser (D-NY) asked, "Is there an index on this? I am trying to go through trying to find sections. There does not appear to be any indexing of where anything is. Is there a master sheet that shows something?" Informed by Representative Trent Lott (R-MS) that side by side explanations or summaries were available, but no indices, Representative Al Gore (D-TN) warned against the validity of the document entitled "Overview Summary," pointing out that while the summary claimed solar programs would be increased in the bill, the figures seemed to indicate just the opposite. "I did not comment on the authorship of those papers," snapped Lott, "I am just telling the members where they can get the committee print or the various explanations of the bills as seen by the authors of the documents."

Substantive debate on the bill proved nearly impossible, as none of the members knew how to refer to specific pages. Representative Obey vented his frustrations: "I do not know how to accomplish this. My first question comes about an eighth of an inch into the bill. We have so many different page seventeens that I do not know how to tell you which one. But on page, the first page seventeen, I guess it says line seven, 'No funds are authorized to be appropriated to carry out section 1524 of the Education Act of 1978.' Can the gentleman from Ohio [Latta] tell me what those provisions are?"

At one point, Speaker of the House Tip O'Neill asked House Minority Leader Bob Michel, "It is my understanding that the gentleman just met with people from the White House and the staff people, who said this is such a mishmash, you ought to pull it off the floor. Is that what the gentleman is leading up to?" Michel responded angrily, "I understand the Speaker suffered a defeat yesterday and it was a pretty bitter pill to have to swallow."

Michel charged that the Democrats had engaged in a "certain form of interception" of Gramm–Latta before it was sent to the Government Printing Office, which had resulted in the bill's state of disarray. O'Neill quickly intervened: "I do not know if such a thing happened or not."

> Michel: I have not even stated the facts. It is quite obvious from the Speaker's observation that he does not know what happened. I will tell him what happened.
>
> O'Neill: Will the gentleman yield?
>
> Michel: Not for a moment, for God's sake.
>
> O'Neill: It is your time.
>
> Michel: It sure as heck is.

The House Minority Leader claimed that a certain member had grabbed the messenger who was on his way to the GPO with Gramm–Latta: "[He] comes up and demands it, takes it from his hand downstairs someplace where you have members of the Democratic Study Group, throws it out on the table and spreads it all around. However, they put it back together, I know the messenger had to wait." Representative Phillip Burton (D-CA) proved to be that certain member. Said Burton:

> . . . I believed in the absence of having more than one copy we should see if the matter would lend itself to some kind of reproduction. Normally . . . we are required to present three or six copies at the desk. . . . That is when we learned it was several inches thick. Once it was ascertained it did not lend itself to reproduction, the papers were then forwarded. . . . There were no papers spread all over. The gentleman from California only tried to make one other assessment, which was in this rather thick, six or seven inches thick, sole copy proposal, whether it reflected anything that had previously been in print and the gentleman from California discovered with complete alarm there was not anything that had previously been in print.

A few of those who had supported the administration on the first resolution refused to go along on the second. Elliott Levitas (D-GA) railed, "I spoke to the President personally before that vote [on Gramm–Latta I] and I asked him did voting for that budget resolution lock in the various assumptions that he had made in achieving those reductions? And he said, 'No, you can achieve them any way you want to. It is the spending level we are concerned about.' "

But the harshest criticisms were leveled at Stockman, not at the President. Speaking of Stockman's refusal to accept the cuts of the House Budget Committee, Representative St. Germain charged, "I suggest this is not a major policy difference but a prime example of David Stockman's monumental hubris, which turns the slightest deviation from the OMB computer printouts into a disaster for our nation." Representative Henry Gonzalez (D-TX) declared, "No one else knows what this substitute contains, no one except the geniuses at OMB, who know nothing but contempt for the legislative process."

The budget also cut the House proposal by $2.2 billion. Passed by a vote of 232 to 193, the package skirted the committee process entirely. The Democrats could only fume. Said Leon Panetta, "We are dealing with more than two hundred and fifty programs with no committee consideration, no hearings, and no opportunity to offer amendments." "It was shocking," reflected Pat Schroeder. "One vote, for one year, for the entire U.S., on almost all of the domestic programs." Elliott Levitas waved a copy of the bill, saying, "It's the 1981 edition of the *Book of the Dead*." And Jim Wright (D-TX), House Majority Leader, insisted, "This isn't a budget document— this is a document of reaction with all the whims and prejudices of a little group of willful men."

It was the longest bill in history and undoubtedly the most disorganized. Indeed, the legislation was so hastily put together it was discovered that a woman's name and telephone number— "Source, Ruth Seymour, 225-4844"—had accidentally been written into the bill. "Is that part of the permanent record?" queried O'Neill. "Maybe that's her golf score," replied one of the bill's sponsors, Delbert Latta.

It took days, even weeks, to uncover some of the hidden provisions in the bill. OMB received sole responsibility for determining the national poverty line. Hispanic groups shuffled furiously through the legislation for three days in a frantic search for bilingual education funding. Congress lost the power to come up with an allocation plan in an energy crisis.

Commenting on the passage of the bill, Stockman remarked, "For once a strategy that was carefully conceived actually materialized." On both points—conception and execution—Stockman was the leading figure. "Stockman did this," said Tip O'Neill. "They turned the whole process over to him. Hell of a way to legislate."

Through the budget cuts, Stockman was able to make policy changes by taking away funds for programs that were mandated by law. Some cabinet members rebelled at this tactic. Anne Gorsuch of the Environmental Protection Agency pointed out in early 1982 that while her agency's responsibility had risen nearly 50 percent (due to the implementation of the Superfund), her budget had been reduced by nearly 50 percent. In another case of what Representative Richard Ottinger (D-NY) termed the "continual whittling down of the legislative process," Stockman directed the Energy Department to shut off funds for the Weatherization program despite congressional appropriation of that money. In effect, claimed Ottinger, many of the cuts "make the best case for abolishing departments or programs by making them totally incompetent."

On March 23, 1981, the Committee of Energy and Commerce released a statement of its objectives. One of those statements could be interpreted as a direct warning to its ex-member, David Stockman. Said the report:

> We are a nation of laws, and under the Constitution the Executive Branch has a responsibility faithfully to execute the laws. If the Administration proposes to make such significant changes in *substantive* law and *national policy*, it should make these recommendations to Congress in the form of legislative proposals. It must not seek to achieve such changes through the back door in the guise of "budget cutting." Any promise to send up legislative proposals later is not justification for acting as if the laws were already altered.

In yet another situation where it appeared men, not laws, were prevailing, the Reagan Administration froze the hiring of federal employees on January 20, 1981, a freeze that included not hiring personnel for Vietnam Veteran counseling centers, despite the fact those centers had been written into law. The Senate passed a resolution overriding Stockman's actions, but Representative David Bonior (D-MI) decided to press the case further by bringing suit against OMB. Said Bonior, "OMB continues to assert that its actions were lawful and can be repeated in the future. The fundamental principles of congressional control over spending are now at stake in this suit." Bonior gave a frightening assessment of the powers of the insulated OMB under Stockman: "The situation politically is that OMB has become increasingly a power center in the government, so much so that people have suggested that OMB is forming the domestic policy of the U.S. government. I don't think that's too much of an exaggeration."

Elliott Levitas, who was chairman of the House Subcommittee on Public Works and Transportation at that time and today is a Washington lawyer, remembers those days most vividly.

> In terms of Machiavellian politics, it was the crowning achievement. In my opinion it was the closest the United States has ever come to having a parliamentary government, in the sense that this program was being presented as the President's—read 'prime minister's'—program and thus the members *had* to vote on it. It was one of the most incredible stories of political power in this country's history.
>
> It wrote into law *David Stockman's* view of what Ronald Reagan wanted, in Ronald Reagan's name!

Within three months of the bill's 1981 passage, the state of the economy was dreary: 10.5 percent interest rates looked like a pipe dream, unemployment was heading steadily upward, and huge deficit predictions were causing some of the previously staunchest supporters of the administration to jump ship. The words of Alexander Hamilton, with whom former Congressman Bob Eckhardt had compared David Stockman, came back to haunt Congress: "In the legislature, promptitude of decision is oftener an evil than a benefit."

---

8 • Man Over the Supply Side

READING A TAX bill is laborious; in all probability writing one holds even less charm. As chairman of the House Ways and Means Committee, Dan Rostenkowski (D-IL) had done more than his share of both in the spring and summer of 1981. Yet the mechanics of fashioning a tax bill paled when set against the hand-holding that the job required. But Rostenkowski was known as a politician with a well-developed sense of compromise. As the tax cut vote neared, many observers predicted a win for the Illinois representative.

The date of the House vote on the tax bill, July 29, 1981, was shared by another momentous event: the wedding of Lady Diana Spencer and Prince Charles. Commenting on the Reagan tax plan, Representative Thomas J. Downey (D-NY) observed, "It is appropriate that we should be debating this bill today; with the royal wedding in the morning, we are debating a bill that will benefit the economically royal in the afternoon."

As Reagan put it, the tax vote came down to whether congressmen were "for" or "agin" the administration. After five months of concentrated work by the Ways and Means Committee, the tax vote was finally on the floor. Rostenkowski had planned an elaborate victory party for that evening, but as the congressional tally board flashed the votes on the Reagan plan, the Ways and Means chairman was forced to admit defeat. Representative Charles Wilson (D-TX) put a sympathetic arm around the dejected Rostenkowski. "Danny, cheer up. It could have been worse." Unconvinced, Rostenkowski asked, "How could it have been worse?" Wilson paused. "Well, he might have come out against f-----g."

Ronald Reagan rode into the White House astride an economic program that promised massive tax cuts, huge increases in defense outlays, domestic spending reductions in the nebulous area of waste, fraud, and abuse, *and* a balanced budget, even a small surplus, by 1984. Reagan's victory was testimony to his success in convincing voters there was a painless way to go conservative. Others remained less swayed, doubting the plan was painless, even plausible. John Anderson declared it could "only be done with mirrors." Jimmy Carter attacked it as "completely irresponsible." And, early in the campaign, George Bush, not yet Reagan's running mate, had dubbed the program "voodoo economics."[3]

Early in January 1981, before Reagan had even moved his desk to the Oval Office, Stockman convinced the President-elect to slash domestic spending beyond the politically acceptable realm of gov-

---

3. Early in 1982, Bush claimed, "I didn't say it. I challenge anyone to find it." Mike Francaviglia of NBC found it—amid old newsreels of the Pennsylvania primary in April 1980. NBC ran the "I didn't say it," and then quickly cut to Bush denouncing "voodoo economics." In a note sent to NBC, Bush came clean: "NBC 1, Bush 0. The context of voodoo economics has been escalated till my hemoglobin count is zero."

ernment excess. Still, the program looked like a pipe dream. In its heyday, the flaws of Reaganomics were obscured by economic assumptions that left most American economists agog. When the public cooled somewhat to that tactic, Stockman deployed his "magic asterisk" (so dubbed by Senate Majority Leader Howard Baker), which denoted future budget cuts and thereby glossed over a grim reality—without those domestic cuts an additional $60 billion would be tacked onto the 1982 deficit. But Ronald Reagan was not conceding to realities, grim or otherwise. When the program was heaped with criticism, Reagan dismissed the cries as the ceaseless squawking of "Chicken Littles."

A year after Reagan took office, the administration and the Republican Party in general were in turmoil. The head of the House Republican Conference, Jack Kemp (R-NY), announced that "Republicans no longer worship at the shrine of a balanced budget." That statement threw half the Republican Party into a dyspeptic frenzy. David Stockman was perhaps the most frenzied of the lot. Over the past few months, Stockman had increasingly come to pay homage to the squared account, willing to sacrifice tax cuts to bring the federal ledger out of the red. For the OMB director, his first year had been a lesson in his self-described search for the "way the world works." That search led Stockman to believe within months after he assumed his post that Reaganomics could be done on paper "with mirrors" but not in the actual economy. Faced with budget deficits that seemingly multiplied while he slept, Stockman cast about for ways to keep the numbers under control. Though ostensibly remaining a team player, Stockman added another item to his own personal agenda that ran counter to Reaganomics: the partial reinstatement of slashed taxes. The upshot of "Stockmanomics," as revealed in part in the *Atlantic* article, nearly cost the OMB director his job. When the curtain opened on the struggle over the Fiscal Year 1983 budget, Stockman reappeared as a fervent, albeit chastened, team player.

At first, supply-siders were openly derided and generally ignored. The label "supply side" was not actually coined until 1976, when the foundling economic theory was christened by one of its most vocal critics, Herbert Stein, chairman of the Council of Economic Advisors under Nixon. Stein found little positive to say about the group in a spring speech on budget balancing. Recalled Stein, "I referred to the supply-side fiscalists, meaning the people who believed that budget decisions affected the side of output but not the demand for output."

The supply-siders had really begun their move into national prominence in the spring of 1975, when Jude Wanniski published an article in *The Public Interest*, the neo-conservative journal. Entitled "The Mundell–Laffer Hypothesis—A New View of the World Economy," Wanniski argued both for a return to the gold standard and for an "older style of economic thought" based on "incentives and motivations." The article intrigued one of Reagan's 1976 campaign workers, Jeffrey Bell, who contacted Wanniski and eventually joined the supply-side team. Bell, who ran without success for New Jersey Senate seats on two occasions, was also instrumental in the selling of Kemp–Roth.

Wanniski had then, and still retains, a good eye for the colorful. A former reporter and, in 1976, an editorial writer for *The Wall Street Journal*, he was always in the market for a new propaganda tool to advertise his theory. Two weeks after Stein's speech, a Wanniski editorial appeared in *The Wall Street Journal* entitled "Supply Side Fiscalists." The name (*sans* "Fiscalists") stuck.

Although Wanniski and Arthur Laffer (often referred to as the "father" of supply-side economics) had been batting around economic theories since 1971, the journalist was not entirely sold until the spring of 1974. Following his conversion, Wanniski set out to find backers in the Ford Administration who could make supply side a political reality.

Ford's economic men were not impressed, although they gave Wanniski a considerable hearing. Undaunted, Wanniski came away with his greatest propaganda tool of all: the Laffer curve. According to Wanniski, Laffer grabbed a cocktail napkin at a Georgetown dinner and sketched out his now-famous curve as a visual aid for Richard Cheney, then a deputy to Ford's Chief of Staff, Donald Rumsfeld. Put simply, the curve contends that higher taxes increase government revenues but eventually discourage production. At some point, taxes are so high, both revenue and production drop. (Although Laffer agrees that is indeed his belief, he does not remember sketching it out on a napkin.)

Meanwhile on the Hill, the supply side was gaining ground. In 1977, former Buffalo Bill quarterback Jack Kemp had collaborated with Senator William Roth (R-DE) on the Kemp–Roth bill, which translated supply-side ideology into legislation. The bill called for a three-year, 10-percent-a-year, across-the-board tax reduction.

For Dustin Hoffman, in *The Graduate*, the word was "plastics." In the Kemp–Roth campaign, the word was "incentives." Indeed, it was the word that lent credence to the bill. Jack Kemp has remarked, "Tip O'Neill has suggested I don't know much about economics. Nonsense! I don't know *anything* about economics. But I'm an expert on incentives." In his book *An American Renaissance*, Kemp traces his expertise in the incentive field to the football field:

> Well, right about now I would say I'm an expert on incentive . . . I played quarterback for about 27 of my 35 years in organized and professional football. I was president of the football players union. I bargained on behalf of the players. I operated in an environment that was basically very marginal, to the extent everything you do in professional football as quarterback is on the margin. You're in the huddle, you get 30 seconds, you call the play. Either it works or it doesn't. Your success is easily measurable, you have three seconds to get the ball, get back and choose a receiver from four or five different possibilities.

Kemp concludes this somewhat baffling analogy by saying, "It's incentive." Later, in the Greider interview, Stockman would have another term for it, one that would cause him much embarrassment.

As their idea began to move through Congress, the supply-siders gathered for mutual support. In the fall of 1977, Wanniski was in Washington working on the final draft of his supply-side primer, *The Way the World Works*. One Sunday he hosted a football party that was attended by a "whole slew of supply-sider types—Art Laffer, [Paul] Craig Roberts, a whole bunch of them." Jack Kemp also came, with House freshman David Stockman in tow. Kemp had given Stockman part of Wanniski's manuscript to read, and the young congressman, according to Wanniski, said he was "intrigued with its propositions." After that, says Wanniski, "Stockman became a regular part of the group which would get together. When I was in Washington and Art was in Washington we would all meet, mostly in Jack's office—thirty or forty of us, and we'd talk about economic reform. Dave was always part of that group."

Stockman later mused to a newspaper reporter, "I guess I always had a strong intellectual bent, so I needed a strong theory of how the world works." What better person, given Stockman's apparent abandonment of Reinhold Niebuhr, to explain that than Jude Wanniski, who was laboring over a book with just such a title. Wanniski insists Stockman was "absolutely committed to the supply-side tax cuts. I don't know if he ever really got the argument down on the gold thing. But the cuts, yes."

But more traditional Republican and business voices were wary. On August 7, 1978, *Business Week* attacked the Kemp–Roth bill as "Irresponsible. . . . Wishful thinking . . . [that] would wreck the country and impoverish everyone on a fixed income."

In 1978, Kemp–Roth made it to the floor of the House, where it was promptly defeated by a vote of 177 to 140. On that occasion as we have seen, Stockman argued that the bill would cause "no credit imbalance, no pressure on the Fed to pump up the money supply and no additional inflation."

Having found his new ideology, Stockman pursued the supply-side line at every opportunity, grabbing a hefty share of publicity for himself in the process. On March 2, 1980, Stockman had an article published in *The Washington Post* headed "Why the Economic Doctors Have Failed." Asking "What is to be done?" Stockman gave a textbook-perfect supply-side answer:

> Cut taxes—across the board and deeply. Stop redistributing income and goldplating the public sector in the guise of demand stimulation. Fix the dollar's value in something grounded in the planet rather than in political institutions—gold, mercury or sweet potatoes. And enroll the defrocked priests of Keynesianism in a job training program—they deserve mercy too.

"Everyone likes to vote to cut taxes," explained Representative Bill Hefner (D-NC) in an early 1982 budget hearing. "I'd like to make it [paying taxes] voluntary." This whimsical observation helps explain why Kemp–Roth—with minor revisions—became party policy in an amazingly short period of time.

In reality, Kemp–Roth was simply a rephrasing of traditional Republican policy: Give tax cuts to wealthy individuals, who will invest their money and produce positive effects that will shower down on everyone—like proverbial pennies from heaven. Couched in the term "supply side" rather than the old label "trickle down," the idea remained the same. Reagan and his staff argued repeatedly that the combination of budget cuts and tax cuts would revive the economy and eventually benefit all. There was no shortage of skeptics. Speaking on the House floor in May 1981, Representative Carl Perkins (D-KY) remarked, "We are being told every day that 'all boats rise with the tide.' My answer is that boats that get sunk don't rise at all."

Even some members of the administration seemed unsure as to the merits of the rising boats argument. Dismissing charges that Reagan's economic plan was a "crude version of trickle-down," William Niskanen of the Council of Economic Advisors explained, "We want to improve the opportunity to become wealthy." Niskanen added, "Any system that promotes the opportunity to become wealthy will generate very wealthy people. My personal experience is that some of the most boring people I have ever met are wealthy. But that is irrelevant."[4]

Ronald Reagan's decision to embrace the tax cuts was, above all, a pragmatic one. The California governor needed the support of Jack Kemp in his early campaigning as well as an assurance that Kemp would not make a leap into the presidential race himself. Representative Newt Gingrich (R-GA), a close ally of Kemp's commented, "Jack Kemp's specific price to campaign for Reagan was that he agree to the tax bill." Kemp himself has admitted that although "there was no formal price involved, it was implicit that there would be a lot more enthusiasm," for Reagan if the candidate endorsed the Kemp–Roth bill. (Once in office, Reagan's advisers did their best to minimize the Kemp–Roth connection. Then White House Chief of Staff Jim Baker announced, "We must make it clear that this is the Reagan tax package, not the Kemp–Roth bill." Admitting that there were only minor differences between the two, Baker exclaimed, "When you call it Kemp–Roth, you tend to crystallize opposition" among the hard-liners. Despite Baker's concern, the name stuck, occasionally being referred to as Reagan–Kemp–Roth, if Reagan's name was mentioned at all.)

By the fall of 1980, supply-side theory had begun to take hold in fashionable Republican circles. A gold-embossed bust of the supply-side hero, eighteenth-century economist Adam Smith, stamped onto a blue silk tie, predominated at Republican gatherings. Paul

---

4. In *Wealth and Poverty*, George Gilder insists: "A successful economy depends on the proliferation of the rich, on creating a large class of risk-taking men who are willing to shun the easy channels of a comfortable life in order to create new enterprises, win huge profits, and invest them again."

Samuelson (author of the most widely read Econ 101 text in the world) revealed that his next edition would at least *mention* the supply-siders, something of a coup for the theory, which was thereby granted a certain amount of academic respectability. And Senator Bob Dole (R-KS), resting comfortably after a minor operation, was given a get-well gift by President Reagan—a copy of Gilder's *Wealth and Poverty*.[5]

Satisfied with his commitment to their cause, a group of ardent supply-siders launched a heavy lobbying effort to have Stockman named OMB director. They were successful. But other supply-siders were not so sure about Stockman's allegiance. In their book *The Reagan Revolution*, influential conservative columnists and dedicated supply-siders Rowland Evans and Robert Novak gave Stockman their cautious approval, "despite his occasional lapses and preoccupation with expenditure reduction."

Still, at the very outset, Robert Novak was delighted to see Stockman heading up OMB. As he told Anne Urban: "The whole idea was that here would be a guy who would be sold as a great budget cutter but in actuality his secret agenda would be tax rate reduction. Here would be an OMB director who, when the crunch came, wouldn't say 'do it through taxes.' To have a tax cutter in that position was considered by the supply-siders to be one of the great coups of our age." Later, when Novak included these revealing items in his column with Evans, his friendship and closeness with Stockman would begin to diminish.

But in the hands of the administration—primarily Stockman's—supply-side theory was not to retain its purity. Despite his professed support for the supply side, Stockman remained an unflagging champion of reducing the size of the federal budget through budget cuts, a position that estranged him from supply-siders.

Supply-side purists like Arthur Laffer and Jude Wanniski believed that welfare payments would shrink naturally with the economic growth inspired by tax cuts. Other supply-siders such as Paul Craig Roberts supported budget cuts because they believed the growth projected by Laffer and his peers was too optimistic and that accordingly the tax cuts would result in tremendous revenue losses that would create a dangerously unbalanced budget. Stockman took

---

5. Within eight months Dole—having lost the faith if he ever truly had it—would be telling good news, bad news jokes that began: "The good news is a busload of supply-siders went off a cliff. . . . The bad news is there were three empty seats."

the position of traditional Republicans like Alan Greenspan, former Council of Economic Advisors chairman under Ford, who pressed for budget cuts on political as well as economic grounds. As early as his 1975 *Public Interest* article, Stockman had declared his opposition to "Using the federal government as an all-purpose instrument of social reform." Foreshadowed in that "Social Pork Barrel" article, Stockman's views became increasingly antagonistic toward social welfare policy over the years.

Coincidentally, Stockman's pork barrel piece appeared in the same *Public Interest* issue as Wanniski's supply-side piece. "That article indicates that Stockman's own personal agenda had been established before any of us met him," Wanniski told Anne Urban. "He was another Alan Greenspan. Greenspan has been one of the biggest parts of the problem that we've had. All he cares about is pushing his own desire to destroy the welfare system. Greenspan is so Ayn Randian that his first objective is to throw the widows and orphans out onto the street, and Stockman has the same Calvinist view of the world—put on your hairshirts and suffer, suffer, suffer."

Stockman's personal agenda became ever more apparent, much to the dismay of his former allies. Indeed, Alan Reynolds, an ardent supply-sider who works with Wanniski, charged, "The minute he took office, he became a monomaniacal budget balancer." Day by day, Stockman shifted the focus from taxes to the budget. Appearing on the "Good Morning America" show on February 3, 1981, just two weeks after the inauguration, Stockman was asked by host Steve Bell, "Would you support holding off on a tax cut, deferring the tax cut until you have got the guarantee on the budget cuts?"

Stockman replied, "Well, I think we need a down payment on the budget cuts, I think we need to have in place by middle or late spring some major changes in entitlement programs and funding levels that we are going to propose."

Later that day, testifying on Capitol Hill, Stockman again stressed that the administration's tax cuts would be "joined" to its budget cuts, thereby implying that the amount of tax cuts would hinge on the spending reductions—an idea abhorrent to supply-side purists and indeed one ultimately rejected by the Reagan Administration. While Stockman was rankling the supply-side network, then Treasury Secretary Donald Regan surprised Washington by coming down firmly on the supply side. "You're holding up business there," scolded Regan, in rejecting the notion that tax cuts be contingent on spending reductions. The taxpayer, insisted Regan, "is entitled to be able to plan taxes and not have 'if' and 'maybe.' "

But part of the plan was already "if" and "maybe": the effective date. A week after the election, the transition team toyed with the idea of asking Congress to make the cuts effective in the spring. During the transition, columnist Novak met Stockman for breakfast. "Stockman told me he thought they might have to redo the tax cut and delay it for six months in order to reduce the deficit," Novak told Anne Urban. "I said to myself, 'Oh my God, I can't believe this.' I said to him, 'My goodness, it's the old tradition of raising taxes to reduce the deficit.' That's when I really started to have my doubts."

The doubts grew. In addition to his black books of budget cuts, Stockman had compiled another set of proposals, which he dubbed "Chapter Two." Aimed at bringing in an additional $20 billion, the proposals were also designed to squelch liberal critics by not only cutting social welfare programs but also closing tax loopholes for big corporations, particularly the multinational oil companies. According to Stockman, the President dismissed all but a suggestion to impose "user fees" on private boats and planes. Undaunted, Stockman later "cheerfully" explained to Greider, "Those were more like ornaments I was thinking of on the tax side. I call them equity ornaments. They're really not too good. They're not essential to the economics of the thing." ("If there is one thing that I have learned in my twenty years of public service," Representative David Obey would later thunder at the OMB director, "it is that equity is not an ornament.")

Robert Novak was not so sure that Stockman's "Chapter Two" cuts ever existed. "In the beginning of the administration he was telling me about that list," Novak told Anne Urban. "I said, 'Great, would you get that list to me so I can run it?' Stockman said sure he would, but he never got it to me, and now he tells people there never was such a list. That's sort of David's style—all smoke and mirrors."

Even if Stockman had succeeded in getting all of the budget cuts he was asking for, he would have still been faced with unprecedented deficits. A true supply-sider would not have been overly concerned, but the OMB director, in the words of Novak, had become an "establishment, Republican, green eyeshade, Herbert Hoover budget balancer."

The campaign to close the deficit took to all possible avenues, increasingly alienating the supply-siders. On January 7, 1981, two weeks before Reagan assumed office, "associates" of the President-elect revealed that the tax cuts would probably be delayed to July or August. The principal economic advisor pressing for this delay was Stockman, who envisioned 1982 deficits of over $100 billion if the cuts were not put on hold. Having conducted a vigorous lobbying effort to have Stockman appointed two weeks earlier, Jack Kemp already found himself in a major policy dispute with his former ally. "I think for both political and economic reasons we should go ahead with the original plan," Kemp told reporters. Eventually, Kemp lost his first battle; the administration put off the personal cuts until July 1, and Congress made them effective even later, on October 1. An inveterate enemy of Stockman's, Paul Craig Roberts (who ulti-. mately resigned as Assistant Treasury Secretary for Economic Policy), subsequently claimed that "The efforts to avoid deficits by delaying the tax cuts have produced deficits brought on by recession." Evans and Novak would weigh in with like criticisms of the OMB director, referring to the severe economic contraction that ensued as "the Stockman recession."

Stockman's old supply-side allies were far from the only critics. The tight money policy that was relentlessly pursued by the Federal Reserve kept interest rates high and discouraged capital investment. In September 1981, Jim Jones, chairman of the House Budget Committee, voiced a common anxiety: "My fear is that the program now put into place by the administration is the equivalent of stepping hard on the gas at the same time you slam on the brakes."

The Kemp–Stockman split grew over whether the maximum tax rate on unearned income would be reduced. The supply-siders wanted it cut from 70 to 50 percent. When the administration decided against the change in deference to the budget deficit, Kemp told *The New York Times*, "I no longer am bound. Obviously, I support the President but I will pursue my own program." Ostensibly a long-time supporter of what Kemp considered a vital portion of the tax bill, Stockman later admitted to having held a startlingly contrary view for quite some time.

On the other side of the ideological aisle, another experienced Stockman watcher was feeling a sense of *déjà vu*. David Cohen, former chief political lobbyist and president of Common Cause, who had known Stockman since his days as an aide to John

Anderson, was aware of Stockman's proclivity for turning on friends
and associates once he'd gotten what he wanted from them:

> Back in the early seventies, we were engaged in a bipartisan push for
> campaign financing reform, and I was working with John Anderson and
> Mo Udall, and Stockman was the bright young staff guy feeding
> Anderson the information on this issue. I didn't realize how much
> Stockman's politics had changed until he was in Congress himself and
> went on the House Administration Committee and didn't fight for
> campaign reform. I don't mean he opposed us, but he could have
> played an active role, and he didn't. It was instructive to me to watch
> him as he stood back on this issue in 1977 and 1978 and declined to
> fight for it. His performance had all the elements of taking a dive.
>
> I saw then, for the first time, that Stockman was not really part of the
> John Anderson wing of the Republican Party, the Barber Conable wing,
> men who may have had differences but had in common caring about
> the party. David Stockman was really just interested in maintaining the
> status quo. I should have caught on when, as I said before, I visited his
> first congressional office and he showed me, with great pride, how he
> had everything *programmed*. Right from the start, he understood the
> power of incumbency, and how to increase it.

Despite his obvious shift to more conservative economics, Stockman was able to remain in Kemp's good graces—a position he
considered very important. "As long as Jack is happy with what's
happening," Stockman would later tell Greider, "it's hard for the
[supply-side] network to mobilize itself with a shrill voice. Jack's
satisfied, although we're sort of on thin ice with him."

Paul Craig Roberts believes that in his budget-cutting offensive,
Stockman was simply looking to grab the limelight from Jack Kemp.
A half-joking comment by Kemp hinted that he shared that view of
his relationship with Stockman. Quipped the former Buffalo Bill
quarterback, "I'm tired of Dave Stockman pushing me off the front
pages. The next thing, I'll be seeing him on the cover of a sports
magazine with his arm cocked back ready to throw a pass."

Meanwhile, almost unnoticed beside the supply-side experiment
was another equally large change in tax policy. This was the
administration's vast business tax cut, which would slice business's
tax bill by accelerating the rate at which it could depreciate
investments. The scheme had its roots in the "Carlton Group"—so

named for the Washington hotel in which a gaggle of businessmen and lobbyists met for weekly breakfast meetings. Foremost among this coffee-and-danish cabal was Charls Walker, head of the American Council for Capital Formation and a former deputy secretary in the Treasury. Other regular attendees included representatives from the Business Roundtable and Fortune 500 companies such as Chrysler.

When the Carlton Group began huddling over business strategies back in the mid-1970s, they probably never dreamed that in a matter of five years they would walk away with unprecedented corporate prizes. But business's influence in Washington steadily increased in the late 1970s. Business lobbyists successfully defeated labor law reform, the establishment of a Consumer Protection Agency, and weakened regulatory agencies that monitored their activities. In 1978, business groups not only succeeded in defeating a set of tax loophole reforms proposed by President Carter, but were able to widen other chinks in tax laws. One reason was money. While corporate and trade association political action committees (PACs) had donated $6.7 million in 1976, by 1980 that figure had shot up to $67.7 million—a 900 percent increase.

Buoyed by their victories, the group set out to make a good thing better. Thus was born 10–5–3. The plan provided for generous depreciation allowances on capital investment—so generous, the provision threatened to do away with the corporate income tax. For many it was too much to swallow, even for some members of the business community. *Fortune* magazine, generally a big business booster, had this to say: "Business's dismal record of putting its parochial interest above the general good is the darkest cloud over Washington's new approach to taxes." Of an earlier investment tax credit, which the Carlton Group had been instrumental in passing in 1978, the *Fortune* article noted wryly, "There is no doubt it has boosted spending on equipment (and the number of doctors driving Mercedes-Benz)."

Jude Wanniski referred to the 10–5–3 plan as the "Idea of the establishmentarians, the pain and austerity boys." Said Wanniski, "These were the same guys who would have *killed* to see Connally elected. When that campaign went down the tubes and Reagan got the nomination, they swarmed around him." Wanniski maintained that 10–5–3 was the "invention of Charlie Walker and the rest of the

Business Roundtable"—which is undoubtedly true. William Niskanen of the Council of Economic Advisors confirmed this. Asked who was behind the business tax cuts, Niskanen replied, "I think as far as I can trace the history on that, nobody except maybe Charlie Walker really knew what was going on." Wanniski agreed: "They shoved it down the throats of the administration," which implies more resistance than there actually was. During his 1980 campaign, Reagan told *The Wall Street Journal* that if given his druthers he would choose to eliminate corporate taxes altogether, "But I know you can't campaign on this. It would be twisted and turned around and everyone would think you are for the capitalist rich."

Reagan, true to his word, did not campaign on eliminating the corporate tax; yet once in office, he pressed for a plan that would do that. The heart of his business tax bill, 15–10–5–3, was little more than a modified version of Charlie Walker's 10–5–3 scheme.

Also known as the Accelerated Cost Recovery System (ACRS), 15–10–5–3 allowed for near lightning speed write-offs for purchases of equipment by business. In the past, corporate write-offs to cover depreciation (also known as the wearing out of equipment) had been done over periods ranging from two to sixty years. If a small truck had an expected life span of five years, the truck was depreciated over a five-year period.

The Reagan plan changed all that. ACRS simplified and expedited depreciation cycles by lumping all capital investments under four headings: a three-year write-off for autos, light trucks, electronic materials, and other short-lived capital; five-year write-offs for heavy trucks, bulldozers, cranes, and other comparable hardy equipment; fifteen-year depreciation schedules for most buildings; and ten years for nearly everything else that eluded the categories above. Reagan did not stop at supporting the ACRS plan. Eventually, he came out in favor of an expensive provision known as tax leasing, which allows companies to buy and sell their tax breaks.

On Friday, June 6, 1981, Reagan made public his tax package in the White House Rose Garden. That unveiling left the business community in a rage when they realized the ACRS plan had been substantially cut. What has come to be known as the "Lear Jet Weekend" (one Senate Finance staff member calls it the "Leer and Jest Weekend") ensued. Top executives from across the country flew in to Washington on Saturday and Sunday, ready to twist any arm available to have ACRS, in its full form, reinstated.

They were successful. On Monday, June 9, the White House capitulated and then, as if to show the business community how truly sorry it was, the administration added still more business sweeteners to its package. The most notorious of those sweeteners proved to be the tax leasing provision. (A March 1982 Treasury Department study showed that in the three weeks of 1981 during which tax leasing was allowed, $11.4 billion in would-be taxes were sold.) Roger Altman of the investment banking firm of Lehman Bros. commented at the time, "The tax bill has virtually phased out the corporate tax in America."

According to Robert McIntyre of Citizens for Tax Justice, over the next decade the business tax plan will cost over one-half trillion dollars—$500,000,000,000. And most of those dollars will be going to those corporations whose assets top $250 million. McIntyre has calculated that just as nearly a third of the individual tax breaks will go to the top 6 percent of wage earners in the country, nearly 80 percent of 10–5–3 will go to the top 1,700 corporations. Those gathering the largest share of benefits from the plan will be the oil (up to $100 billion) and gas and electric companies ($30 billion). Indeed, in the words of Harvard Professor Dale Jorgenson, the administration's business cut will, "to paraphrase Dave Stockman, create a coast-to-coast soupline." And Representative John Seiberling (D-OH) sent out a press release with this observation after its implementation: "There's a joke going around Wall Street. It says that if your company is still paying income taxes, you obviously haven't read the new tax law. Well, it's a joke all right, but the joke is on the rest of the taxpayers."

Though the cuts are designed to provide incentives to business, there is little evidence to show that business is actually reinvesting even half the money it is retaining from these breaks. Economists Robert Eisner and Robert Chirinko of Northwestern University concluded in an early 1980 study for the Treasury Department that "one can get almost any answer one wants as to the effects of tax incentives" from economic models. Based on previous tax breaks to business, the two economists estimated that a scant 40 percent of the breaks would be used to purchase such items as typewriters and trucks. According to Eisner, it would make more sense to "have government buy the new plants and equipment and give them to business." Early in 1982, the Commerce Department issued a dismal projection: investments were expected to be *down* in real terms during the coming year, not up.

Where is the money from these tax breaks going? While the President's Council of Economic Advisors issued a report which stated that the business tax cut plan would have the "advantage of reducing incentives for mergers," the effect is apt to be just the opposite. Encouraged by the administration's lax antitrust enforcement, 1981 saw a record $82 billion in mergers.

Neither the personal nor the business tax cuts were nicked in Congress. Cries of dissent were squelched or hardly taken seriously. Early in May 1981, Senate Democrats offered a proposal on the floor that would have scaled down the size of the first-year personal tax cut by $32.5 billion. "Vote no" was the only argument offered by Senate Finance Chairman, Bob Dole (R-KS). The chamber accepted this pithy advice 61 to 24.

Business lobbyists watched their gains with glee. "There was a time when you practically had to explain to people that capital formation didn't refer to the shape of the Capitol dome," remarked Mark Bloomfield, executive director of the American Council for Capital Formation, in early February 1981. "All you heard about was 'tax reform' and 'closing loopholes.' Those days are gone."

Talk of "reform" and "closing loopholes" waned and then almost disappeared in committee meetings. The administration remained silent on both counts. An exchange between Stockman and Senator Howard Metzenbaum (D-OH), one of the OMB director's sharpest critics, prior to the start of a hearing explained why. "Dave, why can't we do something about closing those loopholes?" the senator asked. "It's not me," Stockman replied. "I think we should close them and broaden the tax base." "Well, then, why can't we do something?" "It's the party line," retorted Stockman. "The best thing you can do is make me squirm. That's part of my job."

Together, the supply-side tax cuts for individuals and the accelerated depreciation plan for business moved through Congress with only the most cursory examination. Over a three-and-a-half-day period in May, the Senate Finance Committee, led by Dole, approved the largest tax bill in history by cutting taxes $700 billion. Throughout, business lobbyists packed the hearing room. Their omnipresence prompted Chairman Dole to remark with a chuckle, "This would be a good place to hold a fund-raising dinner."

Tax reform proposals were not in evidence. (It should come as no surprise that Reagan and his advisers showed little interest in tightening tax loopholes. In 1971, a flustered Governor Reagan admitted he paid no California state income tax in 1970, despite his $73,000 plus income. Jack Anderson took a look at Reagan's financial disclosure statement and concluded that in 1970, Reagan had probably "paid no federal taxes" either. A Reagan staffer denied this, saying the governor had paid "several hundred dollars" in federal taxes that year.) Senator Daniel Patrick Moynihan (D-NY) did manage to pass a measure that closed a loophole for commodity speculators. Some time later, Moynihan offered a provision to reduce the capital gains tax on investments. "I remind the Treasury that I got you $1.3 billion a few hours ago," chided Moynihan. "We already spent that, Senator," replied Dole.

A $700 billion loss in revenues over five years was a staggering drain that Stockman knew would be impossible to cover in spending cuts. Seeing the problem he was facing, Stockman began a subtle drive to compromise on a smaller tax bill in the House. Looking back at the events, Robert Kaiser of *The Washington Post* wrote: "Stockman hoped that the Democratic controlled House of Representatives would moderate the size of the tax cuts and thus the size of the federal deficits. 'Don't worry, the House will bail us out.' This was the slogan at OMB. But the House did not cooperate." Confronted by this and other quotes at a Governmental Affairs hearing on the day after Kaiser's article appeared (October 6, 1981), Stockman protested to Senator Thomas Eagleton (D-MO), "Let me just say *The Washington Post* is having a bad week."

Stockman, of course, could not publicly acknowledge he did not want the House to pass the President's package. But his feelings had been clear for months. In a May 17 meeting with reporters, Stockman sent out a clear signal to the House: "No one writes a sacred text for budget, tax or any other policy that doesn't get some kneading and shaping as it moves through the process." The OMB director also explained that administration "preferred" rather than insisted on the three-year, 30 percent reduction in taxes. "We probably nuanced it incorrectly" in the beginning, admitted Stockman.

The House took Stockman's advice and "kneaded and shaped" the tax package, but in a manner that exacerbated Stockman's deficit problem. Rostenkowski and the House leadership grew so desperate to stop their headlong retreat and post a victory—any kind of victory—on the tax bill that they entered into a special interest bidding war with Republicans that drove up the price of the tax bill to levels that would create the largest deficits in the history of the Republic. (When judging the House Democrats' role in the tax cut controversy, one is reminded of the words of one Michigan state senator: "Now we've got them right where they want us.")

As the months passed, Rostenkowski came to favor legislation embracing many of the elements in the Kemp–Roth bill. It was a matter, according to the Illinois representative, of "whether you want to lose courageously or win." There were two important exceptions in the Democrats' bill, however: their attempt to target the cuts toward those making under $50,000, and a proposal to raise the "zero bracket" (or the cap on tax-free income), a measure designed to aid the working poor. The Democrats also included a "trigger" on the third year of the bill, which would make the third-year cut effective only if the economy had performed as predicted. (Reagan explained that the trigger was a fine idea for those who only intended to live for another two years. When the curtain rose on the July 29 House floor debate, numerous Republicans sported buttons announcing, "I plan to live.")

Rostenkowski and the House leadership held out against the across-the-board feature of the Reagan cut, which in practice favored the top income earner. On that issue, negotiations between the Democrats and the White House broke down.

Reagan launched a personal lobbying effort to push his bill over the top. Late in July, fourteen Democrats were flown out to Camp David for a barbeque and some last-minute politicking. Reagan also summoned wavering Democrats to the Oval Office, where he won their support with warm smiles and a stack of 3-by-5 index cards that doubled as cue cards. When Representative John Meyers (R-ID) told Reagan he feared ballooning deficits, the former actor had an answer from his Hollywood days. Meyers remembers Reagan saying, "Well, when I was in the movies, I'd reach a point each year where after the second movie I'd be in the ninety percent bracket. So I wouldn't make any more movies that year. And it wasn't just me, but Bogart and Gable and the others did the same. We weren't the only ones who were hurt. The people who worked the props and the people who worked in the yard, they were the ones who were hurt." House Budget Chairman James Jones was not convinced. "I want to be honest," he told the President. "I think both tax bills are bad for the economy. I think you and the country are sitting on a real time bomb."

Jim Jones proved to be the exception and not the rule. By the time the tax cut vote rolled around, the whole affair had dissolved into a media event. *The Washington Post's* Thomas Edsall tired of the display, describing it as a "public relations contest conducted before television cameras." Rostenkowski complained, "My problem is that the President can gear up his army with just one television appearance. That's fighting the Army, Navy and Air Force."

On July 29, the day of the vote, rhetoric soared through the Capitol. Using an analogy that pops up at least once a year around tax time, Representative Bobbi Fiedler (R-CA) told the chamber that "just as those patriots long ago threw the King's tea into Boston harbor, we must throw the Rostenkowski plan into the trash heap of useless legislation."

The Democrats, needless to say, had brought plenty of return fire. Said Speaker of the House Tip O'Neill, "It is very interesting what has happened. I think perhaps last week we had this bill won. Literally thousands of phone calls and letters came in. I guess we got everything in the tax bill but a cut for the tax callers, particularly for Philip Morris, Paine Webber, Monsanto, Exxon, McDonnell Douglas, who were so kind to allow the use of their staff to the President of the United States in flooding the switchboards of America."

Since the Democrats had spent the previous weeks trying to outbid Reagan for the support of those companies, O'Neill's words had a hollow ring to them. But the Democrats' gambit had failed. They were unable to weed the big business lobbies away from the Republicans, who matched the Democrats dollar for dollar in tax giveaways. Stockman later estimated that wooing the winning votes to the administration's plan cost an additional $60 million in tax breaks. The concessions included real estate tax shelters and still more provisions to whittle away at the corporate income tax. Although Stockman lent a hand in the bargaining, he later rhetorically asked Greider, "Do you realize the greed that came to the forefront?" The OMB director described the scene: "The hogs were really feeding. The greed level, the level of opportunism, just got out of control." Still, Stockman's ethical misgivings about the horsetrading that had resulted in massive giveaways were the least of his worries.

The oil companies elbowed their way to the front of the trough. While their profits had increased 117 percent in the past two years *(twelve times* that of other industries), big oil managed to rake in a whopping promise of $33 billion in breaks over the next ten years—above the billions in breaks they can expect to receive under the ACRS. Representative Dennis Eckart (D-OH) summarized the situation: "President Reagan gave away cufflinks to gain passage of his budget bill, and now he gives away billions to oil companies to pass his tax bill." Representative Barney Frank (D-MA) protested, "I do not object to the eyes of Texas being upon me; I object to the hands of Texas being in my pockets, because when we put into this bill special provisions for the oil industry that only about fifteen members of this body are prepared to defend on their merits, we make an error."

On the sidelines, one oil lobbyist could hardly contain his glee: "It's a bonanza, no getting around it."

9 • Some Discouraging Words

BACK HOME in St. Joseph, Michigan, in the fall of 1981, almost any man or woman on the street would have told you that David Stockman could do no wrong. Look at the miracle he had accomplished in such a short period of time! But in Washington, certain spoilsports—"naysayers," the President would call them— were beginning to take a harder look at what David Stockman had wrought. Soon they would begin to speak up. But for the moment, and from the outside, Stockman was still looking good.

He, however, knew better, for he harbored a traditional Republican fear of the huge deficits such a tax cut might produce. And all but the most ardent supply siders quickly began to doubt that the tax cuts would produce the economic growth promised. Faced with the prospect of losing over $750 billion in revenues over the next five years, Stockman launched a determined, albeit nearly silent, drive to raise taxes. A scant sixty days after the tax bill had been passed, Senator Bob Dole suggested a three-month postponement of the personal cuts. At the same time, talk of "revenue enhancement"—a tidy euphemism for tax increases—began leaking from the executive branch as Stockman slowly won converts in his efforts to undo what Congress had wrought.

The personal tax cut actually had little to recommend it in the way of increasing investment and saving. In 1981, a family of four earning under $10,000 could expect to save an average of $17 from the cuts. In 1983, when the effect of bracket creep and Social Security increases were taken into account, those making under $10,000 would see an *increase* of $240 in their tax bills, according to a study done by the Congressional Budget Office. When this figure was combined with the drastic benefit cuts for the working poor, there would be little "incentive" to work at all, much less invest and save.

In an interview with Anne Urban, Arthur Laffer observed, "The shocking thing about what Stockman has done is while he has kept the minimum benefits there for not working, he has reduced the benefits at each level of working, which means that unemployment is going to increase dramatically in the ghettos." Indeed, unemployment was destined to rise dramatically everywhere, not only in the inner city. The May 8, 1982, headline of *The Washington Post* relayed the grim news: UMEMPLOYMENT WORST SINCE THE GREAT DEPRESSION.

As for middle-income earners, *The Wall Street Journal*, whose editorial writers had long supported the cuts, ran an article on July 29, 1981, that admitted "Retailers See Public Using Fall Tax Cuts Mostly for Christmas Buying, Not Saving." Explaining that some stores were planning to advertise "tax cut specials," the article quoted Martin Tolep, Woolworth's corporate economist, who predicted, "Virtually all of the increase for families earning $20,000 to $50,000 will be reflected in retail store sales."

Such worries were not apt to bother the administration, as the cuts were aimed at those they felt would invest—those earning over $50,000 a year. The implicit assumption in this skewed form of tax relief was parodied in a March 1981 Doonesbury cartoon: Mr.

Slackmeyer, the administration's economic spokesman, is asked by a congressman, "Wouldn't you agree that the most indefensible aspect of your tax cut proposals is the unconscionable way in which they favor the rich?" Slackmeyer takes issue: "From past experience, we know that the well-heeled are the only class that can be depended on to put their tax cuts into savings and investment." "And the poor?" queries the representative. "Studies show they tend to blow it all at the track."

Asked on February 22, 1981, if he would support a tax bill that provided greater relief for lower- and middle-income workers, Stockman echoed the cry of Mr. Slackmeyer: "That would be totally unacceptable. I would recommend a veto of any tax bill premised on redistributing the tax burden. That will achieve nothing in terms of the economic expansion the country needs."

And the rich, the people that the administration was counting on to turn the country around, were unlikely to do so. More likely was an upsurge in real estate and a run on luxury items. Conservative economist Arthur Burns (later U.S. Ambassador to West Germany) concluded that the tax cuts would do little more than "drive up the price of antiques." Indeed, while the assets of such financial institutions as savings and loans continued to drop precipitously, new forms of speculation—notably options and futures based on the rise and fall of the stock market—were proliferating, siphoning away capital from productive uses.

The business tax cut also quickly lived up to the predictions of its critics. Even with cuts—designed to create jobs and boost revenue-producing capital investment—capital spending dropped in 1982, a victim of recession, unused capacity, and high interest rates. Having done nearly everything but take business by the hand and purchase their new equipment for them, the administration was both baffled and angry with the corporate sector. Treasury Secretary Regan lashed out in September 1981: "We have carried through on our commitments . . . but where is the business response? Where are the new research and development initiatives? Where are the new plants? Where are the expansion plans? It's like dropping a coin down a well—all I'm hearing is a hollow clink." Wall Street retaliated sharply and swiftly. Peter G. Peterson, chairman of Lehman Bros. and a Stockman mentor-to-be, shot back, "The street speaks only on tape—in prices and spreads, and these signals are coming from all over the world. Blaming Wall Street for what is happening is like blaming the waiter for obesity."

"It's no secret that there is a healthy and fierce debate going on within the administration about whether there should be a U-turn," admitted Jack Kemp, referring to the tax question. By other yard-sticks, Kemp was understating the controversy—especially between Donald Regan and David Stockman. The supply-siders had initially been suspicious of the former Merrill Lynch chairman now running the Treasury Department, fearing that he was a Republican traditionalist. But Regan and Martin Anderson, a White House domestic policy adviser, proved to be the supply-siders' heartiest allies among Reagan's inner circle.

Early on in the Reagan Administration, Walter Wriston, chairman of Citicorp, had predicted that, "One of these days, Don Regan is going to eat David Stockman for breakfast." Come late October, the table seemed to have been set. One Treasury official told *The New York Times* that Regan was openly exasperated and angry with Stockman.

President Reagan remained unconvinced as to the merits of "revenue enhancement." Appearing at a Republican fundraiser in New York City, he assured his audience, "Your tax cut will not be rescinded. It will not be delayed, and it will not be reduced." But Reagan exhibited little fealty to his balanced budget pledge. On November 6, the President told reporters, "I've never said anything but that it was a goal. And the eventual goal, whether it comes then [1984] or whether it has to be delayed or not, is a balanced budget." That statement contrasted sharply with one Reagan had made in his September 1980 debate with John Anderson: "I believe the budget can be balanced by 1982 or 1983."

A mixed but interesting chorus of other voices was beginning to make itself heard on the subject of David Stockman. In August, Robert O. "Bobby" Muller, head of the Vietnam Veterans of America, which had just been recognized by the Veterans Association as an official organization, was thankful. He had words of praise for both VA head Robert P. Nimmo and President Reagan ("Ronald Reagan was spontaneous enough," he said, after the President had met in mid-July at the White House with veterans' leaders, "in response to our questions for me to conclude that he's honestly sympathetic and supportive of the Vietnam veteran.")

However, he had no warm words for or about Mr. Stockman. As *The New York Times* reported on August 16:

> At the same July 17 meeting . . . Mr. Muller bluntly complained to Mr. Reagan about David A. Stockman, the director of the Office of Management and Budget, who had sought vainly to limit funds for storefront counseling centers. According to Mr. Muller, he told the President that "Stockman has particularly aggrieved many Vietnam veterans because he opposed the conflict while in college and spent the war years at Harvard Divinity School." Mr. Reagan sat and listened, saying nothing in response, said Mr. Muller.

That same month, consumer activist Ralph Nader, evidently even more "aggrieved" than the Vietnam vets, wrote Stockman a long, stinging letter of general complaint. After scolding him for what he termed "your across-the-board obstruction of the government's statutory lifesaving and disease-reducing missions," Nader wrote:

> Your practice, as Director of OMB, is one of governing by assertion. Since the wide publicity given to your "Manifesto," titled "Avoiding a GOP Economic Dunkirk" may have impressed you with the ease with which your official position can render your ignorance temporarily invincible, you have failed to back up your policies with substantiation. The shallowness of your manifesto and its follow-up can be illustrated by the way you listed critical health and safety standards or proposed standards for recision and totaled up the industry savings without also totaling up both the dollar savings to consumers and the health and safety benefits which these standards bring in turn. Not only do you uncritically accept industry cost figures, you also fail to distinguish between gross or net costs (after tax benefits for example), learning curves for cost reduction over time, how such investments increase both the quality and quantity of GNP and many other factors. These factors are so obvious in the literature that to ignore them reveals more willfulness than technical ignorance.

Nader wanted to know why Stockman, despite the provisions of the Freedom of Information Act, refused to provide OMB's supporting memoranda—"if indeed they exist"—for public scrutiny. As a way of "amplifying what tiny kernel of empathy may be striving to survive within your mind," he suggested a series of "tours" for the OMB director, which, he wrote, "could open your eyes, quicken your conscience and ease your clenched jaw fanaticism toward the injured, the sick, the weak and the poor."

1. Spend an hour with representatives from Allstate and State Farm insurance companies who with their films of auto crashes and how air bags have saved American lives on the highway, can prepare you for an evening spent with highway police accident patrols that go to the scene of fatal highway crashes. . . .

2. To arrive at a better understanding of the need for stronger enforcement of the Clean Air Act, you should journey down Interstate 77 into Charleston and the Kanawha Valley in West Virginia. According to the National Cancer Institute, death rates for cancer and leukemia are among the top ten percent in the country, leading medical specialists to connect these rates to the pollutants emitted from the area's five large chemical plants. . . .

3. Spend a day at the card room of the 85-year-old Hermitage Cotton Mill in Camden, South Carolina. You might not be able to hear the person next to you because of the grinding of the carding machines and your earplugs. Nor will you be able to talk to them through the bulky face-covering respirators that are necessitated by cotton dust levels five times higher than OSHA standards allow. . . .

4. Dr. Donald Rasmussen of the Appalachian Pulmonary Laboratory will be happy to accompany you during a day of treating and examining patients with black lung disease at the Laboratory—located in the Appalachian Regional Hospital in Beckley, West Virginia. . . .

5. To gain some empathy for the reality of workplace noise, you could spend a day watching the forging of crank shafts, axle shafts and front end parts at the Chevrolet Tonowanda Forge, in Tonowanda, New York (near Buffalo). Taking your colleague Jack Kemp with you. Mr. Garath "Stretch" Tubbs, the health and safety representative for UAW local 846, would be pleased to show you around through areas where the noise regularly reaches 105 decibels. On the way back to Washington, you might want to take a small detour and stop off at Love Canal and see what is left of that neighborhood.

6. The Fair Haven Community Clinic at 374 Grand Avenue, New Haven, Connecticut, would welcome your visit to talk to some of the 1000 women who have been able to meet their basic nutritional needs during pregnancy through the Women, Infants, and Children (WIC) program. All of these women are needy; some of them would give birth to sick or deformed children without the benefit of the milk, cheese, eggs and other staples provided by the WIC program. Most simply cannot afford proper cereal or other food for their babies without the WIC vouchers they receive. Talk with Elizabeth Gersten, who heads the program. She will provide some insight on what the 20 percent budget cut—which will lessen monthly caseloads by one-third—will mean to the pre- and post-natal needy women that this program serves.

"Having returned from these short trips to reality," Nader added, "you might muster the courage to go after the bloated corporate subsidies and military contracting waste that you have virtually ignored. Those areas are where the billions of dollars of saving are contained along with enormous economic benefits that accrue from bringing them under national cost-controls."

He concluded with an invitation:

Once again may I invite you to appear at the Public Citizen Forum in Washington at a date and time of your choosing between now and the end of the year. The Forum has hosted numerous Cabinet Secretaries under both the Ford and Carter Administrations. Your speaking with an audience of informed groups would itself be an advisable change from your steady diet of addresses to trade groups and corporate executives. The practice of these citizen leaders asking questions of the speakers should not unduly trouble a person with strong convictions such as yourself; or should it?

Stockman did not accept the invitation.

In September, Evans and Novak had reported in their syndicated column:

Facing the fear of the faithful, Stockman responded in his old role as Reagan's revolutionary. Although he styles himself as a practical politician not chained by visionary dogma, he met faltering faith at the Reagan grass roots with pure supply-side credo. Stockman's frenetic tour (26 performances in four days) confronted anti-Reagan social activists, peace demonstrators, striking air traffic controllers and ERA enthusiasts chanting and picketing at every stop. If such a demonstration could be launched at Mankato, Minn., a month before his budget cuts begin to bite, Stockman pondered what will take place later in big cities. . . .

"I think he's got the right cure," a homebuilder who had just paid $500 for a Stockman reception in South Bend, Ind., told us, "But I wonder if it's going to kill us first." . . . He left those worried Midwestern Republicans feeling better but not wholly reassured. After Stockman promised in South Bend that the prime rate would drop to 8 or 9 percent by the mid-1980s, a manufacturer told us: "That's a 2 percent drop a year. By that time, I'll be ruined." In truth, Stockman believes the progress will be swifter. If not, he knows the chanting pickets outside and the frightened Republicans inside are the foretaste of much worse to come.

The first week of October saw a flurry of negative comments. Both Mo Udall (speaking to the Women's National Democratic Club) and Missouri Democrat Richard Bolling (in an interview with a group of reporters) said that the only way to avoid the mounting deficits that were sure to follow the passage of the tax cuts bill would be to slow them down or to repeal some of the new loopholes. Stockman himself was quoted in *The New York Times* as saying he wouldn't seek further budget cuts, if the economy weakened further, just to keep the deficits from growing larger.

On October 7, *The Washington Post* editorialized:

> In case you missed the first, or second, or third time around, let us say it again: there is something fundamentally wrongheaded and outrageously unfair about the recent changes in welfare law that punish people for working. We are not talking about some abstruse concern of theoretical economics. We are talking about real people who now face the grotesque choice of either quitting their jobs or, by keeping them, losing both income and medical care.

It was hardly just the so-called liberal press that was giving Stockman what for. All during the fall, Evans and Novak had been weighing in with reports that were not designed to bring a smile to the face of the budget director. On September 6, they had embarrassed him by revealing that while he was calling for all of America to climb on a noticeably austere bandwagon, he and Defense Secretary Weinberger were jetting to California via a very first class mode of air travel—Air Force courier jets.

"While the plane stayed in California to await Weinberger's return," they wrote, "another Air Force jet was deadheaded west to pick up Stockman and return him. Cost of a courier roundtrip: $15,000 in fuel alone. To some insiders, the profligate expenditure on such flights shows a mindset in the White House oblivious to personal cost-cutting."

Eleven days later they leveled a far more serious charge:

> A private one-on-one meeting initiated by budget director David Stockman with Rep. Jack Kemp ended with the congressman delivering a lecture against destroying Ronald Reagan's revolution by turning backwards to orthodox, big-business Republicanism.
>
> On the morning of Oct. 14, Stockman turned up in Kemp's congressional office (with no aides present) to explain reports that he was willing to delay next year's 10 percent tax cut by three months. He asserted he was under terrific pressure from orthodox Republican senators, such as Bob Dole (finance committee chairman) and Pete Domenici (budget committee chairman). Stockman asked Kemp: What else can be done to close the budget deficit?
>
> Kemp replied that retreating to Republican follies of the past would be no answer. To delay individual tax cuts while keeping big business tax cuts in force, he said, would be the worst kind of politics. He then urged his old compatriot Stockman to join him in saving Reagan's program.

On November 4, they sent another broadside across Stockman's bow. This one—which said Treasury Secretary Donald Regan's star was in the ascendancy, and perhaps on its way to eclipsing David Stockman's—must have hurt (and, hurt or not, it was an eerily accurate call):

> In the wake of the Reagan administration's failed "September offensive" for austerity, Treasury Secretary Donald Regan is reaching for dominance in economic policy-making by opposing tax increases and downgrading budget deficits. Regan has not won yet. . . . Don Regan, 62-year-old Wall Street barracuda, may be nearing the triumph over budget director David Stockman, 34-year-old congressional boy wonder, that long has been predicted by Washington insiders. But nobody guessed that Regan would be championing supply-side economics against Stockman, the ex-Michigan congressman originally pushed for the Cabinet by advocates of supply-side tax reduction.

The final paragraph must have made unpleasant reading for Stockman, who had been an eager confidant of Robert Novak's ever since he'd been a new congressman. "The Treasury," it began, "wants to shift the debate from fiscal to monetary policy. That reflects this flat assertion in [Paul Craig] Roberts' *Fortune* article: 'The evidence seems clear that money growth, and not budget deficits, explains inflation and interest rates.' He is implying that Stockman's 'September Offensive' not only failed but was an exercise in futility, which is precisely Don Regan's message today."

The suggestion, ever less subtly made, that Stockman was riding for some kind of a fall was beginning to sound like an echo of an echo. The month before Evans and Novak raised Don Regan at the expense of Stockman, Robert Kaiser of *The Washington Post* had all but predicted serious problems. In a long piece on Stockman's first year, Kaiser wrote that the young budget director had had quite a year. And he said that it was "far from over. There are many more battles still to win and lose. Yes, lose. Stockman now loses battles more often than he did in the beginning, back when the new Reagan administration took shape around the bold proposals of this 34-year-old anti-war activist turned avant-garde conservative."

According to Kaiser:

> Stockman tossed phony numbers into the air last winter, numbers predicting better economic developments than were possible. He knew he was doing it, but felt he had to, according to people around him. Now the numbers have to be revised. In fact, Stockman is being pressed to publish an economic forecast in January that is much gloomier than anything the administration has fessed up to yet.

Stockman, said the article, had even begun to show signs of being depressed, but had recently "snapped out of his September blues." It was just as well, for he would need all the good spirits he could muster to handle the next crisis on his personal horizon. And, to make matters worse, unlike the graying economic picture, this one he brought on *entirely* by himself.

David Stockman turned thirty-five on November 10, 1981; a T-shirt proclaiming "I am a team player" on the front and "Treasury Department Supply Siders" on the back was given to Stockman, compliments of Donald Regan, at the weekly breakfast meeting of Weidenbaum, Regan, and Stockman.

Two days later the *Atlantic* story broke, and, tax debate or no tax debate, all of Washington could talk of nothing else.

10 • "L'Affaire *Atlantic*"

VISIBLE FROM the front lawn of the White House, and a short walk from Stockman's office in the Old Executive Building, is the Hay–Adams Hotel—scene of the Saturday morning breakfast meetings of the OMB director and the author of the *Atlantic* article, William Greider. The hotel's restaurant, Le Danielle, is reached by passing through an impressive lobby of carved mahogany. At lobby's end, the dining room is clearly demarcated by one of the largest chandeliers south of Newport, Rhode Island. White linen tablecloths are topped by crystal vases each bearing a single bud rose.

A daytime favorite of the young professional set working in the area's executive offices and hundred-attorney-plus law firms, the restaurant certainly makes one feel as if one has arrived—or is about to. Evenings bring out a slightly older (and considerably wealthier) crowd.

In late 1981 and early 1982, Le Danielle was visited by a small but steady stream of the curious, making it something of a new Watergate. "Business is better than usual, yes," admitted one tuxedoed waiter shortly after the *Atlantic* story broke.

Here amidst all this stately elegance Stockman would eat his breakfast of choice—scrambled eggs and bacon—while over a period of eight months, he and *Washington Post* editor William Greider met, with Stockman saying some decidedly *un*stately things into the journalist's tape recorder.

What prompted Stockman, dubbed by *The Washington Post* as the "vicar" of Reagan domestic policy, to break the very same ranks that he had largely created himself? According to Greider, the arrangement would be mutually beneficial, would have "obvious symbiotic value."

As a congressman, Stockman had readily admitted to feeding the press. While old guard Republicans cast a suspicious eye on the media (Senator Barry Goldwater once denounced those younger

Republicans who "Literally can't go to the bathroom without issuing a press release"), Stockman and his peers, among them Jack Kemp, were anxious to air their views. "We believe our ideas have intellectual responsibility, and we think the press will recognize that. The traditional Republicans probably sensed, even if they didn't know it, that their ideas lacked intellectual responsibility," the OMB director told Greider.

Before Stockman officially was named budget director, he confidently assured the supply-side allies who had won him his position that he had "snared" *The Washington Post*. According to Jude Wanniski, "Stockman began telling us, when he was part of the group, back in 1979 that he was establishing a connection with Greider. He announced this to us as a coup. We said that's great. We wanted journalists who were opposed to us to sit down and listen to us, because the whole thing that keeps us moving is our ability to communicate ideas."

"I can just hear him [Stockman] saying, 'I've got a great connection with the *Post*,' " remarks Greider wryly. "He really managed to snow them." Wanniski, in retrospect, is even less kind: "It was only a narrow pipeline into the administration, so it gives them at the *Post* a distorted view, and it gives Stockman a distorted view on how easy it is to manipulate the capitalist press to his own ends. It all blew up in his face."

But early on, when Stockman's tenure had just begun, the former student of American history accepted the opportunity to relate future American history, with himself at center stage. Ultimately, after having created an economic policy of near-monolithic status, Stockman admitted to Greider that the program he had "sold" contained only one fixed point: the rich would benefit as a result of it. Apparently the ethics of the administration's economic program was a minor concern for Stockman; he viewed the program as a way to cement his name in history.

On October 1, 1981, Representative Thomas J. Downey (D-NY) told Stockman, "I have no doubt that when the history of this Administration is written, you will play a very large role." For David Stockman, these must have been the words he had waited all his life to hear, words that eclipsed any commitment to a particular ideology.

Stockman displayed this lack of commitment when he assumed his position as head of OMB. Although he had relied on the supply-siders to get him the position in the first place, he quickly turned his back on their agenda and allied himself with more traditional economists like Alan Greenspan and Herbert Stein. Conducting the interviews with a *Post* editor allowed the OMB director to do this surreptitiously. Stockman's relationship with Greider let the budget head use the newspaper as a mighty mouthpiece against his intellectual adversaries.

As the anonymous source from the OMB, Stockman used the press to mobilize support for his positions; most notably he focused attention on huge expected deficits in the hopes that panic over those deficits would force a huge tax rise. Stockman was also anxious to use Evans and Novak, the conservative columnists, as a pipeline for his views. Asked whether the OMB director called him with huge deficit predictions, saying "these ought to be printed," Novak replied, "Well, Dave, isn't that crude or gross. It was all done on a very casual basis but yes, he was a source of what was happening."

Upon hearing of the *Atlantic* incident, ex-president Gerald Ford said, "Dave's just a young person and he talked too much." Jude Wanniski, Arthur Laffer, and Robert Novak all mentioned Stockman's age as a primary factor in his philosophical flimflamming as well. But Novak qualified his statement in an interview with Anne Urban:

> It isn't just his age, it's how you live your age. Let me just say that a man of thirty-five can have been married, had children, met a payroll, had his own firm. At thirty-five he is an adult, a mature person. He may not be much, he may be very prosaic, but there is a guy who for fifteen years has had as much responsibility as he is ever going have. Or at thirty-five you can, and I'm not saying this is David Stockman, you can have a guy who has gone to graduate school for fifteen years, never been married, lived in rooms and had an essentially undergraduate life. Never managed people, never led people. Well, his personality is going to be quite different. Now ask yourself—which of those opposite extremes does David Stockman come closest to?

Wanniski was disturbed by Stockman's malleability. Shortly after Stockman's appointment, Wanniski was among those who accompanied the new budget director on a whirlwind tour of Wall Street. "We met with twenty-five top executives from Morgan Stanley [one of the world's largest investment banking firms]," recalled Wanniski, "and I could see that Dave was v-eee-ry impressed. All of these big honchos out to see little Davy Stockman. I've known all of those guys for years and believe me I'd never vote for them, much less take their advice seriously on national economic policy." Asked if he thought Stockman had a mind of his own, Wanniski did not hesitate: "Who, Dave Stockman? No, oh no."

"I think that he is a man with no fixed compass points and I think that he takes on the characteristics of whoever he is near," said Novak. "For example, in the beginning, Stockman was terribly exasperated with Domenici [chairman of the Senate Budget Committee]. He was frustrated by what he called Domenici's obtuseness, his inflexibility, and his tunnel vision. By the time the summer rolled around, Pete Domenici had been transmogrified into the best guy we've got up there. Well, it wasn't Pete Domenici that was changing, it was David Stockman."

Novak also mentioned the Alan Reynolds factor. Reynolds, a strident supply sider, was originally offered the post then held by Larry Kudlow, the man largely responsible for preparing OMB's economic assumptions. In his position at OMB, Kudlow has weathered many a charge of "traditionalist" from less conventional staff at the Treasury Department. Taking into account Stockman's tendency to assume the characteristics of those around him, Novak wondered, "What would it have been like if Reynolds had taken the job? It's a very odd, transitory event in Washington that hardly anyone knows about and yet it might have had an enormous effect, a profound effect on the events that followed. It wouldn't have been possible with a lot of people, but with someone as impressionable as Stockman, it might have." Asked if he felt Stockman was simply an opportunist out looking for the best deal on power, Novak replied, "No, I think it may be much worse than that. I think it may be a habitual inability to adhere to a single standard. In his rather young life, he has changed not just once or twice but has changed his whole orientation on numerous occasions."

Stockman was young—thirty-four at the time he was appointed head of OMB. One of the first of a generation of radical activists to make it big in mainstream politics, Stockman did so, ironically, as a conservative. Beth Shapiro, a former secretary of the Students for a Democratic Society (SDS) at Michigan State, knew Stockman through SDS meetings and rallies. She sees Stockman as "typical" of many she knew in the anti-war movement. When college was over it came time to get on with their lives, they got on with their lives—it was in their best interest to do so. When it was in your self-interest, you were involved. When it wasn't, you weren't. There are hundreds of David Stockman's around," concludes Shapiro. "They're just not quite as successful as he is."

Since his days at Michigan State, Stockman's view of what he refers to as the "way the world works" had undergone a myriad of revisions. Indeed, over the eight-month period during which he met regularly with Greider, Stockman dismissed his old view of the world as envisioned by Jack Kemp and Jude Wanniski as "too simplistic." Compare this with Stockman's statement in a 1979 interview with a *Detroit News* reporter concerning his old anti-war days. Stockman claimed that when he arrived at the Harvard Divinity School, he was disgusted by the "shrill absolutism" of the Left and the "simplistic and idealistic notions that are attractive when you're twenty."

Stockman's pattern has been to favor those abrupt breaks and then recoil in support of more traditional paths. While assuring his supply-side allies that he was still one of their own, Stockman was waging a quiet battle within the administration to have taxes raised. As time passed, he became more and more open about his estrangement from supply-side tenets.

A theory held by many holds that, in all likelihood, Stockman had assumed that by the time the *Atlantic* piece was printed, the administration would have decided to press for higher taxes in order to cover the growing deficit. If that were the case, Stockman's admissions would not have seemed so extraordinary; indeed, he might have garnered an even brighter spot in American history.

But Stockman miscalculated. Although a good many officials had resigned themselves to raising taxes, Stockman had failed to convince the only official who really mattered—the President himself. A source close to Stockman confirms this. "What really screwed Stockman up was the fact that the article began circulating early. Maybe if he had had a little more time, things would have been okay." In the text, Greider says, "The particulars of these conversations were not to be reported until later, after the season's battles were over. . . ." By the time the article appeared, however, the biggest battle of the season had only been temporarily settled in a way that did not bode well for Stockman.

Throughout the time that Stockman and Greider met, the *Post* editor was making good use of the information he was picking up without attributing that information to the OMB director. Peter Silberman, assistant managing editor for business and economic affairs at the *Post*, admitted, "Yes, in a general way, Greider passed information to us. . . . We got a good picture and the paper was well served." Silberman continues, "He would sit down and talk with me or Frank Swoboda of my staff or Bob Kaiser of the national staff or someone like that. We got a feel early on that the administration was really going to push its economic plan. That was very useful."

In October 1981, Stockman must have gotten a feel that Greider's piece might spell trouble for him. Bob Kaiser's article in the October 5 *Post* had begun on the whimsical note of "Juggler, Juggler . . ." in reference to Stockman. Despite any misgivings Stockman may have had about what would appear in Greider's article following Kaiser's piece, the OMB director consented to pose for photographs taken by an *Atlantic* staffer in early October.

On November 10, Stockman sat down for his weekly breakfast meeting with Treasury Secretary Regan and Council of Economic Advisers Chairman Murray Weidenbaum. The week before, Stockman had lost out in the internecine battle over taxes: Reagan had announced he would seek no tax increases. The President had also remarked that he was confident Stockman would go along with that decision because he was a "team player." The day promised at least one bright spot for Stockman—it was his thirty-fifth birthday. As the three sat down to hash out the economic events of the previous week, Stockman was presented with a surprise birthday cake topped with thirty-five miniature hatchets in tribute to his budget-axing efforts.

Hitting mid-life was no great bargain, as Stockman would shortly discover; indeed, before the day was out he would face his first mid-life crisis. That afternoon, Stockman would receive the galleys of the story Greider had written for the *Atlantic*. A cursory glance at those galleys would assure Stockman he was in for some trouble.

Greider spoke with Stockman that evening and relates the two had "an amiable conversation." Whether Stockman asked Greider to change or edit parts of the article is not known, but even if Stockman had asked, it was already too late. Of their conversation that evening, Greider says, "It was obvious to both of us that there was going to be a big fallout—I don't think either of us realized just how big it would be, though."

"Yes," concedes Greider, Stockman was "nervous." According to a Stockman aide, the OMB director was "floored by the appearance of the piece," because, as the aide told *The New York Times*, Stockman thought it wouldn't appear until "well into the middle of the President's term." Greider disagrees with this, maintaining that he and Stockman decided in September 1981 that "now is the time to write the article."

By the afternoon of the tenth, some subscribers of the *Atlantic* had already received their December issue of the magazine; worse still for Stockman, some reporters had managed to rustle up copies. At the end of a press conference designed to smooth over the celebrated dispute between Secretary of State Alexander Haig and National Security Adviser Richard Allen, CBS correspondent Lesley Stahl waved a copy of the magazine in the face of a President who had not been briefed on the issue. Earlier that afternoon, Stockman had sent the article over to the White House aide with a casual "I think you'd better see this" over the phone. Following the President's news conference, harried White House staff finally found the time to examine the article. "My first reaction was that the Democrats were going to use this politically and that it would hurt us politically. It was a credibility problem," said one aide.

By Wednesday morning, much of Washington had managed to dig up a copy of the *Atlantic*. Most of Stockman's 610-member staff at OMB had read photocopies of the piece, made on their boss's machine, which appeared on some OMB desks as if by magic. (When asked how he obtained his copy, one OMB official explained mysteriously, "It was just here." Said another, "Copies did appear.") Over at 1600 Pennsylvania Avenue, White House police were pouring over the December issue of the magazine. Asked where their copy had come from, one officer replied, "Some reporter came breezing through the gate with a whole stack of them and handed us one." Eventually, demand for the article would spur the printing of an extra 70,000 copies.

Wednesday's papers carried little on the story. *The New York Times* relegated Stockman's predicament to page 7, and, similarly, the *Post* itself ran what was ostensibly their "scoop" on an inside page. (According to Robert McCloskey, the *Post's* ombudsman, the treatment of the paper's handling of the Stockman affair "seemed too deliberately inconspicuous—the equivalent of hiding a light under a bushel.")

The events of the next few days demanded more coverage, however. Reagan read the article on Wednesday evening, and, according to one White House aide, "The President was as upset and angry as I've ever seen him."

In addition to being politically explosive, William Greider's article was both informative and readable.[6] The first section began with an account of a visit Greider made with Stockman to Stockman's hometown, shortly before the congressman took over as Ronald Reagan's head of the Office of Management and Budget:

> He was thirty-four years old and looked younger. His shaggy hair was streaked with gray, and yet he seemed like a gawky collegian, with unstylish glasses and a prominent Adam's apple. In the corridors of the Capitol, where all ambitious staff aides scurried about in serious blue suits, Representative Stockman wore the same uniform and was frequently mistaken for one of them.
>
> Inside the farmhouse, the family greetings were casual and restrained. His parents and brothers and in-laws did not seem overly impressed by the prospect that the eldest son would soon occupy one of the most powerful positions of government. Opening presents in the cluttered living room, watching the holiday football games on television, the Stockmans seemed a friendly, restrained, classic Protestant farm family of the Middle West, conservative and striving. As sometimes happens in those families, however, the energy and ambition seemed to have been concentrated disproportionately in one child, David, perhaps at the expense of the others. His mother, Carol, a big-boned woman with metallic blond hair, was the family organizer, an active committee member in local Republican politics, and the one who made David work for As in school. In political debate, David Stockman was capable of dazzling opponents with words; his brothers seemed shy and taciturn in his presence. One brother worked as a county corrections officer in Michigan. Another, after looking on Capitol Hill, found a job in an employment agency. A third, who had the distant look of a sixties child grown older, did day labor. His sister was trained as an educator and worked as a consultant to management-training programs in Missouri that were financed by the federal government. "She believes in what she's doing and I don't quarrel with it," Stockman said. "Basically, there are gobs of this money out there.

---

6. The author would leave *The Washington Post* in 1982 after a stay of fourteen years to become the national editor of *Rolling Stone* magazine.

CETA grants have to do evaluation and career planning and so forth. What does it amount to? Somebody rents a room in a Marriott Hotel somewhere and my sister comes in and talks to them. I think Marriott may get more out of it than anyone else. That's part of what we're trying to get at, and it's layered all over the government."

While David Stockman would speak passionately against the government in Washington and its self-aggrandizing habits, there was this small irony about his siblings and himself: most of them worked for government in one way or another—protected from the dynamic risk-taking of the private economy. Stockman himself had never had any employer other than the federal government, but the adventure in his career lay in challenging it. Or, more precisely, in challenging the "permanent government" that modern liberalism had spawned.

Greider then went on to discuss Stockman's embrace of the supply-side doctrine, an embrace that, at least in the beginning, was downright devout. Stockman told Greider, "The whole thing is premised on faith. On a belief in how the world works." The journalist felt that as Stockman

prepared the script in his mind, his natural optimism led to bullish forecasts, which were even more robust than the Reagan Administration's public promises. "The inflation premium melts away like the morning mist," Stockman predicted. "It could be cut in half in a very short period of time if the policy is credible. That sets off adjustments and changes in perception that cascade through the economy. You have a bull market in '81, after April, of historic proportions.

After briefly sketching the route that led Stockman to Washington, Greider delivered the first of the startling quotes from the Hay-Adams Saturday morning breakfast tapes: ". . . as a congressman, Stockman had worked hard to make certain that his Fourth District constituents exploited the system. His office maintained a computerized alert system for grants and loans from the myriad agencies, to make certain that no opportunities were missed." (This was the kind of calculated exploitation of incumbency that had surprised David Cohen when he first visited Stockman's office.) And then Greider quoted Stockman as saying, "I went around and cut all the ribbons and they never knew I voted against the damn programs."

Having used that, Greider quickly righted the balance by praising Stockman. "Still, more than most other politicians, Stockman was known for standing by his ideological principles, not undermining them. When Congress voted its bail-out financing to rescue Chrysler from bankruptcy, Stockman was the only Michigan representative to oppose it, even though a large town in his district, St. Joseph, would be hurt."

At the beginning of the second section of this very long article, which was entitled "A Radical in Power," Greider explained the terms under which he and Stockman had "collaborated":

> When his appointment as budget director first seemed likely, he had agreed to meet with me from time to time and relate, off the record, his private account of the great political struggle ahead. Particulars of these conversations were not to be reported until later, after the season's battles were over, but a cynic familiar with how Washington works would understand that the arrangement had obvious symbiotic value. As an assistant managing editor at *The Washington Post*, I benefitted from an informed view of policy discussions of the new administration; Stockman, a student of history, was contributing to history's record and perhaps influencing its conclusions. For him, our meetings were another channel—among the many he used—to the press. The older generation of orthodox Republicans distrusted the press; Stockman was one of the younger "new" conservatives who cultivated contacts with columnists and reporters, who saw the news media as another useful tool in political combat. "We believe our ideas have intellectual respectability, and we think the press will recognize that," he said. "The traditional Republicans probably sensed, even if they didn't know it, that their ideas lacked intellectual respectability."

One of the lesser-noticed but nonetheless significant admissions contained in the article was Stockman's explanation of how he had re-programmed the OMB computer that had produced dire economic predictions the month before Ronald Reagan was to give his first budget message. This was one of the actions that would later produce charges of his having "cooked the books." As Greider recounted it:

> Stockman set about doing two things. First, he changed the OMB-computer. Assisted by like-minded supply-side economists, the new team discarded orthodox premises of how the economy would behave. Instead of a continuing double-digit inflation, the new computer model assumed a swift decline in prices and interest rates. Instead of the continuing pattern of slow economic growth, the new model was based on a dramatic surge in the nation's productivity. New investment, new

jobs, and growing profits—Stockman's historic bull market. "It's based on valid economic analysis," he said, "but it's the inverse of the last four years. When we go public, this is going to set off a wide-open debate on how the economy works, a great battle over the conventional theories of economic performance."

So much for the supply-side theories that had, in very large part, gotten him the job. Stockman told Greider, "Laffer sold us a bill of goods." Then he softened the harsh statement: "Laffer wasn't wrong—he didn't go far enough."

Stockman's second major action, according to Greider, was to use "the appalling deficit projections as a valuable talking point in the policy discussions that were underway with the President and his principal advisers."

As Greider put it:

Nobody in that group was the least bit hesitant about cutting federal programs, but Reagan had campaigned on the vague and painless theme that eliminating "waste, fraud, and mismanagement" would be sufficient to balance the accounts. Now, as Stockman put it, "the idea is to try and get beyond the waste, fraud and mismanagement modality and begin to confront the real dimensions of budget reduction. . . . For starters, the new administration would have to go for a budget reduction in the neighborhood of $40 billion. Do you have any idea what $40 billion means? . . . It means I've got to cut the highway program. It means I've got to shut down the synfuels program and lot of other programs. The idea is to show the magnitude of the budget deficit and some suggestions of the political problems."

"Stockman was impressed," wrote Greider, "by the ease with which the president-elect accepted the broad objective" of finding $40 billion worth of cuts. Greider reported that Stockman was well aware it would not be an easy job: "The struggle began in private, with Ronald Reagan's Cabinet. By inaugural week, Stockman's staff had assembled fifty or sixty policy papers outlining major cuts and alterations, and, aiming at the target of $40 billion, Stockman was anxious to win fast approval for them, before the new cabinet members were fully familiar with their departments and prepared to defend their bureaucracies."

Just how far Stockman had taken Greider inside the Cabinet Room of his memory was soon made startlingly apparent:

During that first week, the new Cabinet members had to sit through David Stockman's recital—one proposal after another outlining drastic reductions in their programs. Brief discussion was followed by presidential approval. "I have a little nervousness about the heavy-handedness with which I am being forced to act," Stockman conceded. "It's not that I wouldn't want to give the decision papers to the Cabinet members ahead of time so they could look at them, it's just that we're getting them done at eight o'clock in the morning and rushing them to the Cabinet room. . . . It doesn't work when you have to brace these Cabinet officers in front of the President with severe reductions in their agencies, because then they're in the position of having to argue against the group line. And the group line is cut, cut, cut. So that's a very awkward position for them, and you make them resentful very fast."

A former cabinet member (who requested anonymity) recalls that another reason they became resentful is that Stockman teamed up with former Interior Secretary James Watt in a sort of good cop–bad cop approach that in effect sandbagged the President. "Because he was a Westerner and spoke the President's language, Jim Watt would get his ear, and then Stockman would dazzle him with the numbers. The President would then say, 'Well, if Jim agrees with Dave, then I guess that's what we should do,' and that would be that." And the process worked, said the former official, "until the cabinet members learned their jobs." Others, including another former cabinet officer, downplay Watt's role, but Anne Gorsuch Burford, for one, says, "that's exactly what happened."

After a while, Stockman confessed to Greider, he streamlined the process for better efficiency. He got Ed Meese's approval to form a "budget working group, in which each cabinet secretary could review the proposed cuts and argue against them." As the group evolved, however, it was stacked in Stockman's favor:

> "Each meeting will involve only the relevant Cabinet member and his aides with four or five strong keepers of the central agenda," Stockman explained at one point. "So on Monday, when we go into the decision on synfuels programs, it will be [Energy Secretary James B.] Edwards defending them against six guys saying that, by God, we've got to cut these back or we're not going to have a savings program that will add up."

In general, the system worked. Stockman's agency did in a few weeks what normally consumes months; the process was made easier because the normal opposition forces had no time to marshall either their arguments or their constituents and because the President was fully in tune with Stockman. After the budget working group reached a decision, it would be taken to Reagan in the form of a memorandum, on which he could register his approval by checking a little box. "Once he checks it," Stockman said, "I put that in my safe and I go ahead and I don't let it come back again."

The check marks were given to changes in twelve major budget entitlements and scores of smaller ones. Eliminate Social Security minimum benefits. Cap the runaway costs of Medicaid. Tighten eligibility for food stamps. Merge the trade adjustment assistance for unemployed industrial workers with standard unemployment compensation and shrink it. Cut education aid by a quarter. Cut grants for the arts and humanities in half. "Zero out" CETA and Community Services Administration and National Consumer Cooperative Bank. And so forth. "Zero out" became a favorite phrase of Stockman's; it meant closing down a program "cold turkey," in one budget year. Stockman believed that any compromise on a program that ought to be eliminated—funding that would phase it out over several years—was merely a political ruse to keep it alive, so it might still be in existence a few years hence, when a new political climate could allow its restoration to full funding.

"I just wish," Stockman confided to Greider, "that there were more hours in the day or that we didn't have to do this so fast. I have these stacks of briefing books and I've got to make decisions about specific options. . . . I don't have time, trying to put this whole package together in three weeks, so you just start making snap judgments."

As intriguing as these behind-the-scenes glimpses into the mechanics and the methodology were, they paled in interest value when compared with Stockman's almost incredible revelations that he did not really believe in the theoretical basis of the program he'd been working so incredibly hard to pass and to implement. After having sold the budget figures as being hard and dependable, Stockman confessed to Greider that he had never actually felt that way: "None of us really understands what's going on with all these numbers."

The most startling revelations of all, however, were Stockman's statements about supply-side economics. He told Greider, "*I've never believed that just cutting taxes alone will cause output and employment to expand*" (italics added). All he had done with that statement was to deny the very foundation of supply-side economic theory!

"Stockman himself," wrote Greider, "had been a late convert to supply-side theology, and now he was beginning to leave the church. The theory of 'expectations' wasn't working. . . . For his part, Stockman began to disparage the grand theory as a kind of convenient illusion—new rhetoric to cover old Republican doctrine."

The next statement in the article was one that would be quoted and requoted across the country, but especially in Washington, where many readers would be shaking their heads in sincere disbelief:

> "The hard part of the supply-side tax cut is dropping the top rate from 70 to 50 percent—the rest of it is a secondary matter," Stockman explained. "The original argument was that the top bracket was too high, and that's having the most devastating effect on the economy. Then, the general argument was that, in order to make this palatable as a political matter, you had to bring down all the brackets. But, I mean, Kemp–Roth was always a Trojan horse to bring down the top rate."

Greider's reaction, even in cold print, had a ring of astonishment to it:

> A Trojan horse? This seemed a cynical concession for Stockman to make in private conversation while the Reagan Administration was still selling the supply-side doctrine to Congress. Yet he was conceding what the liberal Keynesian critics had argued from the outset—the supply-side theory was not a new economic theory at all but only new language and argument to conceal a hoary old Republican doctrine: give the tax cuts to the top brackets, the wealthiest individuals and largest enterprises, and let the good effects "trickle down" through the economy to reach everyone else.

If any readers held out hope that Stockman didn't mean what it sounded like he was saying, that he wasn't *really* saying, as Greider put it, "supply-side theory was really new clothes for the unpopular doctrine of the old Republican orthodoxy," that hope would be dashed by the next quote.

"It's kind of hard to sell 'trickle down,' " Stockman told Greider, "so the supply-side formula was the only way to get a tax policy that was really 'trickle down.' Supply-side is 'trickle down' theory."

Those were the biggest shockers, the statements that made Stockman look cynical and manipulative—not to mention dishonest—in the extreme. But they were not the only surprises. There were more.

When the administration played ball with key Republican leaders and promised them concessions that were then announced, Stockman (he told Greider) felt they were only "authorization ceilings," which could be reduced at a later date:

> This codicil of Stockman's was apparently not communicated to the Republicans with whom he was making deals. They presumed that the final figures negotiated with Stockman were final figures. Later on, they discovered that the budget director didn't agree. When in September the President announced a new round of reductions, $13 billion in across-the-board cuts for fiscal year 1982, the ranks of his congressional supporters accused Stockman of breaking his word. In private, some used stronger language. The new budget cuts Stockman prepared in September did, indeed, scrap many of the agreements he negotiated in June when he was collecting enough votes to pass the President's reconciliation bill. In the political morality that prevails in Washington, this was regarded as dishonorable behavior, and Stockman's personal standing was damaged.
>
> "Piranhas," Stockman called the Republican dealers. Yet he was a willing participant in one of the rankest trades—his casual promise that the Reagan Administration would not oppose revival of sugar supports, a scandalous price-support loan program killed by Congress in 1979. Sugar subsidies might not cost the government anything, but could cost consumers $2 to $5 billion. "In economic principle, it's kind of a rotten idea," he conceded. Did Ronald Reagan's White House object? "They don't care, over in the White House. They want to win."

Greider's analysis of what this meant to Stockman's reputation was right on the money:

> This process of trading, vote by vote, injured Stockman in more profound ways, beyond the care or cautions of his fellow politicians. It was undermining his original moral premise—the idea that honest free-market conservatism could unshackle the government from the costly

claims of interest-group politics in a way that was fair to both the weak and the strong. To reject weak claims from powerful clients—that was the intellectual credo that allowed him to hack away so confidently at wasteful social programs, believing that he was being equally tough-minded on the wasteful business subsidies. Now, as the final balance was being struck, he was forced to concede in private that the claim of equity in shrinking the government was significantly compromised if not obliterated.

Greider reported that when the tax cut legislation was at last passed, amid "a final frenzy of trading and bargaining," it actually seemed to shock David Stockman. "Do you realize the greed that came to the forefront?" he asked the *Post* editor. "The hogs were really feeding. The greed level, the level of opportunism, just got out of control." Apparently Stockman had seen, for once, the way the world *really* works.

Two other quotes would be widely repeated. In a reprise of his most embarrassing metaphor, Stockman referred to the final budget measure, Gramm–Latta II, as "a Trojan horse filled with all kinds of budget-busting measures and secondary agendas." And in regard to defense spending, the one area in which he was so clearly defeated by his fellow Reaganites, he told Greider, "They got a blank check. . . . We didn't have time during that February–March period to do anything with defense. Where are we going to cut? Domestic? Or struggle all day with defense. So I let it go. But it worked perfectly, because they got so goddamn greedy that they got themselves strung way out there on a limb."

The more Stockman tried to figure out what had gone wrong with his grand design, the more—according to Greider—"he moved away from the radical vision of reformer, away from the wishful thinking of supply-side economics, and toward the 'old time religion' of conservative economic thinking. Orthodoxy seemed less exciting than radicalism, but perhaps Stockman was only starting into another intellectual transition. He had changed from farm boy to campus activist at Michigan State, from Christian moralist to neoconservative at Harvard; once again, Stockman was reforming his ideas on how the world worked."

Perhaps. But to many people who knew and had dealt with David Stockman, that reading was much too kind.

11 • "That's When the Administration Died"

"I WOULD not be here now, nor would I have worked sixteen hours per day for nearly a year, if I did not believe in the President and in his policies." These were the words of a chastened David Stockman speaking to a hastily assembled White House press corps shortly after publication of "The Education of David Stockman" in the *Atlantic Monthly*. Absent from Stockman's face was what one congressman called that "everpresent smirk that seems to say: 'Here I am, the smartest kid on the block. I know what I'm doing and you don't.' " Following the news conference, a White House aide put matters even more succinctly. "He looked about six inches shorter than the last time I saw him."

One Washington reporter said what was on the minds of many: "Nobody had any idea of the kind of language that Stockman was using. That was the real shocker. Direct quotations assume great importance when presented in black and white. People can say from now to doomsday that it had all been said before"—the position taken by Edwin Dale, Stockman's press secretary and a former reporter for *The New York Times*—"but there was never anything to equal the 'Trojan horse' allusion or the admission about the 'trickle down' theory. That had a stunning impact."

Not surprisingly, Democrats, who had been simmering in defeat ever since June, pounced on the potential impact of the article. Stockman "knew first-hand the fundamental weaknesses of the Reagan program and chose to cover it up," charged House Speaker Tip O'Neill. Senator Gary Hart (D-CO) labeled Stockman's role in the administration's economic debate as "one of the most cynical by a public official perhaps since the Vietnam era." On the Republican side, Representative Jack Kemp professed "deep sadness that my close friend and first choice as budget director has put himself in this difficult position." Kemp also insisted (as Arthur Laffer would reiterate) that Stockman's positions in the article "are contrary to everything Dave has always expressed to members of the House in public and private."

On Thursday morning, Reagan assembled his top aides to decide on Stockman's fate. According to reports, two of the President's "big three," Michael K. Deaver and Edwin Meese urged the President to fire Stockman, as did Reagan's departing political director, Lyn Nofziger. Not long after, as he was leaving the cabinet for the private sector, Transportation Secretary Drew Lewis had one suggestion for the President: "Get rid of Stockman."

Deaver was the most vocal in urging Stockman's ouster; "He was furious," recalls one aide. In Chief of Staff Jim Baker, Stockman had his sole ally. As for the President, looking back, one wonders if the irony of the situation had struck Stockman. While on both defense and taxes the OMB director won nearly all the top officials over to his view, the President stubbornly ruled against Stockman. Now in a situation where, once again, Reagan would rule against most of his inner circle, his decision would save David Stockman his job.

At the time, rather than make a final decision, Reagan canceled a date with Vice President Bush and summoned Stockman to the White House for lunch. By some accounts, Stockman arrived for his meeting anxious to cast blame on Greider, saying the *Post* editor had misled him. Hearing this, one White House aide took Stockman aside and cautioned him, "Don't go in and blame it on the goddamn article. You and everybody else know you made a serious mistake."

Stockman emerged from his November 12 luncheon saying, "I feel like I've been run over by a freight train." Although he made an obligatory offer to resign, Stockman managed to hang onto his $70,900 a year job as budget director. His immediate ordeal was not over, however. Reagan called for a press conference, saying, "I think the press and public should see and hear David's explanation just as I did."

Returning to his office in the Old Executive Building adjacent to the White House, Stockman spent an hour writing a press release, which he later read to reporters. Following that, the OMB director rehearsed his answers to some possible queries he might be faced with at the hands of the press. "A group of us worked up the most likely questions to be asked," explained Ed Dale. "They weren't hard to pick."

Pale and visibly shaken, Stockman appeared before the press and began his statement: "Today at the President's request, I discussed my problem with him." Insisting that "President Reagan believes with every ounce of his strength" in the administration's economic program, Stockman added that "never, ever" had Reagan attempted to mislead the Congress or the American people," or say things that weren't true." Referring to his "careless rambling to a reporter," Stockman confessed, "I have worried, but too publicly, and deeply regret any harm that has been done." The upshot of all of this was that "the President has asked me to stay on the team."

When asked about his lunch with the President, Stockman replied, "I hesitate to use metaphors after the bad luck I've had in recent days. But I grew up on a farm and I might say therefore, that my visit to the Oval Office for lunch with the President was more in the nature of a visit to the woodshed after supper." Questioned repeatedly about his "Trojan horse" references, Stockman gave one cryptic answer after another:

> Well, let me try to explain it this way: A Trojan horse is a—wouldn't be without a brain, and had I recalled that I never would've used that metaphor. I think the facts speak for themselves.

Again in response to a question about "that metaphor":

> I don't think it was a very good metaphor to use and I certainly wouldn't apply it to anything that has happened as we have sought to implement the program.

And in one last exchange:

Q: You think of a Trojan horse as that horse that contained soldiers inside Priam's walls, then in the dark of night were released to destroy Troy.

Stockman: Well. . . .

Q: A device to betray. Right?

Stockman: I can only say that it was a rotten, horrible, unfortunate metaphor. I will not go into literary history to determine its meaning and application.

When asked about his assertion in the article that the Republican tax plan was little more than "trickle down," Stockman opted for obfuscation:

Well, I am not certain what trickle-down means. . . . There is no more, there is no less involved, and I think it would be terribly unfortunate if this phrase, whatever it means—and I would defy anyone here to write an economic essay on its meaning—stands in the way of communicating what we're attempting to do.

If Stockman offered these same explanations to the President, it is a wonder Reagan kept the OMB director on. After the press conference, one administration official said that he had been asked to give four reasons for the President's decision on the condition that the source remain unnamed. First, Reagan had "satisfied himself that Stockman can and will in good conscience continue to advance" the economic program. Second, Stockman was "needed as a member of the President's team." Third, the OMB director was "an extraordinarily capable public servant." Fourth, and perhaps most importantly, Reagan happened to have met with Republican congressional leaders the previous day who considered Stockman "an effective spokesman for the administration." To a cynic, the last three reasons sound as if there was simply no able and/or willing replacement at hand. "Hell," one aide told *Time* magazine, "he's our entire domestic policy staff. What are we going to do without him?" Said another, "David Stockman is this Administration's budget process." When asked if he had been offered the budget post, Phil Gramm replied, "A lot of people ran around here saying I had, but you can believe me, I rained on that parade. That is a job I would not want."

Others suggest that while Stockman absolved Greider of blame beyond "misunderstanding" before the press, he may have fed a different story to Reagan. Of the incident, President Reagan told Barbara Walters on November 25, 1981, "I think David Stockman was not the sinner. He was sinned against. . . . Very frankly, while that article used a few quotes from [Stockman], I think that the real cynicism and doubts of the plan were written by the author and [were] his interpretation." Shortly after the *Atlantic* came out, Stockman phoned Novak:

Novak: He said, "I am not Judas Iscariot"—he used those words.

Urban: How did he explain it to you? What did he say about the article?

Novak: He said nobody would ever say those things—but he said
           them.

Following Thursday's press conference, Stockman headed back
to his office, where he worked until after 10:00 P.M. On Friday,
OMB canceled his appearance on ABC's "This Week With David
Brinkley," scheduled for Sunday. "It would be asking too much to
request his interviewers not to bring up the subject of the *Atlantic*
article," said his press office. Meanwhile, in the premier showing of
his public policy program, David Brinkley was left without a guest.
On the show that Sunday, Brinkley took little care to hide his
displeasure with Stockman, commenting simply that the OMB
director had "backed out." Brinkley concluded by saying the incident would probably blow over for Stockman as the "normal gossip
shelf life is five and a half days in Washington." Outside of
Washington, the fact that Brinkley dismissed the whole incident as
gossip may have been a little shocking. Seeking a language those
outside of Washington could better understand, Lem Tucker of
CBS News observed, "Everything seems clearer now. In fact, the
David Stockman affair may even help give politicians an answer to
one of their greatest mysteries, which is 'Why don't people trust
us?' " (At least two persons outside of Washington did trust Stockman. One was his mother. Shortly after the episode, reports from
Michigan were that Mrs. Stockman was selling buttons that announced: I'M FOR DAVID STOCKMAN.)

An enormous amount of talk and speculation was generated by
the Stockman episode—talk that lasted far beyond five and a half
days. Over the next few weeks, a plethora of observers weighed in
with their assessment of the situation. Roy Cohn, the rarely reticent
lawyer from New York, wanted Stockman "run out of town on a
rail." The *Post* ran twenty "Letters to the Editor" on the topic in a
single day. The co-sponsor of the 1981 tax bill, Senator William
Roth (R-DE), announced that he had invited Stockman to a
Thanksgiving dinner. On the menu: "Trojan horse pâté, Chateau
Hemlock '81, trickle-down consommé, and foot in mouth filet."
Following the meal, said Roth, Stockman would be "offered a
blindfold and cigarette."

Senator Ernest Hollings (D-SC) told Chris Wallace of NBC,
"He's [Stockman] a pathological finagler, and everyone knows that.
He can give answers to anything. And this is no time to be cute."

Russell Baker gave Stockman the "Sore Winner of the Year Award." Stockman, "While maneuvering the President's tax bill successfully through Congress . . . spent a month of breakfasts complaining to a newspaper reporter that the bill was a hoax and a fraud," wrote Baker. For this, Baker continued, Stockman will "receive the traditional H. R. Haldeman crew cut . . . in memory of the man who celebrated President Nixon's landslide victory of 1972 by demanding that all Nixon's aides and cabinet officers tender their resignations." And finally, in February 1982, a Washington modern dance group opened a performance that took its title from one of Stockman's lines in the *Atlantic*: "None of us really understands what's going on with these numbers." While dancers in conservative white shirts and black sweat pants roamed over the stage, the central figure moved about uttering monosyllables like "Cut," "Chop," Shear." The group's artistic director told *The Wall Street Journal*, "The Budget Director hasn't been invited. I felt when he saw what he was doing he would be embarrassed."

There were few allies for Stockman to turn to. In an exchange with Arthur Laffer, Anne Urban asked:

Q: Would you like to see Stockman go?

Laffer: Let me just ask you this: Would you like to have him in charge of your money?

Q: No . . .

Laffer: Well, you've answered the question. The next question is whether you'd like him to handle your country's money.

And Robert Novak:

Q: Would you like to see Stockman go?

Novak: Oh yes, I mean, I've said that.

Q: Who would you replace him with?

Novak: Anybody in the first one hundred pages of the Washington telephone book. . . . Who would I really like to see? From the standpoint of the President I'd like to see anybody who would be loyal to him and not work on his own objectives. . . . I think when the President kept David on he showed a tremendous weakness, an inability to see how the system works, and perhaps even a certain amount of fear.

Although hardly by choice, Stockman had happened upon an opportune time to land himself in hot water. Congress would soon break for the holidays. And it was Congress that would administer the OMB director's true test of survival. Two days after the story broke, Senator Howard Baker was asked if Stockman had damaged himself beyond repair. No doubt with the Hill in mind, the Senate Majority Leader fretted, "That may turn out to be the case. I hope not."

But as events unfolded, it seemed Baker was more skeptical than he let on. According to a November 14 story in the *Post*, shortly before Stockman met the President for his "woodshed" lunch, Reagan asked Vice President Bush to get an assessment of the damage done to Stockman from some senators on the Hill. Bush phoned Howard Baker, who in turn called a dozen or so top leaders in the Senate. The verdict, according to sources, was negative. One congressional aide stated, "The senator told the Vice President essentially this—'The incident has seriously damaged Stockman. It has hurt his credibility and effectiveness, particularly when he has to go up to the Hill and testify.' " Speaking for the Vice President, however, one spokesman denied that Baker had given any ap- praisal—positive or negative—to Bush. Congressional sources in- sisted the Senate leader had. It seems George Bush may have played a crucial role in keeping Stockman on by way of the bottomless briefcase maneuver.

Meanwhile, Stockman, when asked about the *Atlantic* article, acted as if he didn't know what his questioners were talking about. Asked by David Espo on "Face the Nation" whether he expected the Democrats to "treat you gently," Stockman replied, "Well, I don't think anyone should ever expect—expect to be treated gently who is trying to bring about fundamental change, who is disrupting in- grained habits and patterns. . . ." And on January 3, 1982, when Stockman finally did make it onto the Brinkley show, he probably wished he had stayed home:

> *Brinkley:* Mr. Stockman, have you been something like a pariah around the White House since you expressed some doubts about Reagan's economics in the *Atlantic* arti- cle?
>
> *Stockman:* Well, that's for others to judge. I've been working hard. This budget, for—

Brinkley: Well, you can judge that, David.

Stockman: No, I would leave that to others.

In any case, Stockman was not relishing the idea of appearing on the Hill. But in the confusion over the measure to keep the government funded that arose in late November, the OMB head was called in by Howard Baker. Baker told *The Washington Post,* "At first he was sort of unsure of himself, sort of nervous. . . . There were a few good-natured jabs. He handled himself well. After an hour he was going." Throughout December, Stockman shuttled to the Hill to deal with Republicans on various details. The Republicans, Stockman reported, were treating him "very nicely."

But Stockman's diminished esteem was apparent in sometimes subtle ways. A Senate committee staff director told the *Post* that Stockman now had to wrangle with aides, whereas "Before the *Atlantic,* he only met with principals." Some, like Novak, argue that Stockman wielded just as much influence as prior to the incident, saying it was only the OMB director's profile that had all but disappeared.

Few would disagree that Stockman's visibility took a sharp downward turn after November 1981. That occurrence seems to have been a result of a conscious effort on the part of the White House to move Stockman out from center stage and slide in Treasury Secretary Donald Regan. One White House aide commented, "Stockman will continue to testify at budgetary hearings. That has to be. But there's no doubt that Don will be out front—at least for the foreseeable future. Dave's visibility will be lowered. He will be assuming a lower profile." In a House Appropriations hearing at which Regan, Weidenbaum, and Stockman all appeared, some House members took special care to emphasize that Regan was on the rise. Representative Norman Dicks (D-WA) observed pointedly, "As I understand, it, Mr. Regan is the economic spokesman for the administration."

When Stockman did travel to the Hill to deal with Democrats as well as Republicans, copies of the *Atlantic Monthly* were much in evidence in hearing rooms. In his first hearing since the article, Stockman appeared before the Senate Governmental Affairs Committee on February 4, 1982. He received some blows. Senator John Glenn (D-OH) fumed, "Mr. Stockman, we trusted you last year and the public trusted you and we were deceived—deliberately deceived." Stockman replied icily, ". . . the notion that anyone has been misled, anybody has been deceived, anything has been rigged, is absolutely and utterly without foundation. . . ."

"I have no questions for you because very frankly, I wouldn't believe any answers you gave to them," said a disgusted Representative David Obey (D-WI) to Stockman at a House Budget hearing on February 17. Representative Bill Hefner (D-NC) told Stockman, "I have to say that in all fairness, you didn't mislead me on the budget last year, because I didn't vote with you last year. It is nothing personal, I want you to understand." And in that same February 17 hearing, Stockman once again feigned ignorance in an exchange with Representative Thomas Downey (D-NY):

> *Downey:* Do you believe that supply side is nothing more than trickle-down, the old warmed over trickle-down theory?
>
> *Stockman:* I am not sure why you form the question that way. Obviously . . .
>
> *Downey:* Yes?
>
> *Stockman:* That phraseology, like the rather colorful metaphors we have heard from other members of the committee today, is not something that is easy or worthwhile to explain.

Following a question from a *Hartford Courant* reporter, Stockman said he felt he'd "been getting about the same grilling as last year." Asked whether he saw the *Atlantic* as making a difference in his reception on the Hill, Stockman replied, "The only thing it affects are questions from the press like this."

Meanwhile, a number of Republicans were prepared to defend their budget whiz kid, come hell or high water. "In my mind, he's still okay," said Senator Jeremiah Denton (R-AK). Asked why, Denton barked, "That's just my answer." And Representative Lynn Martin (R-IL) confided at the February 17 budget hearing, "I flew in this morning, not with the thought of discussing the economy, but in that the Director needed the protection of some of his fellow Republicans around him."

"In a way, Stockman was asking Greider, 'Can you believe they believed it?' " mused Representative Pat Schroeder. Within a week after the 1983 budget was delivered to the Capitol, it looked as if no one was believing it the second time around. When asked if he had contacted Stockman since "The Education of David Stockman," William Greider replied, "No, when the '83 budget was sent over I thought I might call him, but then I saw the response it was getting and figured he'd had enough trouble."

Eventually, one heard less and less about David Stockman, as the battered budget director deliberately kept a very much lowered profile. The number of articles written about him, once the initial uproar caused by the *Atlantic* article had passed, dropped to a small fraction of what it had been. One former cabinet member, when asked why there was so much less written about Stockman after mid-1982, told us simply, "Because that's when the Administration died."

12 • Trojan Horse Getaway

THE DATE was February 3, 1982, the scene the Government Printing Office—and the mood one of frustration. Reporters and camera crews were growing impatient as they waited for David Stockman to appear for a "photo opportunity" at the ceremonial unveiling of the 1983 budget.

Twenty-five minutes passed. The production line of thirty-five workers stood still. Only one hundred copies of the budget remained to be run off, but the "powers" insisted that the presses be running when Stockman emerged from a nearby freight elevator.

Another fifteen minutes passed. Where was Stockman? One GPO management employee, serving as a public relations man for the afternoon, confided, "He's upstairs having a cup of coffee." At last someone asked the obvious question, "How much would you say this is costing the government?" On hearing this, the unofficial PR man became noticeably less friendly: "I don't think that's a very fair question, do you?" "Of course it's a fair question," interjected another reporter, "but it's not the kind of question you get an answer to in Washington."

Shortly thereafter, the elevator door slid open and out stepped a weary-looking Stockman. The presses rolled. Stockman leaned over and hugged a budget. Then he hugged the last woman on the line, hugged his budget again, and smiled wanly for the cameras. He turned back to the elevator, still tightly grasping his copy of the 1983 budget, and disappeared. As for the budget, it was mostly downhill from there on.

As part of its much-heralded "management initiatives" program, designed to save $20.3 billion in a single year, OMB elected to sell the FY 1983 budget to all but the press, the Hill, and federal agencies, rather than distribute the information gratis to the first 15,000 or so takers. The fifteen-volume set added up to a hefty 2,542 pages with an equally hefty price tag of $61.50. "The chances of that budget going through are absolutely *nil*," observed one OMB career specialist early in February. "The irony is that this is the first year they are making people pay for their copies. People will pick it up, take one look at that budget deficit [$92 billion] and forget about buying it."

By mid-February, the OMB staffer's suspicions were confirmed. Addressing Stockman at the February 17 hearing of the House Budget Committee, an exasperated Leon Panetta said, "I don't think there is any question up here that this budget isn't going to fly as presented to the Congress. I think that anybody who thinks that is the case is nuts. Nobody has come forward and wrapped their arms around us and said this is a winner."

Throughout 1981, Stockman, the President, and the other major administration policymakers had spoken glowingly of the national economic revival the administration's economic plan would produce. Spurred by the unprecedented cuts in individual tax rates and accelerated depreciation, entrepreneurs and businesses would funnel money back from yachts, tax shelters, and mergers into job-producing investments. Predictable monetary policy would moderate interest rates and, in combination with the expansionary tax cut, reduce unemployment. Together with continued spending cuts, these developments, as the administration outlined them in its February 1981 "Program for Economic Recovery," promised a steadily improving budget picture. Hard choices would remain, to be sure, but they would reduce the federal expenditures occasioned by recession, at the same time swelling federal revenues.

Figures in the "Program" quantified the scenario. For 1982, the report projected that the federal deficit would be $45 billion on expenditures of $695.5 billion and receipts of $650 billion. With the economy buoyed by supply-side economic growth, the federal government's share of the GNP would drop from 23 percent in 1981 to 20.4 percent in 1983. In the out-years—1984 to 1986—both the deficit and the government's share of the GNP would steadily decline until, by 1986, government expenditures would constitute only 19 percent of the GNP, the lowest figure since 1966.

If the world that greeted the release of the 1983 budget looked like the economic wonderland contained in those figures, undoubtedly Stockman's second effort would have received a warmer reception. But the world in February 1982 bore little resemblance to that supply-side fantasy, a fact grudgingly made clear by the 1983 budget itself.

In that document, the inability of the administration's economic programs to produce the results that Stockman and the others had promised was reflected in the budget's own numbers. Though still more optimistic than the assessments given by any other forecaster—whether private or the Congressional Budget Office—the numbers still glumly reflected the misplaced optimism of those first months in office. With the economy mired in an intractable recession, the 1983 document admitted that the 1983 fiscal year would not produce the $650 billion in receipts forecast a year earlier but rather $627 billion. And the deep recession would swell federal outlays by $30 billion above the previous year's forecast, producing a deficit of not $45 billion but $99 billion. With the expected economic growth failing to materialize, the budget would consume 23.5 percent of the 1982 GNP, not the 21.8 percent expected a year earlier. As the year went on, all of these revised figures would in turn be revealed to be overly optimistic as deficit predictions steadily soared to uncharted heights.

As the President noted in his economic message appended to the 1983 budget, "the most important setback to [the administration's] budgetary timetable" was the recession. Perhaps the inevitable consequence of the administration's sharp reductions in federal spending and stringent controls on the money supply, the recession was among the most debilitating in postwar American history. Like the deficit, unemployment rose to unprecedented postwar heights, reaching 10.1 percent by the second fall of Reagan's first term.

This massive joblessness, regularly portrayed by the national media, inescapably conjured up memories of the Great Depression. When the Agriculture Department decided in February 1982 to distribute surplus blocks of cheese, the lines stretched so long through the winter chill that many sites ran out. And that image, too, set the atmosphere in which Stockman's second budget was received; in the midst of such pointed suffering, the winners and losers of Reaganomics were thrust into sharp clarity.

Steadily, what presidential advisers termed the "fairness issue" rose to the top of the political agenda. Given the reluctance of political leaders to address issues in even the most mildly class-oriented terms, the development of a sustained opposition to Reaganomics based on its unfairness to the poor was remarkable in itself. The reassessment of Reaganomics as a class, or fairness, issue took place inexorably, on both the intellectual and the emotional level.

Providing ammunition for critics in Washington were the first official studies of the combined impact of Stockman's 1981 budget and tax actions. In February 1982, the Congressional Budget Office released a study showing that 86 percent of the tax cuts would go to those making over $20,000, while those earning below $20,000 would absorb 75 percent of the budget cuts. Even with Reagan's tax cuts, 79 percent of all Americans (those earning under $30,000) would be paying *more* of their income in taxes in 1984 than they did in 1980, according to data from the Joint Congressional Committee on Taxation. For those earning over $200,000, however, the cuts would amount to as much as $20,000 annually from the rate cuts alone, not to mention the generous loopholes. Analysis by the President's own Council of Economic Advisors demonstrated that the extraordinarily generous depreciation allowance passed in 1981 would actually provide a *subsidy* on some business investments.

These facts provided an underpinning to the images of inequity that the administration continually brought to bear on the debate. The President, along with most of his closest aides and cabinet officials, were used to the privileged lifestyle many of them had enjoyed as millionaires in the private sector. Nor did they seem subdued in their revelry, their living of the good life, by the inauspicious backdrop of the highest unemployment in forty years. With remarkable regularity, stories turned up demonstrating the President's devotion to luxury and opulence, while he and his budget director were preaching Calvinistic sermons on the importance of discipline in times of austerity.

It began, of course, with the lavish inaugural (the most expensive ever), the soliciting of corporate contributions to redecorate the White House, Nancy's china, and the President's long and regular vacations. But soon the images proliferated so that it was almost impossible to keep up: the head of the Veterans Administration using a chauffeur when his predecessor, a triple amputee, drove himself to work; the Secretary of Defense spending thousands of taxpayers' dollars to ferry himself and his family to a summer home in Maine; the Secretary of Commerce spending $118,000 to redecorate his office; the Secretary of Health and Human Services and his wife posed on the cover of the *Washington Dossier* (then a social magazine distributed only to the "better" ZIP codes), he wearing white tails and she a burgundy ball gown with long white gloves; the President insisting that his cuts did not threaten student aid while basking in the Barbados sun during an especially cruel Northeast winter. One Chicago area woman with two disabled sons wrote a personal letter to the White House asking that Reagan leave special education programs intact. In reply, Susan Benjamin received (among other things) a recipe for crabmeat casserole.

"Even if it was an error," said Benjamin, "I was appalled by the insensitivity of the White House. Here they're asking us to take budget cuts from all sorts of vital programs and still sending out such expensive recipes. Why, the crabmeat casserole would cost twenty bucks to make, with artichoke hearts and crabmeat at fifteen dollars a pound." Mrs. Benjamin observed, "I could take the pumpkin pecan pie and the Baja California chicken. But with the crabmeat casserole they lost me." The incident generated a "Let Them Eat Crabmeat" campaign by a group representing the handicapped in Chicago. Shortly thereafter, the White House replaced the crabmeat casserole recipe with one for macaroni and cheese. Undaunted, Stockman cut special education programs almost across the board in his FY 1983 budget.

Nor was Stockman personally immune to the lavishness in Washington. In April 1981, the OMB director chartered an Air Force jet to Baton Rouge, Louisiana. In his written request for the plane, Stockman explained that "commercial air travel is neither available, readily convenient or satisfactorily capable of providing the requirements of the mission." That mission—speaking to Louisiana's Sixth Congressional District Business Advisory Committee—cost taxpayers $3,945. (During April of 1981, Delta Airlines records show, they had at least three flights a day to Baton Rouge, at a round-trip cost of $388 for coach passengers.)

In policy decisions, too, the administration seemed incapable of moderating its basic instincts enough to minimize the fairness issue. At a time when satirists and cartoonists were comparing Nancy Reagan to Marie Antoinette, the administration seemed to proclaim "Let Them Eat Catsup" as a matter of national policy. Making regulatory changes necessitated by the administration's cuts in the school lunch program, the Agriculture Department proposed to "accept catsup as a fruit/vegetable when used as an ingredient." Not only catsup but pickle relish would count as vegetables; cake and cookies could be used as bread. Under the new regulations, along with a side of catsup, a kindergartner could be fed half a piece of bread, half a glass of milk, and a quarter of a medium-sized hamburger or soybean substitute.

The proposed rules provided a sure handle on the overall Stockman program, which the budget director himself realized more quickly than his colleagues in the Agriculture Department. Once the story hit the press, Democratic Senators Hollings, Leahy, and Byrd staged a press lunch at which the three sat down to soybean patties, four ounces of milk, a few french fries, and a side of catsup. Even friendly Republicans disassociated themselves. Senator John Heinz (R-PA), whose family owns the H. J. Heinz Company, sniffed, "Catsup is a condiment. This is one of the most ridiculous regulations I ever heard of, and I suppose I need not add that I know something about catsup and relish—or did at one time." Sensing the danger, Stockman squashed the regulations—without so much as a warning to the Agriculture Department. Speaking on a September 27, 1981, "Face the Nation," Stockman referred to "the little catsup episode" and said, "It's true that unfortunately some bureaucrats [at the] USDA ended up with egg on their face. But I must stress the mess in the kitchen was made by the Congress." (Jack Strayer, a close friend of Stockman's, says, "When I heard about this thing with the catsup I just laughed and laughed because Stockman puts catsup on everything—eggs, potatoes, you name it. Dave considers catsup a vegetable.")

With his "Face the Nation" remarks, Stockman sought to distance the administration from the catsup rules by laying blame on bureaucrats and the Congress. But, of course, it was Stockman's own budget cuts that necessitated the change. And, far from being dissuaded by the uproar, he would propose another 9.4 percent reduction in child nutrition programs for 1983, with additional reductions of $800 million slated for 1984 and 1985.

It was impossible for Stockman, or any of the President's aides, to separate the administration from the policy pronouncements coming directly from the White House itself. And indeed they surely reflected the budget director's own personal feelings as well. At a strategy meeting of Republicans, Senator Bob Packwood (R-OR) who was one of the participants, told reporters the President responded to concern over his unprecedented deficits by saying, "You know, a person yesterday, a young man, went into the grocery store, and he had an orange in one hand and a bottle of vodka in the other, and he paid for the orange with food stamps and he took the change and paid for the vodka. That's what's wrong." Given this explanation for hundred billion deficits," Packwood continued, he and his colleagues "just shake our heads." (An Agriculture Department official, Mary Jarrat, observed a few days later in a congressional hearing that change from a food stamp purchase is limited to 99 cents. Noted Jarrat, "It's not possible to buy a bottle of vodka with 99 cents.")

And then there was the President's view on unemployment. Asked how he would stem the surge in black joblessness at a January 19, 1982, press conference, Reagan cited "the local Sunday paper." Said Reagan, "I made it a point to count the pages of help wanted ads in this time of great unemployment. There were twenty-four full pages of classified ads of employers looking for employees. What we need to do is make more people qualified to go and apply for those jobs, and we are doing everything we can in that regard."

What David Stockman had already done in that regard was eliminate the Comprehensive Employment Training Act, designed to teach the marginally employable a skill and send them out into the marketplace. Indeed, in a March 4, 1982, breakfast speech before the Chamber of Commerce, Stockman did not merely say unemployment was a necessary evil, he proclaimed joblessness a positive good. The OMB director told a room packed with businessmen that unemployment is "part of the cure, not the problem." (Asked whether the President agreed with Stockman's statement,

White House spokesman Larry Speakes replied, "Generally, yes.")

One newspaper offered what seemed to be a wry comment on Stockman's attitude toward unemployment. A February 1, 1982, story in the *Hartford Courant* bore the alarming headline: REAGAN FORESEES 10% JOBLESS RATE. Directly adjacent to that headline was a photo of Stockman laughing uproariously, as if highly amused by the President's grim admission.

These disparate images—the poor shivering in line for blocks of cheese and unemployment soaring while the President sunned himself in the Caribbean—began to coalesce even as Stockman's 1983 budget went into the congressional hopper. On March 9, about a month after the budget's release, Representative Marc Marks, a previously unremarkable Republican from Pennsylvania, delivered a remarkable speech on the House floor. Describing himself as "a three-term" Republican from western Pennsylvania who in his own mind "has not made much of an impact on the nation," Marks admitted he had "voted for every major economic program that Reagan and this administration have put forth since coming to power. I have issued press releases and made public speeches in which I have indicated that Reagonomics is worthwhile." Calling on his fellow House members to say "enough is enough," Marks asked, "Are we not concerned that this President has failed to grasp that perception of this Administration's 'regal image'—are we not concerned that the china policy—and the secondhand dress business image have tarnished the statements made by this President that his administration is one dedicated to helping the people?" Marks insisted, "The time has come to stop this massacre!" and "to wonder *out loud*, whether what Senator Packwood said in candor about this President's understanding or his interest in what is happening to our people is not in fact true."

Far more powerful was the documentary by CBS correspondent Bill Moyers entitled "People Like Us." A preview showing of the program led *Washington Post* critic Tom Shales to predict it "could mark a turning point in American public opinion toward the Reagan Administration and its cavalier treatment of the poor." That assertion so alarmed White House press secretary David Gergen that the aide called CBS, asking for equal time under the Federal Communication Commission's Fairness Doctrine (this despite the administration's attempt to abolish the fairness clause), a request that was denied. The show consisted of four segments: Larry Ham, a cerebral palsy victim who had just had his disability benefits cut off with no appeal; Cathy Dixon, who sends her comatose daughter to a nursing home for fear of losing the girl's at-home care; Francis Dorta, who gives up her midnight to 8:00 A.M. job checking audio cassettes at a New Jersey factory in order to go on welfare and receive Medicaid benefits for an operation her son requires; and, finally, a soup line in the basement of a Milwaukee church.

In the course of the program, Moyers asks Gabriel Dorta, a thirteen-year-old boy in need of surgery, "How would you like to earn your living?"

Gabriel: In the middle.

Moyers: In the middle?

Gabriel: Yes.

Moyers: What do you mean?

Gabriel: Like not that rich, I'll just be in the middle. Like, I'll just take care.

Moyers: Take care of what?

Gabriel: Take care of myself.

Moyers: So you don't want to be rich; just want to make your own way?

Gabriel: Yes.

Moyers: What do you dream about when you dream? I—I used to be a thirteen-year-old boy. I remember my dream.

Gabriel: I always dream of taking pictures of my mother, and then go out to buy some more film.

Moyers: That's your dream?

Gabriel: Yes.

At the Milwaukee church, Moyers asks an eight-year-old boy, Michael, how he gets to the church dinners:

Michael: Just walk.

Moyers: You walk? How—How far?

Michael: Fifteenth and Orchard.

Moyers: How long does it take you?

Michael: Sometimes about thirty minutes.

Moyers: About thirty minutes? What does your father do?

Michael: He cleans up the house sometimes and looks for cans.

Moyers: Does he have a job. He doesn't—

Michael: He's trying to find one.

And finally, in a discussion with the priest of the church, Moyers mentioned, "President Reagan said, 'We really are taking care of the truly needy.' What's your response to that? The priest replied, "Simply the fact that the American citizen who can say that is blind."

And there were a hundred other things—large and small—to drive the point home. Reagan spent $1,000 for riding boots while insisting welfare families possess no more than $1,000 in personal belongings. The "Car Book," a widely praised guide on the safety and quality of automobiles, was abruptly discontinued, while Nancy Reagan had a sixteen-page glossy booklet printed on "Easter at the White House." And Ronald Reagan, vowing to stop this "fiscal joyride," boarded a private helicopter bound for a Camp David barbeque.

On Capitol Hill, another, more parochial form of resentment added to Stockman's problems. The budget director's tour de force in 1981 had left many representatives and senators feeling less like legislators than small children being led by the hand. Stockman's strong-arm tactics on the 1981 reconciliation bill won him the battle, but one battle was not the whole war. Institutional pride had been wounded. "We got kneecapped by Stockman last year," snapped one angry House Democrat. "Believe me, this year it isn't going to happen again."

Beyond the psychological bruising Congress took during reconciliation, many members were sincerely concerned that the process had allowed the White House to usurp legislative power. In an October 6, 1981, hearing before the Senate Governmental Affairs Committee, Stockman considerably understated a crucial factor in the voting on Gramm–Latta II by saying, "Some members of the Congress were concerned that they were voting for something that they did not entirely understand." Testifying at that hearing, House

Rules Chairman Richard Bolling (D-MO) noted wryly, "A conservative President and a conservative Congress are in accord [as] to ends, a drastic contraction of the public sector. Let us not quibble, therefore, over means." Observed Bolling, "If we are to be reduced to automatons, permitted only to ratify a Presidential legislative agenda, which has been premasticated by an all-powerful Executive, the American people, with some justice, may address themselves to the question: 'Why should we support with our tax dollars, this overly expensive anachronism?' " And it was all too clear who Congress held responsible for the damages wrought. In an October 1 House Budget hearing, Representative Leon Panetta exclaimed, "My God, the Gramm–Latta amendment was designed by you [Stockman] and Mr. Gramm. If it didn't include all of the pieces, it wasn't Congress' fault, it was the White House's fault." Representative Bill Nelson (D-FL) had also had enough:

Nelson: If OMB wrote Gramm–Latta—

Stockman: That is not true. Mr. Gramm and Mr. Latta wrote Gramm–Latta II.

Nelson: I would assume with heavy consultation.

Stockman: We all consult.

For the Congress, the chaotic passage of the administration's reconciliation package in July 1981 was only the beginning of Stockman's affronts. Republicans as well as Democrats grew offended. During the congressional conference to iron out the differences in the House and Senate versions of the reconciliation bill in 1981, Stockman had forcefully pressed Senate Republicans to accept the House version. The OMB director hoped in this way to minimize debate that might endanger any portion of his package. But the Republicans refused to be bound lock, stock, and barrel to the 860 pages of scrawl that constituted the House bill. At one point, according to a House Democrat, Senator Ted Stevens (R-AK) grew so irritated at Stockman's pestering that he told the OMB director to "Get the f—k out of here."

Stockman retreated only as far as his typewriter. Unprompted, the OMB head dashed off a seventy-seven-page memo to Senate Republican leaders reminding them of the cuts he wanted made. That memo angered some and amused others. In the former category was Leon Panetta. "So far, luckily, no one is paying much attention to it," he said. "That way we may be able to get something done." In the latter category were the legislators who thought they had made deals to save their pet programs from cuts. Many who had voted with the President found their own projects axed in the Stockman memo. "It surprises me," said Representative Ralph Hall (D-TX). "I have the impression [we had a deal] but I can't honestly say they gave me any assurance."

Stockman's seventy-seven-page directive was a mere prelude to the pressure he would apply in later months. A few days after the conference had begun, the OMB director accused the House Appropriations Committee of sabotage. Claiming the committee's spending exceeded the White House targets by $1.5 billion, Stockman told reporters the House's action "threatens the [White House] fiscal plan, it threatens the deficits." According to Stockman, the President would think hard about vetoing various appropriations measures. "It'll probably come to that," warned the OMB head. A House Appropriations aide told *The Wall Street Journal*. "It really comes down to the fact that they [OMB] don't like our spending priorities." "If they'd keep total outlays under what we've requested, I wouldn't give a rip," retorted Stockman.

Congress largely ignored Stockman's threats. Anxious to avoid the sauna that is Washington in August, the conferees stepped up their work and limped back home. Throughout the congressional recess, interest rates remained higher than mandated by Stockman's economic assumptions. These soaring rates were the prime reason for a revised version of expenditure estimates—from $704.8 billion in July 1981 to $722 billion in September 1981.

And Stockman was not ready to let the difference of $17.2 billion fall through the cracks. When Congress returned after Labor Day, Stockman greeted them with yet an additional demand: Cut another $13 billion from the fiscal 1982 budget and approve a package of $3 billion in tax hikes. Again, in the budget reductions, Stockman sought to eliminate most of the concessions House members had extracted from the White House in exchange for a "yea" vote on Gramm–Latta II.

Appearing on the September 27 edition of "Face the Nation" just three days after Reagan had announced the new budget cuts he was seeking, one of the show's commentators, Fred Graham, tried to pin a wily Stockman to the mat:

Graham: . . . we are hearing that some of the—particularly some of the Republican Congressmen felt that you have reneged on promises that were made to them when you got the first round of cuts; that certain programs such as Amtrak would not be cut further. Did you make that commitment and have you reneged?

Stockman: I think given the kind of fiscal situation that we face—a budget that has enormous momentum—that we can never promise that a program will not be cut next year or the year after.

Graham: But did you? Did you?

Stockman: Well, I'm just saying that the government's been running on a credit card for ten years and the bills are now coming in. And if it takes cuts in areas that we hoped to avoid before, then we're going to have to make those cuts. . . .

Asked on the same show if an $8 or $9 billion spending cut would suit him, Stockman replied, "No, I don't think that would be acceptable," and insisted that the deficit had to be kept to an exacting $42.5 billion. Reminded that one of his colleagues, Secretary of Commerce Malcolm Baldrige, had said that Wall Street would see little difference between deficits of $42.5, $46.5, or $47.5 billion, Stockman stuck by his guns: "Well, I think it would be a big difference."

Sixty seconds later his resolve came unglued. Responding to a question from columnist David Broder, Stockman said, "Well, the answer . . . is valid in the sense that you don't have to hit forty-two or forty-five. But the larger point is the direction of the deficit has to be steadily down this coming year and in subsequent years. . . ."

Broder: So that your real point is not to hit the forty-two or forty-five as you've just said.

Stockman: Absolutely not. It's to keep the deficit moving down. . . .

Broder: So that if the deficit should end up perhaps at forty-eight or forty-nine, you would feel that you had basically achieved your goal.

Stockman: If the deficit is coming down, I would feel that we've achieved our goal. You can't look—

> *Broder:* Why didn't you just say that then rather than torture the—
> go through all the torture of specific cuts aimed at the
> specific numbers?

Perhaps the Congress sensed that Broder and Baldrige were right
and the economic gains of reducing the deficit by $13 or $16 billion
were not worth the political pain of tacking on yet more budget cuts
so quickly. After a year of shattered initiatives, Congress reassem-
bled its institutional pride and let the administration know that the
budget cuts, as presented, had little chance of passage in the House.
Realizing the odds for another win on the Hill were minimal,
Reagan compromised, announcing at his fifth press conference, on
November 10, 1981, that the White House was scaling back its
requested cuts to $8.5 billion and was dropping the tax proposals
entirely. Despite scaling back the budget reductions, Reagan promised to veto any "budget busting bills."

Thus was David Stockman twice rebuffed. He had lost out
entirely on $4.5 billion of his expected budget cuts and failed
entirely on his bid to raise another $3 billion for the government
coffers through increased taxation. And, if anything, these second
round cuts were destined to be even more painful than the original
bill, which sliced $35 billion from the federal budget—a "political
nightmare," in the words of Senator Mark Hatfield (R-OR).

By the time the new round of cuts got to the House floor in mid-
November, Congress was starting to wind down for another holiday
break. One provision in the bill, inserted by the House, concerned
dairy price supports. Over four years the House version was estimated to cost $500 million more than Stockman or the Agriculture
Department found acceptable. On November 14, Representative
Paul Findley (R-IL) offered an amendment on the floor to cut the
supports back to Stockman's original plan. During the two-hour
debate that ensued, the arguments for and against were all too
familiar—despite a front-row seat, Representative John G. Fary (D-
IL) managed to sleep through most of the proceedings.

While the debate may have been familiar, the White House
handling of the matter was most unusual. In the past, the executive
lobbying staff had performed with the precision of a fine orchestra
comprised of well-tuned instruments. On this occasion, it was
difficult even to discern the melody Stockman and his cohorts were
playing. Agriculture Secretary John R. Block was out of the coun-

try. Findley's original amendment was shouted down by voice vote on the floor while the unknowing representative stood out in the hall trying to explain his proposal to an inquiring reporter. Findley quickly devised yet another amendment that differed slightly from the first. To no avail. He and the White House lost that roll-call vote, 255 to 153.

Representative Barney Frank, a liberal Massachusetts Democrat, found himself in an unlikely alliance with the White House on the issue, leading the fight to slash the dairy program with Findley. Frank was not impressed by Stockman and company's lobbying techniques. As he told *The Washington Post*: "The Administration is just in a shambles. They have a terrible time making tough decisions. They have a terrible time being consistent. They just made no effort to work their troops at all."

While the Senate cut an additional $6 billion (only $4 billion by Stockman's estimate), the House found none of the cuts OMB wanted in their debate on November 16. Indeed, there was a great deal of confusion over *what* OMB wanted. Following several hours of frustrating negotiations off the House floor, Representative Les Aspin (D-WI) was still baffled. "I'd be happier if I knew where these cuts were coming from," he said.

From David Stockman's point of view, the timing of the bill was slightly embarrassing: six days earlier his confessions in the *Atlantic* had landed on the newsstands and found their way into the hands of every member on the Hill. Jim Jones was not amused:

> He [Stockman] concedes in that article that they really did not know where their numbers were coming from and we have in this room right behind this chamber, OMB trying to explain how they have come up with the numbers they have furnished to the minority right now, and they cannot explain it. It indicates that they are doing what they did in the spring. . . .
>
> That article also states that one of the strategies [of OMB] is to spread confusion, have a lot of different budget bases, and a lot of different cuts from different bases so that we never quite know what they are talking about. The strategy is to spread confusion. I think that's what may be going on today.

And a number of moderate Republicans in the House (known as "Gypsy Moths" in the Hill vernacular) were none too happy with the promises Stockman had reneged on. Silvio Conte, ranking minority member of the Appropriations Committee, sounded as if he had run out of patience with the executive branch. "There is no justification for backdoor, meat axe cuts," maintained Conte. In the end, eighteen Gypsy Moths bolted the Republican Party and voted with the Democrats, giving that much-beleagured party a 201–189 victory over the White House. The House leadership was elated. For the first time since Ronald Reagan had taken his place in the Oval Office, they had managed to win on a major issue.

Their elation was short-lived. OMB contended the House cuts only amounted to $2 billion on the $8.5 billion requested. After much haranguing back and forth, Reagan cut his $8.5 billion request in half, demanding at least another $2.5 billion from Tip O'Neill's chamber. The President vetoed the bill sent from the Hill at Stockman's urging, and sent the problem back to the legislative chamber. (It was at this point, recalls one House Appropriations aide, that he heard reference to the "White Whine House.")

Shortly thereafter, on November 22, the government technically ran out of money. Congress convened on Sunday at 1:00 P.M. Silvio Conte was even less understanding than he had been a week earlier: "All I can say after twenty-four years here is that it's a hell of a way to run a railroad." The Sunday meeting lasted far into the night but produced negligible results. On Monday, Reagan shut down all but the most essential government services, sending most of Washington's workers home for the day. The House capitulated and made the $2.5 billion in cuts. But as Stockman and the White House would discover, their bullying on the Hill would command a steep price tag.

A week after passage of the budget bill that keep the government going, Reagan lost a key member of his congressional lobbying team, Max Friedersdorf. Accepting a pay cut of $10,000 and a consular post in Bermuda, Friedersdorf announced his resignation effective January 2. "He's just had a hard year," explained one White House official. He had also been the person best able to smooth over the congressional feathers Stockman was so adept at ruffling.

13 • Dueling Elephants

STOCKMAN WAS also faced with a third major source of resistance to his 1983 budget: the rest of the Reagan Cabinet. Unlike 1981, his cabinet colleagues did not docilely accept the budget director's sweeping reductions. Perhaps emboldened by Stockman's confessions in the *Atlantic,* and certainly more secure in their understanding of the government minutiae in which Stockman excelled, the officials fought many of Stockman's efforts in intra-administration squabbling that the President frequently had to arbitrate.

Appearing on "Face the Nation" in September 1981, Stockman had seemed confident that agency heads were again ready to follow his lead. Said Stockman, "On the big issues, on the important things, we're united, we're working together, and we're headed towards the same goal."

But again for the OMB director, wishing did not make it so. By the end of December 1981, the complaints of four cabinet officials, angry over the proposed cuts in their already bare-bone departments, had found their way into the press. And before another six months had passed, a fifth would join their ranks.

Among other proposed reductions, the OMB director had scheduled Education Secretary Terrel H. Bell's department for a hefty 27 percent cut from 1981 levels. In a letter leaked to the press, Bell wrote Stockman that "cries of outrage from the education community" were already being heard over the expected 12 percent funding cuts. Faced with the prospect of trying to explain a cut more than twice that amount, Bell asked that he and Stockman meet to consider "the political realities."

Commerce Secretary Malcolm Baldrige soon joined the parade. By November 28, his troubles also became public in a leaked letter to the *Post.* Asked to eliminate three Commerce offices designed to promote American exports, an angry Baldrige wrote Stockman: "These services are not like an Erector set that one can fool around with on the living room floor and quickly build up again . . . there is no way that I can go along with the recommendations." Baldrige also made obvious his unhappiness over Stockman's continuing efforts to rush through cuts before agency heads could respond. And, apparently, Baldrige would have none of it. "You sent your memorandum over Thursday," wrote the Commerce Secretary, "giving us the weekend to reply to extremely far-reaching recommendations and leaving us with the impression that they were perfunctory at best."

No stranger to disputes with Stockman, Energy Secretary James B. Edwards skipped the leaked memo and met directly with the press on December 10. Faced with employee reductions of 22 percent, Edwards exclaimed, "You'd think that I was the one resisting the cuts and in reality I'm here to close the place down. But even a closeout needs manpower."

With the defection of Health and Human Services Secretary Richard Schweiker, the rebels made four. In a letter that also found its way into the hands of *The Washington Post*, Schweiker took Stockman to task for the OMB director's sharp reduction in Head Start funds. Begun in 1965 as part of Johnson's war on poverty, the program gave preschool training to inner-city children. Funded in 1982 for about 374,000 children, the program was widely considered a success. Indeed, early in 1981, Reagan labeled Head Start one of seven essential services for the truly needy to be exempt from cuts. Clearly, David Stockman felt otherwise. Said Schweiker, "I believe the President appropriately placed Head Start as one of the 'safety net' programs." Of an OMB proposal to reduce the Centers for Disease Control by nearly a fifth, Schweiker protested the reduced funding would "erode our ability" to limit "infectious and other diseases."

With the regular budget appeals process back in place after the chaos of 1981, challenges in 1982 promised to be the order of the day. From December 10 to 23, the President was scheduled to review the pleas that had gone unresolved. One OMB employee explained the difference in the work to be done from the past. "By now, we would usually be down to eight or nine really tough issues [within a department] that would have to be decided by the secretary, the director and maybe the President, and we would have disposed of eighty or ninety other issues. . . . There are still eighty or ninety issues on the table. I think it's because nobody here [at OMB] is willing to be reasonable."

And when the administration's positions were finally ironed out, the battle was just beginning. In a congressional "preview" of the budget on February 6, 1982, which would appear in full form the next day, Stockman admitted "the whole thing will be difficult." Others on the Hill, Republican leadership included, insisted the whole thing would be next to impossible.

Republican whip Senator Ted Stevens admitted he was "sort of in a state of shock" over the deficit figures. Senator Robert Dole, chairman of the Finance Committee, said, "The Republicans I have talked with are frightened about the deficits." A generally talkative Pete Domenici, Senate Budget Committee Chair, had "no comment." Contacted at home with the flu, Senate Majority Leader Howard Baker agreed only to say something the following week.

The next day, Friday, February 7, members received their full sets of budget volumes. Those volumes arrived with "Embargoed for Release until Monday, February 10" stickers prominently displayed on their covers. But in the Government Printing Office bookstore, in OMB press secretary Ed Dale's words, "Things just went wrong." Copies of the budget were sold without the embargo stickers. Reporters dropped their official budget copies and scurried to buy the unrestricted ones being sold on the GPO racks. Both the *Post* and the *Times* served notice to the White House that they intended to run budget stories on Sunday, using the information over the weekend. On Saturday, at a press briefing on the FY 1983 budget held at the State Department, Larry Speakes announced that the administration was lifting the embargo. At least one editor didn't buy Ed Dale's explanation for the mix-up. That newsman described the early media release of the budget data as "the Friday afternoon syndrome" of letting bad news out at the start of a weekend. "The markets are closed, there are fewer reporters to follow up on the story, and Saturday papers are poorly read," explained the editor.

Members on the Hill, fearing deeper domestic cuts and tax hikes in an election year, found the news very grim. In an unconcerted action, many members turned to cutting defense spending as a possible way out of Stockman's work. "When hawks like me are talking about cutting military spending," said conservative Senator

William Armstrong (R-CO), "you know something is in the wind." Meanwhile Republican House freshman Larry DeNardis exclaimed, "The education budget is scheduled for a thirty percent reduction at the same time the defense budget is going to be increased fifteen percent. That's absolutely indefensible."

The fifth administration figure who refused to take Stockman's 1983 budget cuts without a fight was Anne Burford (then Gorsuch) of the Environmental Protection Agency. At this point a full year away from the concatenation of events that would result in her resignation, Burford had come aboard the Reagan team rather late and was trying hard to get a handle on her department.

In her book detailing her stormy tenure at EPA, *Are You Tough Enough?*, Burford tells of her first impressions of Stockman:

> I don't know exactly what caused the lengthy delay in appointing me to head Ronald Reagan's EPA. But I find it very hard to resist the temptation that David Stockman had a lot to do with it.
>
> One of the most brilliant young men I have ever met, David Stockman is also one of the most driven and calculating. And when he gets fixed on an idea, he does not easily let it go. It is a matter of record that he hates the legislation that established the Environmental Protection Agency. In fact, he hates EPA period.
>
> David has the soul of a conservative—at least I think he does. . . . To this day he remains very strongly opposed to the legislation that EPA is charged with implementing. And though that may be correct from a conservative point of view, that won't make the agency go away.
>
> It has always been my feeling that Stockman was instrumental in delaying the decision on my appointment—and perhaps that of others, too. I believe this because in the leadership vacuum that resulted, he did an awful lot of the running of the agency. He proposed the first budget, and he drafted legislation that changed the water laws with regard to grants for sewage treatment plants. He had all that done by the time I got to town. I agree that these very dramatic changes were necessary, and it was David Stockman who got them through, not me. I think he would have been perfectly happy to continue running the agency—through the budget—forever.

In attempting to explain why the press was hard on her, Burford claims that there was "a form of guilt by association that we neither liked nor deserved." She writes:

If the Watt Factor and the Reagan Agenda were not enough, there was another important element—the Stockman Presence. I had barely heard of the former two-term Congressman from Michigan before I came to Washington, but I certainly heard of him once I arrived. And heard of him and heard of him and heard of him.

As he wasted very little time showing, he was one of the two or three most powerful men in the administration. As head of the Office of Management and Budget, he began by telling the Cabinet and the rest of the agency and department heads (with the initial exception of the military) just how much they would have to spend. And there was to be no arguing with him. His budget figures were not suggestions; they were pronouncements. And the matter-of-fact way he testified on the Hill about the coming slashes in spending did not always sit well with the heads of important committees, many of whom, I would soon learn, would then take out their ire on the official in charge of the about-to-be slashed agency or department. And if that official were still awaiting confirmation, then look out.

Eventually, of course, Mrs. Burford was confirmed. But her troubles with David Stockman did not end once she took over the reins at EPA. She and he fought a pitched battle over the cuts he wanted to make in her Fiscal Year '83 budget. What so annoyed Burford was that she had played Stockman's game the first time around, only to learn he wanted to make a second round of cuts. As she tells it in a chapter entitled "Little King David," she is

proud of the fact that I have always stood up to David Stockman. One of the central differences between my administration and that of all my predecessors at EPA was that I insisted on getting personally involved in the budgetary process. My comptroller, Morgan Kinghorn, an excellent civil servant and a superb comptroller who has seen all of the agency's administrators, was initially startled to see me get so involved. But he became a real ally, and he helped me steady my lance as I galloped off for my encounters with David Stockman and his minions at the Office of Management and Budget.

Burford wrote:

The way the budget process had worked in the past was that OMB would give the agency a number, and the five major program directors—AIR, WATER, TOSCA, RCRA, Administration, Research & Development, and Superfund (after 1980)—would sit in a room, and whoever had the biggest stick would come out with the biggest share. In contrast, the budget we constructed for fiscal 1983 . . . was the first EPA budget ever to be based on programmatic objectives, needed manpower, and dollars in each programmatic area down to the five-man office level out in the field.

And I held an extensive two-day hearing for each programmatic area. The head of each program had to survive my grilling about the whys and wherefores of his or her proposed allocations. As a result, and to understate it, I knew what that agency was doing. . . . I knew my agency cold, down to the smallest local levels. . . .

I knew we were in for a battle of the budget with David Stockman because once he burned me the first time, I refused to play the game by his rules. The way it goes is that you play a little charade on the public and the Congress by which you both look good and King David remains on top of the power heap.

The "dance" began in the spring when Stockman or one of his top aides called and said, "I'm whispering a number in your ear; this is your target." And then you get a budget together that comes very close to that number.

Shortly after I took office I got a call from Stockman's aide Fred Khedouri. He said, "This is your whispered number."

I didn't complain, nor did I, as most of the other "players" do, inflate it. I submitted a budget that met that figure, or came very close to it. Of course that meant that we could do only some of the things we wanted to do in TOSCA, for example, but that's the way of the world, especially in Washington.

In late summer, by which time we had most of the budget put together, [Fred] Khedouri called me with a different figure. *Lower.*

Well, there were a few things we thought we could postpone . . . so once again I went along. It meant developing an entirely new budget, which is hardly a simple process, *but we did it because we thought we were doing the President's bidding.* [italics added]

We sent our reconstructed budget back to OMB, and it came back in *pieces.* It wasn't cut, it was shredded. And we had been using David Stockman's own revised "bottom line" figure!

They hadn't just lowered the figures, they had made programmatic decisions! They had eliminated offices here, added others there, cut six and a half people in one obscure office, but added ten someplace else, and axed dollar amounts all over the lot. Their alterations represented management and policy decisions, not budgetary decisions.

For example, they eliminated one of the existing offices within the Water area, but added an Office of Federal Compliance, or some such title, which was an attempt (laudatory under other circumstances) to eliminate some of the duplication of environmental regulations that exists among the various federal agencies and departments. That kind of decision was hardly within the scope of OMB's function.

Burford—who says, "It takes a lot to get me angry"—had had it. She decided to appeal. As the first step in what she calls "an interesting example of reduced democracy," she took her first appeal to Stockman himself. After a forty-minute meeting in which Burford thought she had presented her case very well, Stockman, who took no notes and said little, got up and announced, "Thank you very much. That's the way it's going to be." And he left the room.

That got her *real* angry. She asked to appeal to the Budget Appeals Board, an act of near heresy. That body consisted of James Baker, Ed Meese—and David Stockman. According to Burford, "David Stockman was in the interesting position of being both your prosecutor and your judge."

> That appeal went well too. The panel restored quite a bit of what I wanted. But I was very disappointed on two counts. One, they cut fifty million for Superfund. It made little sense to cut the Superfund totals, that money had been collected in taxes from industry, and was already earmarked, like Social Security, to be spent from that special fund, not from the general fund, which meant it would not add to the federal deficit.
>
> I knew I had to ask for the maximum with Superfund. If I didn't, then I would have had to go before the Congress and explain why I wasn't spending that money. And they and the media would see it as part of a nefarious Reaganite anti-environmental plot.
>
> The other point I felt strongly about involved what I viewed as a credibility issue for the President. In 1981 Stockman had gotten Congress to agree a $2.4 billion appropriation for Sewage Treatment Plant Construction Grants. Although it hadn't been carved in stone anywhere, there was a general agreement on the Hill that that would be the annual amount appropriated for that purpose for the next four or five years.
>
> This was only the second year of the program and Stockman wanted to cut that figure to $2 billion. I felt very strongly that not only would the President be hurt, but even if we did ask for less the Congress was going to appropriate $2.4 billion anyway. So what was the point?
>
> I decided to appeal to the President. And that stunned David Stockman.
>
> The meeting was attended by me, David Stockman, President Reagan, Ed Meese, Jim Baker, Craig Fuller, and Ken Duberstein, the

White House congressional affairs person, among others. Thank God for Mr. Duberstein. At one point, after I had made a heartfelt pitch for the Sewage Treatment grant funds, he spoke up and said, "Mr. President, Anne's right. There's a general consensus on the Hill that you agreed to $2.4 billion, not just this year but next year too. And you're going to get it. But you're going to establish a credibility problem for yourself if you ask for less."

The meeting ended and I went back to my office. Before the day was over the President called me personally to tell me that I had won.

I got substantially everything I asked for. I did not get the amount for Superfund that I wanted, but I got a far greater amount than Stockman or the Budget Appeals Board would have allowed me. And I did get the $2.4 billion for the Sewage Treatment Construction Grants program.

Near the end of our conversation, the President said, "Okay, Anne, that gives you pretty much what you wanted. But you will have to give a bit, too. We have to throw David a bone."

The bone was a slight reduction in the budget for research and development.

As a result of her battle with Stockman, Burford "lost a great deal of respect for him." As she put it, "What bothered me the most was that when it was all over, he was *personally* angry that I had won. To me, that indicated a character flaw. Several people have suggested to me that I created a mortal enemy that day."

As mentioned briefly above, James Edwards, the first Secretary of Energy, was another Reagan appointee who battled with Stockman. In fact, the battle extended to Edwards's chief lieutenants, one of whom, Dr. Shelby Brewer, has no qualms about voicing what he terms his "perspective on David Stockman's presence in the Reagan Administration."

Brewer, then the DOE's Assistant Secretary of Energy for Nuclear Energy, was the point man on the Reagan Administration's nuclear policy. He had been appointed by President Reagan in 1981, and one of his assignments was to remobilize one of Stockman's least favorite federal projects, the Clinch River Breeder Reactor. He recalls, vividly, a particular lobbying trip on behalf of that project. "I was in the office of a congressman from Louisiana, and I gave him my reasons why I felt he should vote for the project, and suddenly I realized he was giving me a very odd look. I asked what the matter was, and he replied, 'That chair you are sitting in is still warm from the last person who was sitting there, and he was telling me to vote *against* the project. His name was David Stockman. He called it Baker's boondoggle. [a reference to then Senator Howard Baker of Tennessee, where the project was to be located].' "

Dr. Brewer goes on:

Ronald Reagan had very strongly endorsed the project, publicly and repeatedly, but at the same time David Stockman was *against* the project on the Hill. Wherever I went, I found the fingerprints and the footprints of David Stockman.

To put this episode in context, remember that President Carter had tried to terminate the project . . . and the project lay dormant for those four years, with the meter running. Cost went up about one billion dollars because of the Carter delay. President Reagan reversed the Carter policy in 1981 and ordered the project remobilized. That we did, and I streamlined and fast-tracked the project. I was concerned about cost, and all of the nonessential featherbedding that tends to cling to any federal undertaking, so I included a cost ceiling, and together with industry, designed a financial proposal that would relieve the taxpayer of almost half of the remaining cost by securing private sector investment. The issue with Stockman seemed not to be so much a *fiscal* issue but a policy issue—the justification of the project as a rational technological pursuit—but the boss [President Reagan] had spoken, and that should have been that.

Brewer continued:

And that seems to be core of the problem so many Reagan appointees had with David Stockman: his agenda seemed to be driven not by genuine fiscal conservatism and not by the usual comptroller role of managing financial operations—his attention was focused instead on policy and political choices—which was not his job. He was out of his wigwam. There was an irresistible itch there to recast the President's agenda, to interdict the policies and priorities of the White House policy staff and the cabinet. And his policy and political notions and actions were fundamentally at variance with the President's and those of the men and women the President appointed to implement his policies.

Reagan appointees by and large were fiscal conservatives when they entered office and they set about voluntarily to shed budget. We were not embarked on a spending spree. Thrift was not invented by David Stockman. In the case of the nuclear programs, I cut the budget forecast inherited from the Carter Administration in half. Then we cut it in half again by getting the waste management program user-financed through legislation, and off the taxpayers' backs. But despite all that—which was accomplished without Stockman's help—there emanated from OMB a sort of policy oversight pretension, second-guessing on appropriateness of nuclear power. The OMB's political whims and fancies just sort of seeped out of there like a damp vapor. And this ambiance carried the faint odor of Mr. Carter's Administration, which nagged, fretted, micromanaged, overspent—and *failed*.

Asked for his reaction to Stockman's revelations in the *Atlantic* magazine article, Brewer responded quickly: "If he had been working for me in a business or political situation, he would have been shown the door that same day."

Brewer feels that neither Stockman nor his people were truly on the President's team: "Throughout the first term, there was a general sense that David Stockman was out of step with the President and the President's agenda. He and his people seemed to be trying to create an illusion that they could manipulate the President. One of his assistants once told me, 'I know what's in the President's head before he does and better than he does.'"

Dr. Brewer is in accord with Anne Burford's point about Stockman and his people becoming entrenched while it took so long for secretaries and assistant secretaries to get nominated, approved, and on the job:

Another thing that worked against the efficiency of the Reagan Administration was that the appointment process was so badly strung out. In many cases, assistant secretaries didn't get installed until nine months later, and by that time things were going pretty much Dave's way. Governor Edwards [Energy Secretary James Edwards had been a governor of South Carolina] essentially was alone for the first six months in terms of carrying the administration's water. During all that time he was constantly being belabored and undermined by David Stockman and his staff of non-appointees.

Stockman's assistants in OMB were not presidential appointees like secretaries and assistant secretaries in the various cabinet departments, who were nominated by the President and confirmed by the U.S. Senate. They were accountable for nothing. They were not responsible for managing large enterprises. Nor did they have to formulate complex policy positions and defend these positions before Congress and the public. They were immune from those discomforts, but they still harbored fantasies that they called the shots. This play-acting was an enormous pain in the neck for those of us who were on the point, and accountable, and caused the administration embarrassment time after time.

Asked to summarize his opinion of David Stockman, Dr. Brewer said, with no hesitation, "I've always believed that having him on the team was like backing a Trojan horse up to the Reagan Administration."

In one of the most startling revelations in Anne Burford's book, she includes a scene recaptured by Dr. John Hernandez, who became her second-in-command. Also involved were two Stockman aides, one of whom, Fred Khedouri, was also mentioned by Dr. Shelby Brewer as working *against* the President's nuclear energy program. (As mentioned earlier, Khedouri, a very bright University of Chicago graduate, once worked for Ralph Nader.)

At the time, Hernandez was in the running for the top job at EPA, and to that end he met with the Stockman aides. As he tells it:

> My meeting was with Glenn Schleede, the number three man at OMB, and Fred Khedouri, OMB's budget director for EPA. I went into that interview very cautiously because I knew that these people wanted to make a lot of major cuts at EPA. So I was quite reluctant to say anything that I didn't believe in, in way of philosophy or approach. I was absolutely terrified of becoming the head of EPA and all that mess it was in, so it was in the forefront of my mind all during that meeting that anything I said to those guys I would have to live with if I became the administrator.
>
> And, finally, at one point, Fred Khedouri leaned over in his chair, and kind of quiet like, but dead serious, asked, "Would you be willing to bring EPA to its knees?"
>
> I was so startled that I kind of just laughed, as if I couldn't believe he said that. But he had said it, and I just demurred.
>
> And when Anne was selected head of EPA instead of me, I was very much relieved.

Burford adds, immediately after Dr. Hernandez' account:

> John Hernandez never asked me if I had been asked that same question. I wish he had. I had not been asked the question. It would have been helpful to me to know that Stockman's people had asked it of him. Had I known, I would have gone to the President and demanded Stockman's resignation. But as Hernandez later told someone, he simply didn't want to know the answer—in case it was yes. I have

thought about this startling and sickening bit of information a lot since learning of it, and I am convinced that this attitude toward EPA, and therefore toward the environment, was behind a lot of the problems I encountered. But knowing the question was asked, and knowing who asked it, and knowing whom he worked for helps me to understand some of the things that happened to me and my people in the years that followed.

Not too surprisingly, Stockman had his critics outside his own party in regard to the 1983 budget. Although the figures were toned down from the last budget's, the number of its critics had by no means lessened. James R. Schlesinger, an acting budget director under Nixon, warned in a *Washington Post* article, "This budget's numbers require the same care in interpretation as reading the entrails of a goose." Some of those interpretations were a 3 percent growth rate in FY 1982 and a roaring 5.2 percent in FY 1983, an 1982 unemployment rate of 8.9 and then 7.9, interest rates at 11.7 and 10.5, and an inflation rate of 7.2 to 5.5. Schlesinger could scarcely conceal his disgust with the new figures and with OMB:

> All of this represents a serious blow to the credibility of the budget process within the executive branch. The OMB, unloved but broadly respected for its integrity, has long been a government pillar. Its debauchment represents the needless wastage of social capital. The Congressional Budget Office may well enjoy the satisfaction of providing the only credible official estimates in town. . . .

Stockman's first formal appearance on the Hill after his *Atlantic* interview hit the stands concerned a safer topic than budget reductions. Appearing before the Senate Governmental Affairs Committee, Stockman discussed the "New Federalism," a once-trumpeted initiative sent down from the White House that became largely viewed as so much smoke and mirrors by both parties in the legislature. Senator Dole commented, "Every president wants to find something to get out front with but the economy can't be subordinated and he knows that." Pete Domenici said simply, "It can't take the place of fiscal policy issues."

The "New Federalism" was essentially block grants on a large scale. The crucial attractiveness of the idea (at least for Stockman) was that prior to sending funds for programs back to the states, the OMB director proposed to slash the funds. Speaking at the February

4 hearing, Senator Henry Jackson (D-WA) was unimpressed. "We have over eleven percent unemployed [in Washington State], and I must say to go out and explain to people about Federalism as they are unemployed and going broke, raises a modest question of timing." Jackson concluded by asking, "And when you go out and start talking, Mr. Stockman, about New Federalism, how do you eat it?"

Senator Bill Bradley (D-NJ), appearing on "The Week With David Brinkley," observed, "I thought the President's federalism approach was a relatively interesting diversionary tactic, diverting attention away from the highest unemployment since the Depression and interest rates that are preventing families from buying homes and driving small businessmen to the brink of bankruptcy." Mayor Charles Royer of Seattle explained, "There's an old budget saying, called the shift-and-shaft theory of budgeting, which is to move responsibility but not move the means to pay." Some on the Hill were simply jealous of their prerogatives. "Hell," grumbled one House Democrat, "I should have run for the state legislature if that's where they're going to be doing everything."

Either the New Federalism was an outstanding diversionary tactic or, more likely, there was simply no one in Washington ready to do anything about coming up with a budget in the months that followed. From February to mid-May 1982, negotiations on the federal ledger consisted of broken promises, severed negotiations, and (arguably) fear. Addressing Stockman at a House Budget hearing on May 5, Representative Jim Mattox (D-TX) relayed a common frustration: "I think we are fiddling, not while Rome burns, but while the American economic system is burning." Speaking on the House floor on March 9, Representative Robert Walker (R-PA) assured his peers:

> America has been breathlessly waiting to see what the House is going to do on the Potato Research and Promotion act, and today we are going to take that bill up. There was another bill scheduled that dealt with the Hoboken pier, but of course that had to be pulled off the calendar. I know that millions of Americans are going to be disappointed to learn that fact.
>
> We may not be able to deal with the issues as big as the Hoboken pier or other important issues like balanced budgets or busing or school prayer, but let there be no doubt, when it comes to small potatoes, this Congress measures up.

And there were the horror stories concerning OMB's work that trickled in. Ostensibly intent on bolstering incentives, OMB's cuts in benefits to the working poor, according to Alice Rivlin of the Congressional Budget Office, would put nearly one-third (or 63,000 families) back onto the welfare rolls. Jack A. Meyer, a scholar at the American Enterprise Institute, was not generally one to lecture the administration. But in a May 25 column in *The Washington Post*, Meyer called for "A superior—and more humane—approach that substitutes graduated assistance for the all-or-nothing approach and views marginal assistance to the working poor as a prudent social investment in their future self-sufficiency."

As it turned out, Stockman's credibility problems had only just begun with his *Atlantic* ramblings. While Stockman claimed in early 1981 that by reducing the federal work force by 43,000 persons the administration would save $1.6 billion, the Government Accounting Office (GAO) had a significant dispute with the OMB director's figures. The GAO viewed the savings as up to $1 billion on the optimistic side. In a report released in February 1982, it stated, "OMB officials could not provide any documentation to support their projected savings or the extent to which they considered offsetting costs."

Stockman's admissions in the *Atlantic* had damaged his effectiveness on the Hill, a fact the White House could not seem to forget. In a *Washington Post*-CBS News poll reported on November 25, 1981, respondents were asked, "Did the reports of the Stockman magazine article give you a more favorable or less favorable impression of Reagan's plans for the economy?" Of the 66 percent who had heard or read about the article, 7 percent answered more favorable, 54 percent viewed Reagan's plan less favorably, 32 percent claimed it made no difference, and 7 percent held no opinion.

There was more than a faint odor of distrust wafting through Capitol corridors. Representative Les Aspin listened to Stockman testify at the House Budget hearing on February 17, 1982, scratched his head, and then rewrote his own version of what Stockman had said:

1. The Democrats have no alternatives and their alternatives would have been worse if they had been adopted last year.

2. The President's programs have reduced inflation significantly,

but the unemployment is the fault of the previous administrations (presumably Democratic) and besides, the President's program hasn't had time to work yet.

3. Nobody's expected this recession, and furthermore economists have been predicting it for years. In fact, it was long overdue. We should rejoice that it finally arrived so that we can recover from it.

On March 15, *Business Week* weighed in with a story that should have sent Stockman scurrying to pick up an unemployment check. One top Reagan official told the magazine, "On a scale of 0 to 100, Stockman's credibility rates a 3." Another aide explained, "His problems are much worse than we supposed." And a Senate aide was quoted as saying, "If Reagan's program goes to hell—and chances are 50-50 that it will—he'll need a scapegoat to execute in public—that's where Stockman comes in."

Jack Kemp was willing to let Stockman be, on the condition that the budget director stick to the numbers and keep his nose out of the tax question. "Stockman is only a budget director and he's acting like he's running a finance ministry at OMB," Kemp was quoted as saying in March 1982. The New York representative's words were less a personal warning to Stockman than an insistence that the White House keep David Stockman under control. Rumors that Kemp was keeping "plants" in meetings with Stockman to wait for a slip-up on the part of the budget director were dismissed by a source close to Kemp as "ridiculous." According to the Hill aide, "those stories came from OMB. Stockman's buddies are spreading that stuff around so that if Stockman gets in a tight spot he can claim Kemp rolled him."

The conventional wisdom had it that Stockman would not last long as budget director. Of course, as so often happens, the conventional wisdom would turn out to be wrong. And that, as Stockman was learning the hard way, was really the way the world works.

14 • The Out-Years

To THE consternation of his critics, on both sides of the aisle, David Stockman would remain in government as Ronald Reagan's director of OMB until the summer of 1985. But although he would continue to churn out budgets that called for sharp cuts, in some cases even sharper than the ones he'd managed to inflict in his first and most famous budget, it simply wasn't the same. Media coverage lessened dramatically; a quick glance at the *Reader's Guide to Periodical Literature* would reveal that from 1983 to the time he left office, there were about 80 percent fewer articles written about him. He simply wasn't the "good copy" he once had been.

The administration got around the problem of Stockman's tarnished reputation on the Hill by transforming James Baker's role into a cross between Max Friedersdorf's and budget director. Baker was increasingly mentioned as the biggest of the big three at the White House—and from Stockman's point of view, if he had to keep his profile low, James Baker was not such a bad intermediary. Not only was Baker the sole adviser of the President's top three to urge Reagan to keep the budget director on post-*Atlantic*; Baker also adhered to traditional economic theories that were compatible with Stockman's new-found love for the austerity style of old-boy Republicans.

When the President's 1983 budget came out of OMB, Baker organized the infamous gaggle of budget negotiators, dubbed the "gang of seventeen," and generally rushed around town with minimal success. Representative Tony Coelho (D-CA) was not impressed by the spectacle. "Jim Baker is fabulous. He has been trying to orchestrate the cover-up of their own problems and put it on the lap of the Democrats. When Democrats turned down Jimmy Carter's budget, he submitted another one. That's what Reagan ought to do."

Based on their experiences in 1981, many Democrats were skeptical of the administration's intentions. "There's been tremendous concern from the very beginning that these negotiations are a trap," explained Representative Leon Panetta. "They [the White House] extract concession after concession, and then at the last minute, either the President walks away from the deal, or they make a demand they know we can't accept. . . . Either way there's a tremendous risk, they can make Tip O'Neill the fall guy." And, despite Reagan's televised appeals, which had worked so well in the past, the public supported Congress. In a *Washington Post*–CBS News poll reported on April 30, 1982, a majority of 59 to 29 percent wanted Congress to work its will on the President's budget.

Meanwhile, on both sides of the Hill it was common knowledge, as Senator Domenici readily admitted, that OMB's budget "won't pass." Alternative budgets multiplied like rabbits. By the end of May, the Reagan plan, the Senate plan, the Aspin–Panetta and Pritchard plan, the House Budget Committee, and the Obey plan were all very much in evidence on the Hill. One beleagured congressman, Representative Roy Dyson (D-MD), reported receiving calls from his constituents who told him to "Support the bipartisan budget." According to Dyson, "I say, 'Which is that?' and they gulp and say, 'Well, you know which one it is.' "

Back in February, Senator Pete Domenici (R-NM) had sat down and come up with a budget all his own. The Senate Budget Committee chair's version differed from Reagan's substantially, advocating large tax increases, a smaller defense buildup, and a freeze on most national programs. At the end of the month Domenici presented his plan to congressional leaders, who were hardly overjoyed but not as negative as they had been about the White House plan. For the time being, the White House was not budging, however. Asked if the President had shown any willingness to accept any congressional proposals, Domenici replied, "None at all."

By early May, the White House had edged its way into a position between a rock and a hard place. Jim Baker's "gang of seventeen" had met for nearly forty hours over the course of a dozen meetings and come to few (if any) conclusions. Then, on May 6, the Senate Budget Committee voted 20 to 0 to throw out the President's package. Faced with this stark rejection of his initiatives, Reagan finally decided it was time to talk compromise. Over the next few hours, something akin to a mad scramble ensued. As the afternoon waned, Domenici laid out his proposals—nearly the same ones he had presented in February. Senate Democrats demanded to know if the President was behind the Domenici plan. Faced with those requests, Domenici excused himself and returned to announce that he had talked with Reagan. According to the senator, Reagan said, "I am for it. I will do everything I can to see that it is passed and becomes law." The Domenici measure passed along party lines, 11 to 9. Senator Ernest Hollings opted against the proposal but was much impressed with Domenici's tactical and diplomatic skills. Noted Hollings, "If I were the chairman and I had an intransigent President and a tricky director of OMB [and was still able to negotiate], I'd say that's a pretty good act."

On the House side, wringing of hands and gnashing of teeth were the order of the day. House Republicans sitting on the Budget Committee were fearful of calling for a vote on the President's plan, as their party leadership was almost unanimous in admitting it would never make it out of the hearing room. Even some of Reagan's staunchest supporters flatly denounced the plan. Representative Mickey Edwards, who once commented that his 1980 support for Reagan was worth it because Stockman had snared the OMB post, dubbed the 1983 plan "a turkey." House Minority Leader Bob Michel admitted some of the domestic slashes in the package were "politically stupid."

At a May 6 hearing of the Budget Committee at which Stockman appeared, Representative Lynn Martin (R-IL) spoke bitterly of the Democrats' failure to come up with any alternatives and insisted "we [the Republicans] have got to hear from the other side." As it happened, House Budget Chair James R. Jones was out of the room and Representative Mike Lowry, a good-natured Washington stater, was presiding. Ever aware of the comic side to any situation, Representative Bill Hefner (D-NC) listened to Martin's exhortations and interrupted ever so innocently: "Is it in order to move on the President's budget at this time?" He was told, in mock seriousness, that it was not.

As it turned out, later that evening David Stockman and Ronald Reagan finally capitulated to the wishes of House and Senate leaders. According to one House Budget expert, the White House wound up settling for a 1983 budget package that bore "very little resemblance to what was originally proposed. The Republicans forced an almost entirely different package on them." That the President eventually came out of the proceedings looking like a winner was testimony to what *The New York Times* called his ability to "seem in control."

Two days later, on May 8, Reagan gave a radio talk insisting that Congress "get off the dime" and pass the GOP's budget alternative. In an Olympian session, which lasted from late afternoon of Thursday, May 27, to the early hours of May 28, the House tried; the results fell short. With three budget proposals before them, the House members would have none.

From his California ranch, Reagan made phone calls to urge passage of the budget of his second choice but was apparently less than convincing. "Yeah, he called me, but it sounded like he was just reading his lines," said one Republican. The ultimate obstacle to the adoption of any budget were conservative Republicans who were loath to embrace $100 billion plus deficits, just as they had refused to sign onto David Stockman's projected deficits. As a sign of their opposition, conservatives voted "present" on all three plans—a tactic that made success on any of the three impossible.

The Republican alternative, which mandated deficits of $99.3 as opposed to the $122 billion in the official Reagan plan, was destined to fare better. Vice President Bush and others trooped to the Hill to lobby for the package. In an impromptu meeting with moderate Republicans, according to one participant, Bush responded to fears that cuts in the alternative were too severe and would raise the ire of constituents by saying most people had no idea what was in the budget. "I've never heard someone talk to members of Congress like that," concluded the Republican House member. The Republican plan was adopted 220 to 207.

Shortly after the vote, Minority Leader Bob Michel put through a transatlantic call to Reagan, who was staying at a castle on the Rhine. Sounding decidedly underwhelmed, Michel waxed less than enthusiastic over the Republican victory. "We pulled it off," he told Reagan. "It was a very nice win."

Nice win or no, it was nowhere near the success the President and David Stockman had scored the year before. In the Senate, the White House assumptions had been almost summarily dismissed by the same committee that had heartily embraced OMB's numbers the last time around. In the House, OMB's budget never received a single vote for or against—largely, one suspects, because of the embarrassment such a vote would have brought to the White House.

In 1981, David Stockman's well-laid plans had come off with barely a hitch; in 1982, there was no repeat performance. During his confirmation hearing on January 8, 1981, Stockman had said, "The Budget process, and the process of economic policy formation in the broader sense, must always be a cooperative endeavor between the executive and legislative branches. The cost to the nation of a breakdown in that relationship can be severe and sometimes irreparable." Had Stockman heeded his own advice, he might have had better luck with his 1983 budget.

At the start of 1982, Stockman was having even less success on the other side of the ledger. Despite marshalling support from nearly all of the President's advisers, Stockman had been unable to convince the President to include the OMB director's proposed tax hikes in the 1983 budget.

A House Republican aide probably mirrored Ronald Reagan's thinking when he told *The New York Times:*

> What we want to avoid is having some poor slob get a pink slip at the plant because of the recession. So he walks across the street to Joe's bar for a brew and he finds he can't afford it because the Republicans have raised excise taxes on beer. He can't get a cigar because the Republicans have raised excise taxes on tobacco, and he can't afford to drive home because the Republicans have raised excise taxes on gasoline.

Ultimately, the Republican Party was unable to avoid the hikes. When forced to choose between living with mind-boggling deficits and raising taxes to cover those deficits, mainstream Republicans opted for deficits. While the administration sought nearly $13 billion in additional taxes in its 1983 budget (nearly half of that through "improved tax collection and enforcement"), the problem of swiftly increasing deficits continued to loom large. In the end, it was not a mere $15 or $20 billion remedy the GOP requested, but nearly $100 billion—the largest revenue-raising measure in history coming close on the heels of the largest tax cut measure in history (one that had virtually eliminated the corporate income tax).

Throughout the first half of 1981, Reagan had remained firm in opposing any significant "revenue enhancement" measures presented to him by Stockman, et al. In his January 26 State of the Union message, Reagan had warned:

Higher taxes would not mean lower deficits. . . .

Raising taxes won't balance the budget. It will encourage more government spending and less private investment. Raising taxes will slow economic growth, reduce production and destroy future jobs, making it difficult for those without jobs to find them and more likely that those with jobs will lose them.

By August 10, 1982, Reagan had either changed his mind or his speechwriters. At a meeting with Republican congressmen to drum up support for his three-year, $98.3 billion tax increase, Reagan charged: "Those who are opposed to it cannot hide from the fact that they are supporting increased deficits and higher interest rates." And in an August 16 televised appeal, the President called the increase "a price worth paying for lower interest rates, economic recovery and more jobs."

The Chief Executive faced an equally weighty problem in terms of his public image. It was beginning to look as if he had come to Washington to raise the deficit. Prior to his taking command, the largest deficit in history had been in 1976 under Gerald Ford, weighing in at $66.4 billion. Before Stockman's budget had even cooled from the presses, it became clear that the '83 deficit would top $100 billion. The irony was not lost on Washington observers, Democrats and Republicans alike. One GOP strategist described Reagan's dilemma, "He built a career campaigning against deficits and now he has the biggest deficit of all." (By the end of Ronald Reagan's first term, his administration's combined deficits would exceed those of all former Presidents', also *combined*, from George Washington to Jimmy Carter.)

Supply-siders and conservatives were all too unhappy with the tax increases they sensed in the offing. Not a few members of the anti-tax contingency blamed Stockman for releasing inflated deficit predictions as a way of forcing tax boosts. On April 19, 1982, Representative Clarence Brown (R-OH) had made public a letter to the President in which he charged, "Growing evidence suggests that the Office of Management and Budget estimates for the fiscal 1982 budget may be overstated by as much as $30 billion." In a pointed reference to the *Atlantic* article, Brown continued, "I can't help wondering whether your economic agenda is once again being undermined by doubts about your program within your own administration."

Once the five-month drama of passing a 1983 budget had been played out, the submerged issue of tax increases assumed center stage. Bob Dole, 1982 tax cutter extraordinaire, became 1983's tax booster. In neither year did he seem entirely convinced as to why he was doing what he was doing. Appearing on "Meet the Press," Dole was asked:

Q: Senator, how do you answer Congressman Jack Kemp, who says that the President is making a dramatic U-turn? Last year he was decreasing taxes, in accordance with supply-side economic philosophy; this year, he is increasing taxes, apparently departing from supply side economics.

Dole: Well, I've said in response to that, we're not trying to make a U-turn; we're just trying to avoid going over the cliff.

Asked to comment on the 1981 tax cut, Dole replied, "I never really understood all that supply-side business." His comment had a familiar ring to it.

Following Dole's lead, the Senate had voted 50-47 on July 26, 1982, to seek $98.5 billion in additional taxes over a three-year period. Dole took the occasion to send out a no-nonsense message: "If the Democrats fail to act [on the tax hike] in the House, we have a campaign issue that just won't stop. It's suddenly in the lap of Tip O'Neill. The future of this economy is now up to House Speaker Tip O'Neill."

Despite much evidence to the contrary, a good many other Republicans found it expedient to blame the need for tax boosts on the Democrats. David Stockman was one of those Republicans. Speaking at an August 18 breakfast meeting with reporters, the OMB head insisted Democrats were guilty of creating the deficit, thus, "They have more responsibility to vote for the revenue bill."

The House vote promised to be close. Two days before the final tally was taken, Representative Dick Cheney (R-WY) commented that anyone who thought otherwise "has been smoking something." Minority Leader Bob Michel, a supporter of the measure, thought otherwise but for less than concrete reasons. "I know we're going to win. I've got that visceral feeling."

In order to whip their own troops into shape, the Republican Party resorted to heavy arm-twisting and arguably, reputation tarnishing. Jack Kemp, in a series of quotes attributed to unnamed officials in the White House, was painted as a stubborn obstacle to setting the country right. The rumors flew fast and furious that congressmen would be denied reelection financing from the Republican National Committee if they refused to cast a yea vote on tax increases.

The pleading and pressuring was destined to pay off. On August 19, by a vote of 226 to 207, the House accepted the tax hike over the protests of Jack Kemp and his allies. Standing before his fellow representatives, Kemp explained to no avail, "I'm as loyal as anyone in this room to the President. I don't think loyalty requires a sacrifice of conscience, principles and belief."

A few hours after the House vote, the Senate gave the measure its final seal of approval, largely along party lines.

For David Stockman, the decision to raise taxes came nine months too late. Had that vote been taken in November of 1981, his comments in the *Atlantic* might have seemed like revelations, not heresy.

On the Hill, as in the White House, the image of the infallible whiz kid was crumbling. Pete Domenici, chair of the Senate Budget Committee, had seen fit to adjourn an August 3 hearing early and thereby stave off any more angry confrontations with the committee's guest, David Stockman. Prior to adjournment, Republican Senator Mark Andrews had told Stockman, "I'm getting damn sick of getting it both ways." And Senator Donald Riegle of Michigan, who had often sparred with Stockman, had also come out swinging:

Riegle:　Mr. Stockman, we have an extremely serious problem today and that is that you have brought us a dishonest budget projection and you did exactly the same thing last year.

Stockman:　Well, Senator, let me observe that I get this lecture from you every time I get up here.

Riegle:　You deserve it every time because the problem repeats itself over and over again. . . .

In early September, Stockman became embroiled in a dispute with Congress over a spending bill. By September 10 the controversy had heated up to the point where Democrats and Republicans alike were expressing outrage with the OMB director. On September 11, *The Herald-Palladium*, a newspaper serving Stockman's hometown, ran a front-page article topped by the headline STOCK-MAN'S FOES SUGGEST HE QUIT.

By chance, that story coincided with "David Stockman Day" in the Fourth District of Michigan. Eighteen months earlier, Stockman would have returned home in triumph. On September 11, 1982, the festivities in honor of the home-town boy were just past the moment, more akin to consolation than celebration.

According to the South Bend, Indiana, *Tribune*, a paper read by many in the nearby Fourth District of Michigan, Dave Stockman Day promised to be a big event. Concerned, apparently, with security problems, local Michigan officials asked the Secret Service in Washington to provide help. "Maybe it's an overreaction," said the city manager of St. Joe, "but he has not been the most popular person in the world."

Stockman arrived on a chartered jet, bringing with him Jennifer Blei, whom he would marry in February of 1983, and an OMB aide. As it turned out, he'd picked a good time to leave Washington: that afternoon, a Republican congressman had complained, on the floor of the House, that he was "sick and tired of David Stockman and his mirror acts."

Earlier in the week, the coordinator of the event had estimated it would draw 5,000 to 8,000 people. But hardly more than 200 showed up to meet Stockman, have their picture taken with him, and eat a five-dollar Kentucky Fried Chicken box lunch on the grass of Lake Forest Park. While the crowd of enthusiastic well-wishers was nowhere near as large as the organizer had hoped, neither was the crowd of anti-Stockman demonstrators as numerous as the city manager had feared it might be. There *was* a surprisingly well-attended counter-demonstration across the river in Benton Harbor, billed as a Democratic Hog Roast, of which a newspaper woman who had been covering the Fourth District for eighteen months said, with evident surprise, "This is the first Democratic event I have ever covered."

At a late afternoon press conference, at which an impolite reporter held up an advance copy of the book that William Greider had written based on his *Atlantic* article, Stockman was asked for further comments. He replied, "I don't think I have anything new or revealing to say about that." (Perhaps he had already begun to think in terms of "saving" good lines and comments for a book of his own.)

That evening there was a banquet, a $50-a-head fundraiser for the State Republican Party, preceded by a cocktail party held in a room at Lake Michigan College. An air of good feeling prevailed in the closed-to-the-press gathering. The chairman of the State Republican Party came out for a moment to talk to the reporters and commented, "If Dave were selling jock straps, I'd tell everyone else to get out of the jock strap business." Mrs. Carol Stockman arrived to an enthusiastic welcome. Old friends showed up from as far away as California, lending the evening more of an air of a class reunion than a political fundraiser.

After the dinner, there was a moment of high drama—a call from Ronald Reagan. The call was piped-in over the loud speaker system, and everyone could hear clearly as the President said, "Dave never lets me call unless I call collect." After some words of admiration, and numerous references to Stockman as the Fourth District's "favorite son," Reagan said, "I'm sorry I can't be there tonight, but this is my weekend to mow the lawn at the White House."

Then it was Stockman's turn. Never a strong or polished speaker, Stockman had improved somewhat, but on this night, in spite of the fact that the audience could hardly have been more friendly or receptive, he sounded rather flat. He began his remarks by saying, with the President still on the phone, "I'll see whether or not that regulation that said you were supposed to mow the lawn this weekend can be changed." After a proper presidential chuckle, Reagan signed off.

At one point in his remarks, Stockman leaned forward and declared, "Just think back on eighteen months ago, how utterly out of control [Washington] was . . ."

He ended up his speech by denouncing *The Washington Post*, Tip O'Neill, New York City, and a few other institutions generally considered to be liberal. And then, amid much applause, Dave Stockman Day was over.

III

THE
STOCKMAN
LEGACY

15 • "It's Delicious,
It's Delightful,
It's De-Regulatory!"

Despite its boasts about pioneering a more rigorous, analytic approach to regulation, the Reagan Administration has in fact moved willy-nilly to deregulate without having the faintest idea of the actual cost to the public. The Reagan White House has promoted the thesis that voluntary action by industry works and that modifying the behavior of the general public—for example, asking them to voluntarily wear safety belts—will reduce death and trauma without new product designs or installation of engineering controls. But the administration has not published any evaluations demonstrating that the health and safety standards they attack either do not work or are less effective than nonregulatory approaches. The serious analyses that have been made outside the White House confirm the time-tested notion that preventive remedies are far cheaper than treatment after harm has already occurred.

JOAN CLAYBROOK, *Retreat From Safety (1984)*

The main prevention program of the Reagan Administration is one designed to prevent industry from paying the cost of doing business.

DR. SIDNEY WOLFE, Director, Health Research Group

Government exists not merely to serve individuals' immediate preferences, but to achieve collective purposes for an ongoing nation. Government, unlike the free market, has a duty to look far down the road and consider the interests of citizens yet unborn. The market has a remarkable ability to satisfy the desires of the day.

GEORGE WILL

RONALD REAGAN'S campaign pledge to "get government off the backs of the people" might well have been rephrased—based on the administration's record—to read "get government off the backs of business." And few administration figures typified that rephrasing, by their actions, more than David Stockman. As Anne Burford, Dr. Shelby Brewer, and other former administration officials have pointed out, when it came to deregulation, Stockman hit the ground sprinting. By the time the President released his famous Executive Order 12291 three weeks after his inauguration, Stockman was into the first curve; by the time some of the cabinet members were finally in office, Stockman had already lapped them.

And the word was out to the business community that the atmosphere in Washington had most definitely changed. In a speech, Boyden Gray, a lawyer who left a private practice that had serviced big business to become legal counsel to Vice President Bush, reassured the U.S. Chamber of Commerce that his office was in their corner:

> If you go to the agency first, don't be too pessimistic if they can't solve the problem there. If they don't, that's what the Task Force [Vice President Bush's Task Force on Regulatory Relief that had been set up in March of 1981] is for. Two weeks ago [a group] showed up and I asked if they had a problem. They said they did, and we made a couple of phone calls and straightened it out, alerted the top people at the agency that there was a little hanky-panky going on at the bottom of the agency, and it was cleared up very rapidly—so the system does work if you use it as sort of an appeal. You can act as a double-check on the agency that you might encounter problems with.

Executive Order 12291 and the Task Force on Regulatory Relief were alike in their intended impact—elimination or relaxation of regulations. In effect, the order gave power over regulations previously held by the separate agencies to David Stockman's OMB. And it also gave OMB an enormous new power: the authority to require wide-ranging analyses of proposed new programs, reviewing current programs, and postponing and eliminating existing regulations. Democratic Senator Albert Gore said of this shift of power, "The critical question is, who makes the decision on the substance of a regulation? Is it made in the agency where the procedural safeguards are present, or is it made in OMB, outside those procedural safeguards?"

The answer to that question, Joan Claybrook writes, is now quite clear:

> By dint of its historical authority to set the president's budget agency by agency, and its responsibility to control paperwork and approve government requests for industry data, the OMB is now in total control—of agency budgets, agency information, and agency regulatory decisions. This enormous power has been harnessed by the Reagan OMB (Stockman, DeMuth, and Tozzi) and the White House (Reagan, Bush). Empowered as no other White House office ever has been, Reagan's OMB set about working behind the scenes in concert with regulated industries, to eliminate government safety and environmental standards, often with only passing regard for the agencies' statutory obligations.

The "Tozzi" Claybrook mentions is James Tozzi, OMB's Deputy Director of Regulatory Affairs until 1983, when he went into private consulting. He had, however, been in government long before David Stockman arrived on the scene. Tozzi was well aware of the importance of the new power. In a fall 1985 interview, he said, "The authority to review all the other federal regs made OMB the most powerful agency in the government. There wasn't anything that could compare to that power." Tozzi, who has a Ph.D. in economics, and who entered government service through the military, had come to OMB in 1972; by the time Stockman got there eight years later, he had a relatively long history of dealing with the conceptual and actual predecessors of regulatory reform. He got his job with Stockman after a long meeting in which he promised to prepare "an agenda for deregulation, and a hit list for regulatory reform."

Stockman made Tozzi the second in command (deputy director) of Regulatory Affairs, and James Miller (today the head of OMB) the director. Tozzi says that Miller, he, and another OMB official "drafted the famous Executive Order on Regulatory Reform."

Tozzi and Stockman apparently worked well together, with the former all but relishing the power they shared. In *Are You Tough Enough?*, Anne Burford paints a picture of Jim Tozzi that is not without begrudging admiration, a portrait much different than the one she paints of Tozzi's boss, David Stockman:

Then there was the matter of Mr. Jim Tozzi, an intriguing gentle-man, a genuine character given to dark suits and thin-lipped locutions, a man to whom a limo was never a limo but always a "stretch." Talking with him was always an experience in jargon-building. Tozzi, who has since left government for the greener pastures of lobbying (when he left, he opened up his closets to reveal enough free booze to give a huge going away party, which he did, and which rated a story in the *Washington Post*), had the slot just under Chris DeMuth [who had taken over for James Miller when he left to head the FTC, the job he held when Reagan asked him, in 1985, to succeed Stockman] at OMB, and it was generally believed that he was the one who did all OMB's regulatory reform work.

I first met Tozzi when he came in to interview for the job as my regulatory reform head. I could never figure out why he would have wanted that job when the one he had already was far more important. Later I concluded that he was really interested in getting a look at me and my shop for his general information and use. He was that kind of guy.

About halfway through my time at EPA we found ourselves in a real crunch. We were under a court order to release some pollutant guidelines for pharmaceutical manufacturers. We had done our work, and then submitted the guidelines to OMB for their review as required. The manufacturers had put on a lot of pressure for certain changes, which we had resisted, but the court order deadline was swiftly ap-proaching, and there was still no word from OMB. Finally, they told us that they weren't approved, though OMB would not put it in writing, as required by the Executive Order, which might have allowed us to buy some time from the judge. This despite the fact that an Executive Order said that if OMB held anything past a certain length of time, they had to put their objections in writing.

All Tozzi would tell us was, "They're not approved." That continued to be OMB's response right up to the last minute. It was the night before the deadline, my last day to obey the court order and sign and release the regs. It got so dark in my office that we could see the moon outside. Finally, John Daniel [her chief of staff] said, "Anne, I recommend you sign the regs without OMB's approval."

We called OMB to tell them what we were going to do. I called Stockman, who had surprisingly little to say, and John called Tozzi. Tozzi didn't say anything for a few moments after he'd heard the news. Then he said, in a quiet voice, "Daniel, I hope you people know there's a price to pay for this, and you've only begun to pay."

John Daniel was so startled that he asked Tozzi to repeat it so he could write it down, and when he had, he said to Tozzi, "Thank you very much. I'll give this to the Administrator right away." He did, I signed them anyway, and we all had a good laugh, because it was such typical Tozzi. But now, looking back, maybe we should not have been laughing.

Joan Claybrook, president of Public Citizen (founded by Ralph Nader in 1970), and formerly President Carter's head of the National Highway Traffic Safety Administration, started studying the Reagan Administration as soon as it began to take shape. In 1984, she and the staff of Public Citizen published the results of that scrutiny as *Retreat From Safety*.[7]
In the Introduction she writes:

Every day, the Reagan White House makes decisions of critical importance to the health and safety of the American public. [The following] are but a few examples. They illustrate the failure of the Reagan government to diligently implement and enforce statutes enacted by Congress to address the documented hazards of our technological society—dangerous drugs, polluted air and water, toxic chemicals, unsafe car design and engineering, and countless other known, significant risks.

Rather than bolster the federal health and safety regulatory agencies in their work to protect the public, the Reagan administration, animated by profound ignorance and rigid ideology, has inflicted severe damage on these unique institutions of our society. The agencies no longer respond to the needs of unorganized victims of technological hazards. Instead, they service the business executives and stockholders who are responsible for the hazards—a radical shift that can be traced to January 20, 1981, the day Ronald Reagan assumed the presidency.

The examples selected from the many possibilities afforded by the Reagan Administration involve such crucial agencies as the Occupational Safety and Health Administration (OSHA), the EPA, and the Food and Drug Administration.
Example A. No one told James Harris or Robert Harris (unrelated), both of Bakersfield, California, that any of the chemicals they were working with were dangerous. But when they were exposed to a fraction of an ounce of ethylene dibromide, or EDB, it triggered a swift process that would end with their gruesome deaths. James Harris's co-workers stripped him to his underwear and hosed him down with water. Despite their attempts to save his life, he died

---

7. The full text of Claybrook's Introduction is reprinted in Appendix B, pp. 269–288.

three days later. Robert Harris did not get out of the hospital alive.

The warnings had been sounded for EDB for over a decade, even within the Reagan Administration itself, but the government, specifically the Occupational Safety and Health Administration, ignored them until it was too late for Americans like James and Robert Harris.

They almost came too late for David Smith of Minnesota, who worked weekends fumigating grain in a flour mill. Within an hour of getting some liquid fumigant on his hands he was feeling very dizzy and complaining that his "whole body felt numb." By the time he got to the ground floor of the mill, he had to crawl into the locker room because he couldn't walk. He was rushed to the hospital, where he spent five days in intensive care; at one point his pulse rate—which normally beats 72 times a minute—dropped to 29.

The federal government has a sad history of ignoring the warning signs about this drug, as a September 1983 NBC special on the subject of EDB pointed out. The National Cancer Institute labeled EDB a carcinogen as early as 1974, and research since then has revealed that it can cause male sterility and birth defects. Even though NIOSH (National Institute for Occupational Safety and Health) recommended in 1977 that exposure levels of EDB be significantly reduced below the existing level of 20 ppm, nothing was done.

Four years later, the debate began anew when the Mediterranean fruit flies were sprayed with EDB. The loudest complaints came from unions whose workers had to handle the drug, and from the AFL-CIO itself; in September 1981 these groups petitioned OSHA to set a temporary emergency standard that would greatly reduce the level of exposure. Thorne Auchter, OSHA's head, and a man who would compile a distinctly unenviable record of dilatory actions, sat on the petition for three months before saying no. He said OSHA didn't have enough information about the amount of exposure or just how many workers were involved. He expressed his doubts that defending a lower level of exposure to EDB would stand up in court.

As Joan Claybrook wrote in *Retreat From Safety*:

In 1982, J. Donald Millar, director of NIOSH, urged Auchter to reconsider this decision in face of the "mounting evidence" of EDB's toxicity. But Auchter again refused to budge. Meanwhile, the government's own research began to provide more damning evidence against EDB. One study performed by EPA refers to the risk of cancer from EDB as being "among the highest the agency [has] ever confronted." Another EPA study showed that at OSHA's current maximum limit of exposure to EDB (20 ppm), death from cancer could be expected for 999 out of every 1,000 workers. A risk assessment prepared by David Brown from Northeastern University in Boston showed that at 10 ppm (half OSHA's limit), approximately 270 workers out of 1,000 would probably develop cancer. The National Cancer Institute also conducted a study using 10 ppm as the exposure rate and found that 40 percent of the rats developed cancer. This is particularly surprising, because in these types of studies the animals are usually given massive doses to approximate a lifetime of human exposure.

In March 1983 it was learned that some attorneys in the Labor Department had written to Auchter in October 1981 stating their belief that "a respectable argument could be made [in court] in support of the ETS [emergency temporary standard] and that we would have a reasonably good chance of success."

House Appropriations Committee member David Obey asked Mr. Auchter why he hadn't issued the ETS. Auchter admitted that his own lawyers had found that EDB met the test of "grave danger" (as Auchter put it, "Ethylene dibromide is a bad actor"), but he still hemmed and hawed, claiming that to have issued the new standard would have thrown "our whole standards activity into total disarray."

Six months later, another congressman had had it with Mr. Auchter. California Democrat George Miller called a hearing to find out why OSHA and EPA had not done anything about EDB. Again, Auchter mentioned his fear of losing in court, to which Miller all but yelled: "It was a question of whether you wanted to go to court on workers' behalf. Those workers came to you and asked you to take a risk. What would have been the harm if you lost? Your pride? Your agency's batting average? The bottom line is you did nothing and workers are still being covered by a twelve-year-old standard everybody agrees is inadequate."

Auchter responded that he had sent out an "alert." That document turned out to be a three-page warning—not the *thirty-three-*page health hazard alert prepared by his own staff, a document that gave workers some very specific suggestions on how to protect themselves from the chemical. Auchter said he had "simplified" the memo so workers could understand it. When she heard this, Robert Harris's widow said, "I don't think they had the right to omit one iota of information. They had a duty to make available all information they had; they are partly responsible for Robert's accident."

Mr. Auchter still maintained that an emergency standard wasn't necessary, citing as his reasoning the fact that worker exposure is seasonal and intermittent. Eventually he could resist no longer, and late in September 1983 both OSHA and EPA proposed new EDB standards, with OSHA even admitting that "risks from EDB exposure appear to be far greater than for any other hazard that OSHA has regulated in the past."

Before the situation could be righted, David Stockman's people made one more attempt to delay things. OMB temporarily held up OSHA's proposed new standards. And it removed the requirement for medical testing for some exposed workers on the grounds that "it is not clear how these tests will reduce the cancer incidence of EDB exposure." As a result, OSHA announced it would be six months before a new standard lowering the permissible exposure to 0.1 ppm. could be issued.

Finally, the public began to hear about the issue. NBC said in its September 25, 1983, report on EDB: "For more than six years, federal officials have known EDB is a potent cause of cancer and one of the most poisonous pesticides in existence, yet have done little to control its use. More EDB is used now than ever before to kill insects that feed on crops. Because of this, it is now showing up in alarming amounts in oranges, grapefruit, and grain. But federal officials have kept these findings from the public."

Today the situation is improved, but that improvement took far too long—and cost lives that should never have been lost.

Example B. The term "acid rain" is a sharply evocative one, drawing up images of unrelenting devastation, but the meaning of those images can be clarified if one thinks of the more prosaic definition: man-made pollution. Composed largely of sulfur and nitrogen oxides that are transformed chemically in the atmosphere before falling back to earth as acidic rain, snow, or dry particles, acid rain destroys life in freshwater lakes, contaminates sources of drinking water, may damage forests and crops, and certainly affects microorganisms. It affects commerce, particularly sport fishing. According to the Natural Resources Defense Council, the state of

Maine has at least five salmon rivers that are so acidic that the young fish are endangered, and the food chain upon which plants, animals, and humans depend is disturbed.

It is estimated that acid rain does $5 billion worth of damage each year in the eastern United States alone. And Congress's Office of Technology Assessment reported that in northern and central Wisconsin and the neighboring Michigan highlands, close to half the 2,200 lakes are already becoming acidified, jeopardizing the state's $6 billion annual tourist industry.

One of the most important elements of the acid rain debate is its effect on our relations with Canada. In fact, it has become a major irritant in that relationship. It is estimated that while only 10 percent of the acid rain falling in the Northeastern United States comes from Canada, about half of the rain that affects their lakes is from the U.S. According to Harrison Wellford, one of the first to be called a Nader's Raider and a former official in the Carter Administration, who now represents the Canadian government on acid rain, further Canadian reductions may be contigent upon "reciprocal action" in the United States. And therein lies the problem.

As Claybrook writes in *Retreat From Safety:*

Up to now, the Canadians have made all the sacrifices; the US has only talked. The Reagan administration has taken no action on acid rain. Instead, it promised to do more research and analysis, while simultaneously easing restrictions on the industrial boilers that emit sulfur dioxide. Until recently, the EPA even refused to call acid rain by that name. It preferred "nonbuffered precipitation." The administration was finally forced to acknowledge what everyone else knew: acid rain exists, it is caused by sulfur dioxide emissions, and it wreaks severe economic and environmental damage. . . .

In July, 1983, after William D. Ruckelshaus had succeeded Anne Burford as administrator [of EPA], the National Academy of Sciences issued a report concluding that a reduction in pollution from industrial sources would reduce acid rain. The report recommended a cut of 50 percent in sulfur dioxide emissions from coal-burning power plants and other industrial sources in the eastern part of the country. David Schindler, a biologist at the Freshwater Institute in Winnipeg, whose research supported the report's findings, stated that a reduction of sulfur emissions by half would shrink the area affected by acid rain by three-quarters. While Ruckelshaus promised to have a recommendation on acid rain for the president by September, 1983, he stated in October that no such recommendation would be forthcoming, and that no time-table had been set for one.

Her final sentence regarding the subject of acid rain has a familiar ring to it: "The delay is believed to be the result of strong opposition from high-level members of the White House staff, including OMB director Stockman."

In January 1986, six months after Stockman left office, Drew Lewis, Ronald Reagan's first Secretary of Transportation and the man he chose to conduct a joint U.S.–Canadian acid rain study, completed the nine-month project. After admitting, in his transmittal letter, that "acid rain is both a serious environnmental problem and a transboundary problem," Lewis told the President, in the preface to his recommendations,

> Both nations want to see progress on acid rain. For such progress to be possible, and if it is to result in part from the work of the Special Envoys [Mr. Lewis and William G. Davis, his Canadian counterpart], then our recommendations must be realistic. They must not ask either country to make a sudden, revolutionary change in its position. They must not call for immediate abandonment of major policy stands. They must instead point the way to a resumption of fruitful bilateral dialogue and constructive action that will help us relieve the stress that this issue has created, and reduce the flow of airborne pollutants across our common border.

According to the press release that accompanied the joint report, "the report makes three key recommendations: 1) the initiative of a five year, five billion dollar program for commercial demonstration of clean coal technologies; 2) a commitment to ongoing cooperative activities, including bilateral consultations and information exchange; and 3) a greater emphasis on carrying out research essential to resolving transboundary acid rain issues." As weak and dilatory as these recommendations are, there is no word from the White House as to whether or not they will carry out the recommendations.

One wonders how David Stockman views the Lewis-Davis report. It is not hard to imagine him being moved to compose one of his famous "Dear Colleague" letters to excoriate the executive branch for even considering the idea of spending $5 billion on a "transboundary" environmentalist-inspired pork barrel that would cause undue hardship for the dear old corporate America he has come to love so well. In Stockman's congressional days, that was exactly the kind of thing that used to send him right up the office wall.

Here are some more examples, briefer ones, of David Stockman and OMB's reg-busting ways, as described by Claybrook in *Retreat From Safety:*

> The executive order [12291] not only provided the administration with the ostensible legal rationale for seizing power that formerly belonged to regulatory agencies, it ushered in a new era of regulatory subversion in which regulated industries and sympathetic government officials could broker deals and violate the law without any public record of the transactions. The examples abound:
>
> - On behalf of the tire industry, the OMB pressed the National Highway Traffic Safety Administration (NHTSA) to eliminate a treadwear rating system of great value to consumers.
>
> - EPA's former chief of staff, John E. Daniel, testified before Congress that "the OMB stalled, tried to reverse, or altered EPA regulations on water quality, uranium mill tailings, and air quality standards." OMB also leaked proposed regulations to the regulated industry so it could bring tremendous pressure on EPA.
>
> - OMB blocked the Occupational Safety and Health Administration's proposed regulations for the labeling of chemicals in the workplace. After six months, OSHA administrator Thorne Auchter was so angry that he asked beer magnate Joseph Coors, a key Reagan political supporter, to intervene with the vice-president to allow issuance of the proposed regulation. Auchter wanted a weaker federal regulation to preempt tougher state labeling laws.
>
> - In 1982, the FDA and HHS secretary Richard Schweicker wanted to require aspirin makers to label their product with warnings about Reye's syndrome, a disease causing convulsions and sometimes death in children who take aspirin when they have chicken pox or the flu. But OMB official James Tozzi intervened on behalf of aspirin makers and stopped the FDA from informing the public. . . .
>
> - On November 7, 1983, Christopher DeMuth sent EPA administrator Ruckelshaus a letter chastising him for interpreting the Toxic Substances Control Act too narrowly and for making "excessively conservative decisions" about potential risk of toxic substances. Several EPA proposals, including one on acid rain, had been stopped by OMB. DeMuth complained that the agency "can and

should be more willing" to tolerate some risk in new chemicals "without imposing either controls or testing requirements. Presumably, some risks should be regarded as reasonable.

"Few of the Reagan deregulatory initiatives could have been secured," Claybrook points out, "without a protective veil of secrecy to hide procedural improprieties. That is why, once OMB had established itself as the point of access for regulatory decisions, its top officials became extraordinarily secretive about its reviews of agency regulations. They refused to disclose to the public or press which regulations they were reviewing, which ones they insisted be changed, or to document their *ex parte* (private, off-the-record) contacts with regulated industries for inclusion in the agency dockets."

Then Congressman (now Senator) Albert Gore of Tennessee leveled a serious charge against OMB, stating, "I think it was no accident that only thirty days after a secret meeting between OMB and the Chemical Manufacturers Association, the hazardous waste disposal regulations were ordered by OMB to be reviewed . . . that shortly after a secret meeting between the Air Transport Association and the OMB, air carrier certification rules were designated for review by OMB . . . that shortly after a secret meeting between OMB and the American Mining Congress, the Interior Department's rule on extraction of coal was postponed indefinitely."

In October 1983, Robert Nelson of the Democracy Project released a report that listed thirty-five significant instances of disregard for the requirements of the Administrative Procedures Act of 1946 (which requires public access to the regulatory process and disclosure of information). He concluded that "secret and preferential influence is now characteristic of Reagan's regulatory process."

That same complaint, especially as it related to David Stockman's OMB, would persist—and grow stronger. In fact, it would be one of his chief legacies. Three months after he left office, the House Committee on Energy and Commerce's Subcommittee on Oversight and Investigations would release a scathing report on what it termed "OMB interference in agency rulemaking" in relation to EPA's asbestos regulations. According to subcommittee chairman John Dingell (D-MI):

> Unfortunately, a major abuse highlighted in our report, and noted in our Subcommittee inquiries since 1981 [the year Stockman took over

OMB] continues unabated. This is the unlawful interference by the Office of Management and Budget in the EPA's rulemaking process pursuant to Executive Order 12291. This Order, issued on February 17, 1981, established for the first time a centralized, enforceable mechanism for presidential management of agency rulemaking activities, thereby marking a major departure from previous presidential efforts to control administrative leavemaking.

The report transmitted herewith chronicles the OMB's secret and heavy-handed interference with two draft proposed EPA rules designed to protect the public against the cancer risks posed by ongoing asbestos production, use, and disposal. The report is highly significant because it lays bare OMB's obstructionist activities. It demonstrates how the OMB caused the EPA to adopt an ill-founded interpretation of the Toxic Substances Control Act which would tie the agency's hands in controlling one of the most well-documented human carcinogens. It reveals how the OMB's interference already has caused a delay of more than a year in the promulgation of EPA's proposed asbestos rules. It shows how OMB sought to impute, behind closed doors, a *discounting of lives* [italics added] approach, which would severely restrict the federal government's ability to protect the American public against cancer-causing chemicals.

Under this discounting approach, the OMB's cost-benefit analysis of the proposed asbestos regulations computes human life at a base value of $1 million—and then discounts that value over the 30 to 40 year latency period for asbestos-related cancer. This arbitrary and callous discounting methodology would reduce the value of life to a figure as low as $22,500, thereby undervaluing the benefits of health and safety regulations and thwarting the regulation of many toxic substances evaluated under the cost-benefit criteria of Executive Order 12291.

In making his point that the order was subject to "serious fraud and abuse," Congressman Dingell introduced the asbestos case study and said it perfectly illustrated how the order "can easily be circumvented in a review process which is shrouded in secrecy, unbounded by statutory constraints, and accountable to no one." He stated, directly, "The report reveals how the OMB is engaging in a pervasive and unlawful scheme to displace agency rulemaking authority."

Dingell was nothing if not blunt:

However, OMB has acted in blatant disregard of this statutory scheme. Instead of utilizing a process which relies on the EPA's expertise and broad public participation, the OMB has substituted a process which allows green-eyeshaded OMB officials to manipulate cost-benefit numbers to impose their will behind closed doors. While Congress expected everyone to play by the same rules, the OMB has rewritten the rules to give itself a special advantage. It engages in secret communications with agency officials and outside parties, leaving other interested parties on the sidelines watching a different game. A regulation may be blocked through the OMB's clandestine intervention at the behest of a particular industry while limiting the presentation of opposing views by other industry representatives and the general public who might benefit from the proposed rule. This secret process is simply incompatible with a regulatory review process purportedly designed to promote rationality in decisionmaking.

In concluding, he touched on a complaint that has been heard ever since the Reagan Administration started having its way with the regulatory bodies: too many important regulatory decisions are being made by people who were never elected to public office. "If the OMB's unlawful interference is not restrained, we [the Congress] will continue to legislate to protect the public from hazardous chemicals but our hard-won battles will be nullified by faceless bureaucrats in the Office of Management and Budget."

Three months after Dingell's report was made public, in early 1986, Federal District Court Judge Thomas Flannery ruled against the EPA, in a case brought by the Environmental Defense Fund over delays in implementing the Resource Conservation and Recovery Act (RCRA). Once again, the villian was the OMB. "Plaintiffs contend," wrote the judge, "that EPA's ability to promulgate the regulations was further prevented by the unlawful interference of the Office of Management and Budget."

These are the facts, as explained by Judge Flannery:

Congress set March 1, 1985, as the deadline for promulgating the regulations. OMB commenced its review of the proposed permitting standards on March 4, 1985. Since these were not "major rules" under the meaning of EO 12291, EPA anticipated that OMB would complete its review within 10 days. On March 15, 1985, EPA staff briefed OMB staff on the proposed regulations. OMB refused to clear the regulations and on March 25, 1985, notified EPA that it was extending its review of the proposed regulations. OMB apparently wanted EPA to gather additional information prior to promulgating the regulations even though it would delay the process. By April 10, 1985, EPA had still not received any formal comments from OMB.

By April 12, 1985, it was clear OMB had serious differences with EPA over what regulations to propose. At a meeting of April 16, 1985 between EPA and OMB staff members, OMB sought significant changes in the proposed regulations in four areas. The idea, apparently, was to shift the goal of the regulations away from EPA's philosophy of containing all leaks of waste disposals to OMB's philosophy of preventing only leaks of waste that can be demonstrated by risk analysis to threaten harm to human health.

Internal disagreement within OMB further delayed OMB's consideration of the regulations. Some OMB staff members apparently felt OMB should not be dictating substantive policy decisions to EPA while others felt the precedent being set an important one for OMB review of other RCRA regulations.

In finding for the plaintiffs, Judge Flannery said, "Promulgation of regulations 16 months after a Congressional deadline is highly irresponsible. . . . Therefore, it is ordered that the regulations be promulgated by [June 30, 1986]. Failure to do so would be capricious and would merit stronger equitable treatment." And the judge went on to say that the fault in the matter was not EPA's, but, clearly, that of OMB.

Thus the regulatory legacy of David Stockman lives on. Indeed, it does so in the work of a three-year-old organization known as OMB Watch. Begun out of a communal protest movement by a variety of nonprofit organizations that feared the effects of an OMB proposal to prohibit government-funded organizations from lobbying with those funds, OMB Watch has survived as a permanent watchdog of the Office of Management and Budget. While many similar organizations spend all their time on the Hill or in court, OMB Watch spends all its time concentrating on—OMB. It doesn't miss much.

In its October 3, 1985, newsletter—three months after the departure of David Stockman—OMB Watch reported:

On Tuesday, September 24, 1985, the Senate Governmental Affairs Committee held its confirmation hearing for James C. Miller III, the nominated successor to David Stockman as OMB Director. . . .

Nearly half the hearing dealt with OMB's enhanced regulatory powers. Both Republican and Democratic Senators expressed concern about: (a) The secret style in which OMB operates; (b) OMB's ability to formulate policy without consulting Congress; and (c) The reach OMB has in almost all aspects of government operations.

For example, Senator Dave Durenberger (R-MN) complained, "Now the OMB director is . . . a central player—keeper of the numbers, carrier of the President's message on Capitol Hill, policymaker in his own right." He added, "What we're asking for is to get cut in on the policy. We're just getting stiffed all the time. And in the process . . . the public gets stiffed."

The newsletter also quoted Senator Albert Gore as saying that OMB had blocked regulations required by Congress "on numerous instances." And Senator Thomas Eagleton said, "The truth is that OMB is displacing agency discretion. OMB is a regulatory juggernaut."

"The most powerful statement," according to OMB Watch, "was written testimony submitted by Representative Guy Molinari (R-NY), in which Molinari lashed out at OMB:

[. . . the issue is OMB's] subtle but decisive takeover of the decision-making process of our government agencies to the point where it is now the determinative, though unaccountable, factor in agency policy decisions. . . . this nominee stands to command an apparatus whose far-reaching operations are shrouded in secrecy and unbounded by statutory constraints. . . . Today . . . we face a serious threat to the separation of powers principle which has served as a cornerstone of our government. . . .

And for that, in very large part, America has David Stockman to thank.

16 • Cooking the Books, and Other Domestic Skills

TYPICALLY, it was I. F. Stone, the radical journalist turned scholar, who got off the best line about David Stockman. After observing him throughout the first Reagan Administration, Stone told John Greenya, "Apparently the only thing from the Gospels that Stockman learned at the Harvard Divinity School was, 'Whoever has will be given more, but the one who has not will lose the little he has.' "

Agonized admissions to friendly reporters aside, if Stockman was displeased with the way the world had worked for the last four years, he had done nothing, by 1984, to dissociate himself from the record of Ronald Reagan—the man who had raised him to national prominence—the record for which he was chiefly responsible. In 1984, however, apparently recognizing that his image could use a little polishing—especially since he had cut off almost all interviews with print journalists after the Greider article—he granted an interview-cum-dinner with himself and his new wife, Jennifer Blei Stockman, in their carefully appointed condominium apartment in the Dupont Circle area of northwest Washington (her apartment, prior to their marriage).[8]

The interviewer was Lois Romano of the "Style" section of *The Washington Post*, a rather unlikely place for David Stockman to allow himself, with or without a new wife, to appear. (According to Robert Novak, Stockman had given no interviews since his plunge in the *Atlantic*, cutting off cold reporters for whom he had been a regular source for years, and making it a practice to "guest" only on the major Sunday-morning-type news shows and never to do radio interviews.)

Romano, a tough interviewer with a sharp pen, was a chancy choice for Stockman, but apparently he felt the "human side" publicity might be helpful to his generally perceived image as a cold, workaholic loner. Also, the budget director had promised the reporter ever since his engagement was announced that he would grant such an interview, and he kept his word.

"David Stockman," Romano's May 24, 1983, article began, "a man so often perceived as an icy ideological zealot, has a new program these days: marriage."

It continued:

He seems to approach it with the fervor of a religious convert, not unlike every other crusade he has been on in his life—from his days as an anti-war activist to his year at Harvard Divinity School, where he

---

8. They would later give this up for a home in Potomac, Maryland, an expensive Washington suburb increasingly attractive to the nouveau riche. For all its pockets of charm and history, the Dupont Circle area of northwest Washington remains far too funky.

once fancied a run at the clergy, to the right-wing fiscal policy of supply-side economics. . . .

During a recent dinner at their Dupont Circle condominium, David Stockman talked about the couple's Royal Doulton china pattern, and how he has even restructured his workaholic habits to be a good husband. Instead of staying at the office late he comes home at 7 P.M. to be with Jennifer, and rises at 4:30 A.M. after 5 1/2 hours sleep, to get the paperwork done.

They talk about starting a family soon—perhaps having two children, never only one. They finish sentences for each other. When he singes a well-known economist, calling him a "little twirp," she reprimands: "Sweetie, that's a slight exaggeration." And he backs off. On weekends, they go to the Safeway. Together.

"David's whole demeanor and body language change around her," observes a friend and political ally. "He becomes much more boyish, a little less confident, more like a kid. David seems to be either a 64-year-old graying senior statesman or an 11-year-old boy."

If he's obliged to attend a political dinner without his wife, an OMB staff member notes, he sulks.

"There's a definite sense of commitment," explains Jennifer Stockman as her husband devours crab claw appetizers. "You function as a unit. David is so involved in every aspect of our life. Like the personal finances. Even grocery shopping. We plan those kinds of things. We go together."

"There *are* functional reasons," interrupts David Stockman, speaking in typical Stockmanese. "She can't carry the bags."

"This is a far cry," Romano observed quite accurately, "from the public perception of a callous David Stockman, the human adding machine. White House aides, the joke goes, huddle around his heart during summers to keep cool."

It *was* a very different Stockman, but not all the revelations were of the sort to make readers feel more kindly toward him (and his new wife). A discussion of their once-a-week maid—who had worked for Mrs. Stockman before the marriage—had a ring of condescension about it. One wonders how David Stockman, who had lived a graduate student type of existence for so long in Washington, related to having a maid—and if he ever got to know anything about her and her life other than the fact that she did not like the new vacuum cleaner they bought for her after "she asked for one for six months."

Near the end, the article offers interesting speculation on Stockman's future. "David Stockman once said he has never needed to write a resume. And there is almost as much speculation on his future as there is on whether Reagan will run again. Jack Kemp thinks Stockman will 'end up as a successful Wall Street business-man, only to be surpassed by his wife.' White House aide and friend Richard Darman speculates that Stockman is not interested in money, only policy.

" 'What do you mean by that?' [Stockman] says when asked if Darman's insights about money were accurate. 'I'm not a fanatic. I'm interested in public policy and economics and government. That's not to say you can't make money doing it. Not in govern-ment, but a lot of people make money advising. It's probably the most lucrative business there is.' "

And that is the business he is in today—at a reported salary of one million dollars a year with the Wall Street brokerage firm of Salomon Brothers. Jack Kemp was a good forecaster, though it remains to be seen if Mrs. Stockman will ever outearn her husband.

It may be instructive to note that when Lois Romano asked Stockman about money, he responded by saying he was "interested in public policy and economics and government." All theoretical concepts, as opposed to "people." One is reminded of the young lady, mentioned earlier, who questioned the unchanging nature of her relationship with the young David Stockman in the early 1970s, a question that caused him to say that "I guess I'm more interested in issues than in people."

Coincidentally, less than a month after the "Style" section article on the happy couple appeared, *The Washington Post* ran a very different kind of article about David Stockman and his policies in the paper's "Outlook" section, entitled "Stockman Is Still Cooking the Numbers. Now he wants us to believe Reagan is fair." The author was Robert Greenstein, director of the Center on Budget and Policy Priorities.[9]

"David Stockman is at it again," wrote Greenstein. "After he confessed to rigging the computers in 1981 to make the prospective Reagan deficits shrink, one might have thought that the budget director had had his fill of numbers juggling. But it was not to be.

---

9. The full text of Greenstein's article is reprinted in Appendix C, pp. 288–294.

This time, of all things, Stockman has been fiddling with figures in the hope of demonstrating how *fair* the Reagan administration is in its treatment of rich and poor."

According to Greenstein, "Stockman unveiled his latest statistical wizardry before the Congressional Joint Economic Conference last month. He came fully equipped with charts, each to illustrate a remarkable assertion. Claim 1: The poor have been affected only marginally by Reagan administration budget cuts. . . . Claim 2: Large parts of programs for the needy weren't serving the poor anyway. . . . Claim 3: The wealthy really were not the big winners in the 1981 tax cut act." Writes Greenstein, "It was an impressive performance, even if it was based on some peculiar evidence."

He went on to explain:

> Start with Stockman's contention that actual spending for low-income benefit programs in fiscal 1982 and 1983—plus Reagan's proposed spending for fiscal 1984—is only 5 percent below the levels sought for these years in the last Carter budget.
>
> Here Stockman has deftly made use of the high unemployment experienced under the Reagan administration in an effort to bolster his case. The costs of a number of these basic benefit programs vary with unemployment levels—when more people are out of work, the number of households qualifying for the program multiplies and program costs rise. By one estimate, for example, food stamp costs rise about $600 million for every percentage-point increase in the jobless rate.
>
> The Reagan budget numbers Stockman cited reflect the impact of 10 percent unemployment on the costs of these programs. By contrast, the Carter budget numbers used by Stockman were calculated back in 1981, based on projections that unemployment would average only about 7 percent in the 1982–84 period. The result: Stockman was able to use the additional costs in the Reagan budget stemming from higher unemployment to make Reagan's spending levels look closer to Carter's—thereby making the Reagan cuts look smaller than they actually are.

Greenstein, in a tone of barely muted anger, went on to illustrate what Stockman had done with the numbers for Medicaid and subsidized housing. He pointed out that Medicaid budgets are based on projections of inflation in health care costs rather than on projections of the *overall* inflation rate. Using the proper formula— which Stockman did not—"you discover that the Reagan Medicaid cuts are about $2 billion dollars deeper for the 1982–1984 period—

or more than double what Stockman indicated." He called Stockman's manipulation of the subsidized housing numbers "equally egregious," pointing out that Stockman had played fast and loose with the numbers for the fixed costs for inflation, jimmying the Reagan figures up and the Carter figures down: "This bit of legerdemain made it appear that Ronald Reagan—whose administration has cut billions from new appropriations for subsidized housing, raised rents for all 3.5 million families and elderly persons living in subsidized units, and reduced the number of new low-income housing units being constructed or rehabilitated by more than half—actually spent more on these programs over the past two years than Carter would have."

He then poses the central question:

> How significant are Stockman's manipulations? A new Congressional Budget Office analysis shows that as a result of the last two years of budget reductions, fiscal 1983 expenditures for the low-income benefits programs were cut $5.2 billion below what they would have been had no changes been made by Congress. Stockman's chart, however, showed a reduction of only $1.7 billion. In other words, Stockman made two-thirds of the Reagan cuts disappear.

> Next, Claim 2: that large chunks of benefits have been going to persons far above the poverty line. Indeed, Stockman maintains that before Ronald Reagan came to the rescue, average workers were being taxed to bring welfare families up to virtually the same standard of living as themselves.

> Specifically, he contends that in 1981, 42 percent of all benefits in these programs went to families over 150 percent of the poverty line, and that 150 percent of the poverty line for a family of four that year was $13,390—or 92 percent of the median annual income for employed workers.

> The misuse of statistics is particularly striking here. First, Stockman has compared 150 percent of the poverty line *for a family of four* ($13,390) to the median income for an *individual* worker. Sorry, but you can't do that. The real numbers go like so: The median income for a family of four in 1981 exceeded $26,000—not $13,390—and 150 percent of the poverty line is about half—not 92 percent—of the median income for a comparably sized family.

As for the third claim, that the wealthy were really not the big winners in the 1981 tax cut, Greenstein again pulls back the veils, covers the mirrors, and blows away the blue smoke:

Stockman carefully limits his definition of the wealthy (without informing his audience) to the top two-tenths of 1 percent of all taxpayers,
those with incomes of more than $200,000 a year. This suited his
purposes admirably: With so few taxpayers defined as wealthy, their
aggregate tax benefits would not look so large. The sizable tax benefits
going to the much larger number of taxpayers in the $50,000 to
$200,000 range were simply excluded from his calculations. Moreover,
Stockman omitted the fact that the elite group he did define as wealthy
did receive, on average, a whopping $22,000 apiece just from the
changes in tax rates—before even counting the new tax shelter opportunities. Ronald Reagan himself saved $90,000 on his taxes last year
because of the 1981 act. His after-tax income went up almost as much
as if his salary had doubled.

Mr. Greenstein concluded with a double-barreled point:

Stockman's manipulation of the numbers makes rational debate on
these spending issues more difficult. But perhaps most significant is the
new dimension that Stockman has added to the much-discussed "fairness" issue. For what can raise more basic questions about whether this
administration is fair than when one of its principal officials—with
access to data, staff and resources that few others in this town possess—
utilizes this power to right the terms of the debate and misrepresent the
nature of his administration's policies?

The classic irony involved here is that David Stockman was, as
we saw from his revelations to William Greider, equally adept at
misrepresenting his faith in those policies to the very administration
he served.

In the third year of the first Reagan Administration, syndicated
columnist Carl Rowan wrote, "The nation must be thankful for the
Center on Budget and Policy Priorities and a few other groups who
care enough to dredge the truth out of the mountain of budget
documents, charts and graphs that are supposed to confuse the
public and Congress to the point that they can't figure out who is
getting shafted."

The organization Rowan singled out for this high praise, the
Center on Budget and Policy Priorities, identifies itself as "a
nonprofit research and analysis organization founded in late 1981
and located in Washington, D.C. The Center specializes in analyses of federal policy issues, including issues relating to the federal

budget, federal programs and policies affecting low and moderate income persons, defense spending, and tax policy."

The director of the Center on Budget and Policy Priorities, which is supported by grants from foundations, is Robert Greenstein, the same man who wrote the June 19, 1983, *Washington Post* article quoted above. Fifteen months later, a group called Interfaith Action for Economic Justice (whose members are "mission boards or program units of national religious agencies working together for just and effective US food and agriculture, health and human services, and development and economic policies") published a study done by Greenstein and his staff of the actual effect of the 1981 domestic budget cuts engineered by David Stockman.

End Results: The Impact of Federal Policies Since 1980 on Low Income Americans is a no-nonsense report built on valid "raw" numbers—definitely uncooked—that wastes no time in getting to its sobering point. The opening section, which is entitled "The Resurgence of Poverty in America," begins:

> One test of the moral fiber of a society is its treatment of people who are less fortunate. Today, as we examine the condition of our nation, one clear fact stands out—poverty is again a major issue in America. The Census Bureau announced in August 1984 that the number of Americans living below the poverty line had increased by over nine million— or 35 percent—in just four years from 1979 to 1983. The proportion of Americans now living in poverty is now higher than at any time since 1965. More than one of every seven Americans is now poor.

The report included some startling—and depressing—statements:

> —During the same 1979–1983 period, the number of children below age six who live in poverty jumped 51 percent. Today one in every four American children under age six (and one of every two black children under six) is poor.

> —The Census Bureau found that these steep increases in poverty show up even if non-cash benefits such as food stamps and Medicaid are counted as income. No matter how poverty is measured, the number of poor Americans (most of whom are children, elderly or handicapped persons or women with children where no father is present) grew by more than nine million in just four years. This represents *the largest increase since the poverty figures began being collected in 1960.*

—Studies by a variety of government agencies and private organizations have documented sharp increases in the number of Americans who are experiencing difficulty obtaining adequate food. One study of emergency food agencies across the country found that between early 1982 and early 1983, the number of people seeking emergency food aid grew by over 50 percent at more than half of these agencies—and doubled at a third of these agencies. Most emergency agencies were forced to turn away some people or to limit how frequently the same needy family could obtain food. Subsequent studies by the U.S. Conference of Mayors found that the number of people seeking emergency food aid continued to grow throughout 1983.

—In Chicago, doctors at Cook County Hospital found striking increases between 1981 and 1983 in the number of young children admitted for health problems linked to poor nutrition. The doctors also found that 30 percent of the children under age two coming to the hospital's emergency room had abnormally low growth, and that half of these low-growth children suffered from inadequate nutrition.

—In early 1984, even the President's Task Force on Food Assistance, a group widely criticized as partisan and predisposed to support Reagan Administration policies in this area, announced that it had found hunger to be a "real and significant problem throughout our nation."

"The rise in poverty," the report goes on, "hunger and homelessness requires a close look at federal policies of recent years and at the policy choices facing the nation in the future. The actions taken—and the future courses to be charted—in the areas of budget cuts, military spending, and tax policies have a profound impact on the lives of those at the bottom of the economic ladder."

In the sections that followed, the report gave further evidence of the real impact of the budget reductions on low-income families, specifying the actual, real number reductions in the "basic programs to provide food, shelter, health care and other necessities" such as food stamps; Medicaid; Aid to Families with Dependent Children; low-income housing; public service employment; job training; low-income energy assistance; Legal Services; compensatory education for disadvantaged children; and the general reduction in health programs. The picture was one of devastating impacts across the entire spectrum of social programs.

The Reagan Administration's famous "safety net" excuse was obliterated with two quotes, the first from Martin Anderson, a

White House domestic policy adviser, and the second from David Stockman. Anderson, in a July 1983 speech, said, "Providing a safety net for those who cannot or are not expected to work was not really a social policy objective. The term 'safety net' was political shorthand that only made sense for a limited period of time." And, according to a *Washington Post* story in early December 1983, Stockman said, "It [the list of programs said to constitute the safety net] was a happenstance list, just a spur-of-the-moment thing that the press office wanted to put out."

According to *End Results:*

> The budget reductions of the 1980s have been concentrated heavily on programs for poor people.
>
> Programs targeted on low income individuals and families comprise less than one-tenth of the federal budget. Yet as every authoritative independent study has shown (from the studies of the nonpartisan Congressional Budget Office to the analyses of the Urban Institute, a highly respected, nonpartisan research organization), these programs are where the deepest cuts have been made. The definitive analysis on the dimensions of the cuts, an August 1983 study by the Congressional Budget Office (CBO), shows that programs targeted primarily at the poor were cut $57 billion over the four-year period from fiscal year 1982 through fiscal year 1985 (after adjustment for inflation and unemployment). The CBO data also show that low income programs were reduced *more than twice as deeply* (in proportionate terms) as social programs not concentrated on the poor. Overall, the low income programs bore nearly one-third of all cuts made anywhere in the federal government, even though they constitute less than one-tenth of the budget. No other part of the federal budget was cut so sharply.

One of the most shocking things in the Interfaith Action report is the section entitled "It Could Have Been Worse" laying out the numerous requested cuts that were turned down *by Congress* (which masked Stockman's cruelty)! And they credit David Stockman with the statement that during its first three years in office, the Reagan Administration sought spending cuts twice as large as those Congress eventually passed.

Some of these rejected proposals would result in sharp cuts in the WIC (the Special Supplemental Food Program for Women, Infants, and Children) and ended prescription nutrition supplements for 750,000 low-income pregnant women, infants, and children found to be at medical risk; ended or reduced food stamp benefits for 92 percent of the elderly and 94 percent of the working poor on the program, those with incomes *below half* of the poverty line; sharply raised rents for poor families and elderly people in public or subsidized housing if they received food stamps, a slash that would have caused the rent of some of the country's absolutely poorest families to *double* over the next decade; cut the low-income energy assistance program by a *third* at a time when natural gas prices were shooting up; cut the budget of the highly successful compensatory education for disadvantaged children by over a billion dollars a year; and completely abolished the Work Incentive Program and the effective Legal Services program for 35 million poor people.

As the report pointed out, "The severity of these unsuccessful proposals illustrates a basic point: these programs have already been cut deeply; they cannot be reduced further without causing especially serious hardship." In support of that conclusion, it quotes no less an authority than budget director David Stockman, who told *Fortune* magazine in early 1984, "Some think there are vast pockets of fraud, waste and abuse out there. In fact, nearly every stone has been turned over." Yet that hardly stopped him from trying, fiscal year after fiscal year, to wring blood out of those same stones.

Thanks to the work of Greenstein's group, the press began to pick up on the story of what Stockman had really been doing. On June 6, 1983, *The New Republic* editorialized about Stockman's "duplicity," pointing out that while Stockman had "disappeared for a time" following the *Atlantic* affair, "on May 4, before the Joint Economic Committee of Congress, we had a performance worthy of the old David Stockman."

> Mr. Stockman told the committee, "I unequivocally reject" assertions that fairness has been violated by domestic program cuts, Mr. Reagan's tax cuts, or defense increases. Such ideas were either "total misrepresentations of the truth" or "a fundamental misunderstanding" of Administration policy. With what turned out to be shamelessly distorted numbers, Mr. Stockman went on to claim that the Reagan tax cuts did not disproportionately benefit the rich.
>
> Mr. Stockman produced one chart showing that six major social programs had been cut only 5 percent below Carter Administration levels. Mr. Stockman's calculations were cunning. He did not use actual budget figures for either Carter or Reagan, but "constant dollar" estimates obtained by factoring in unemployment and inflation. All the

factoring worked to Mr. Reagan's advantage—lowering Mr. Carter's spending levels by using Carter-era unemployment and inflation numbers, and raising Reagan levels by using Reagan-era numbers.

According to the magazine:

> David Stockman deserves to be taken back to the woodshed, and this time, President Reagan ought to be taken with him. . . . President Reagan's statements are no more dependable than Mr. Stockman's. . . . If Mr. Reagan thinks working people are better off because poor people are worse off, somebody has fed him bad numbers once again. Wages have come down as much as prices during the Reagan Administration, leaving the average American with virtually no increase in purchasing power, and far less than occurred during the Carter years. One group clearly has benefited, though. Two-thirds of the population thinks of Ronald Reagan as the rich man's president, and they're not wrong.

In the less than eighteen months since *End Results* appeared, Robert Greenstein and his Center on Budget and Policy Priorities have continued to pour forth studies—using "good" numbers—on the disastrous effects of the so-called Reagan Revolution on those Americans least able to help themselves. In November 1983, it updated its list of harsh cuts that Stockman–Reagan had proposed but failed to get through the Congress. This time it added several new ones, under the heading "The Reagan Administration's Most Draconian Cuts": cuts of over 50 percent in financial aid for needy students; cuts of over one-third in basic social and education services for low-income and black families and children; reductions of more than 50 percent in job-training programs; and reductions of 28 percent in child nutrition programs for low-income children— on top of earlier reductions of 20-30 percent in these same programs.

In September 1984, the Center put out a thirty-five-page pamphlet entitled simply *Fact or Fiction, An Analysis of President Reagan's Statements on Fairness, Spending and Taxes at His Recent Press Conferences and Before the Republican National Convention*. Here are some of the presidential utterances that the document, by a careful use of studies done by the Center and by others, refutes:

> "Not a single fact or figure substantiates the charge that administration budget policies have harmed the poor."

"Social programs have been expanded, not reduced—more people are being helped and more money is being spent."

"Administration tax policies have benefitted low income workers the most."

"The wealthy are now bearing a larger share of the federal income tax burden."

"Black unemployment has been declining at a faster rate than white unemployment."

"The poorest families are receiving more food stamps."

"Poverty has increased at a slower rate under the Reagan Administration than under the Carter Administration."

And, perhaps the most incredible:

"Deficits were out of control in 1980, but since then the administration has started to tighten the federal budget."

Other, like-minded groups were now following the Center's lead. In October 1984, the Center for the Study of Social Policy took David Stockman to task for his testimony and presentation before the House Ways and Means Committee on September 20. Its report began:

In 1980, George Bush coined the phrase "voodoo economics." He was, of course, referring to Ronald Reagan's ambitious but naive plans of simultaneously increasing spending, reducing taxes and balancing the budget. The Administration's "supply-side" theory has since been discredited: the recovery may be robust but it is undoubtedly Keynesian. Today, four years after Mr. Bush's comment, the voodoo continues. The casual misuse and misinterpretation of statistics has become something of a hallmark of this Administration. In fact, on several occasions, statistics have been intentionally misused or distorted—incidents far less excusable than gaffes at a press conference.

The report closed with the observation that:

In short, Mr. Stockman has used statistical trickery to support a claim that turns out to be false. Not only are Reagan's policies unfair, but his Budget Director's testimony are [sic] dishonest attempts to cover the facts. This is not the first time that Stockman's statistical claims have been discredited. In OMB's 1983 publication entitled "Major Themes and Additional Budget Details: FY 1984," Stockman also used statistical gimmicks to support his claims. Several researchers pointed out the distortions in his numbers. Now he has done it again. But this time he has gone even further: he has refined his dishonesty so it is exceedingly difficult to detect. This constitutes a near abuse of power by the director of a powerful executive agency, with scores of statisticians and mounds of data at his disposal.

Most importantly, he has further undermined not only his credibility, but the credibility of government itself as an objective source of vital information. The viability of a democracy rests on the decisions of an informed public. Mr. Stockman's attempts to mislead and misinform the public are corrosive to the democratic character of American government.

About this same time, another well-respected source rebutted the President and his budget director. The House Budget Committee staff prepared a document that, like *Fact and Fiction,* focused on a statement from the executive branch and then carefully dissected it, showing it to be patently false. For example, it rebutted the President's statement, made in his acceptance speech at the Republican National Convention on August 23, 1984, that "The biggest annual increase in poverty took place between 1978 and 1981— over 9 percent each year. In the first two years of our administration, that annual increase fell to 5.3 percent. And 1983 was the first year since 1978 that there was no appreciable increase in poverty at all." Or Stockman's assertion, also made before the House Ways and Means Committee on September 20, that "there is no basis for the charge that Reagan Administration policies have ruptured the nation's social safety net. On the contrary, in 1983 the social safety net was broader, deeper and more generous than ever before."

The titles of some of the releases and reports put out by Greenstein's center in 1985 are self-explanatory: "Stockman Mischaracterizes FY86 Nutrition Budget"; "Poverty Rate Shows Disappointing Drop; Income Inequality Widens"; and "Proposed Cuts in Low Income Programs Nearly Double What Stockman Acknowledges." Finally, in November 1985, the Center on Budget and Policy Priorities released a document entitled *Smaller Slices of the Pie,* which updated all of its previous work. It is subtitled "The Growing Economic Vulnerability of Poor and Moderate Income Americans."

Former HEW Secretary Arthur S. Fleming summed up the importance of the report in his brief Introduction:

The Center on Budget and Policy Priorities has produced a report that will help change the very terms of the debate in this country over poverty and economic vulnerability. Between its covers, the careful reader will find a complete and disturbing portrait of the all too real human conditions, not only of America's poor, but also of all Americans who remain vulnerable to a single development that could force them into poverty—developments such as the loss of a job, or illness or death in a family.

The data presented in this report are also a graphic indictment of governmental policies at both federal and state levels—policies that have taken from many who are poor or vulnerable, while giving to the wealthy and many large corporations. This approach could have serious consequences for the future of our country.

Fortunately, we now have the Center's detailed analysis of past policies and current conditions. This represents a first step toward correcting these problems; but it will require renewed commitment from all Americans—poor, rich, and middle income alike to restore the American dream. Many of us already working to these ends regard this report, along with other work from the Center on Budget and Policy Priorities, as a crucial resource to aid in this task.

Several passages taken first from the Introduction and then from the conclusion of *Smaller Slices of the Pie* indicate the importance of its content:

Today, poverty is higher than in any other non-recession year in nearly two decades. Equally important, the gap between the incomes of affluent Americans and those of low and moderate incomes is growing and has now reached its widest point since the end of World War II. Important changes in the fabric of American society seem to be taking place.

And, from the conclusion:

The data presented here on the economic status of low and moderate income Americans indicate that we are now witnessing a rather ominous series of developments. The gaps between lower and upper income families are widening, poverty rates have increased, disproportionate reductions have been made in programs for the less well-off, benefit levels have declined and program coverage has contracted in many of the most basic assistance programs, rent burdens for those of limited means are increasing, and federal tax burdens on the growing number of those who work but are still poor have soared. . . . The nation faces many tough choices in the years ahead, including choices on how to reduce the federal deficit and restore a better trade balance. But one of the most fundamental decisions facing the society is whether to allow the trends described in this report to continue and to permit the further deterioration of the economic status of low and moderate income Americans. This question deserves to be given as much attention and accorded as high a priority in the years ahead as any other issue before our nation.

In January 1986, Robert Greenstein sat down and discussed, for use in this book, his observations about his work—and about David Stockman:

"What consistently gets missed, and where Stockman and the Reagan Administration *really* get off the hook, are the things they proposed that didn't get enacted. We did a two- or three-page piece entitled 'The Ten Most Draconian Cuts That David Stockman Proposed That Didn't Get Enacted.' They are amazing. It is true that by 1984 Stockman was moderating on the low-income stuff; though he proposed further cuts, they weren't of the depth of the earlier proposals. What happened is that some of what they proposed in '81 didn't get enacted, but the most severe stuff was in '82, the [FY] '83 budget which came out in February of '82. He got less than a fifth of those low-income cuts. When you look at the cuts he proposed in '82, they *dwarf* the stuff that was enacted in '81. They are extraordinary in their depth and their severity, and how they would hit some of the poorest families in the country. And that's probably why they weren't enacted. The people on the Hill, including most of the Republicans, couldn't stomach them.

"The reputation Stockman has is that he wanted a balance in all the cuts. And it's certainly true that he was willing to look at taxes, and he was willing to go after non-low-income domestic programs, but the depth to which he was willing to go in low-income programs up through 1982 is something that really has been missed.

"Why? If you look back at 1981, the low-income cuts during '81 got very, very little attention until after they were enacted and took effect. The administration got away with—and it fooled the national press corps—this 'truly needy safety net' rhetoric. To anyone who knew the programs, an analyst who looked at them, it was very clear that this was a bunch of nonsense, that the cuts *were* targeted in the low-income programs, and they were going to push people into poverty. There should have been no mystery about it.

"When they actually were enacted, and stories started appearing in late '81 and early '82, about the hardships they were causing, this was a shock. Part of what I am saying is that the low-income people's constituency is so weak, politically, that the real situation doesn't really penetrate until after cuts are really enacted and take effect. But the proposed cuts which did not get enacted did not fail because of David Stockman; he pushed them. They failed to get enacted because of the Congress. He is as responsible for them as he is for the ones that passed."

Robert Greenstein seems almost bemused at the number and nature of the domestic cuts that Stockman tried unsuccessfully to impose, but which, for some reason, seem to have been forgotten by the press. A prime example is the cuts that were proposed in Social Security in the FY '83 budget, which Greenstein terms "a massive, massive assault on Social Security."

One recent item about Stockman intrigues Robert Greenstein, and seems to sum up his opinion of the former budget director. In his careful way he refers to it, several times, as "interesting." Clearly, he considers it to be crucial.

"There's that interesting thing [Senator Daniel Patrick] Moynihan said a few months ago about [the budget deficits] being a purposeful plan. And he says that Stockman told him that there was a conscious plan to build up the deficits to then provide a basis for gutting social programs more than they originally would have been able to. My recollection is that Moynihan said Stockman told him that, and that Stockman has not commented on it, but neither did Stockman deny it."

(Senator Moynihan, one of David Stockman's original mentors and one of the people responsible for Stockman's first Washington job, declined several requests to be interviewed for this book.)

According to *The New York Times*, on July 10, 1985, Senator Moynihan told reporters at a news conference, "The plan was to have a strategic deficit that would give you an argument for cutting back the programs that weren't desired. It got out of control."

Stockman's response, made through a spokesman, sounded almost flip: "I can't remember any such conversation. I say only that I have a reputation for candor and Pat has a talent for embellishment."

17 • Final Impressions

A COROLLARY to the lines from St. Luke quoted by I.F. Stone at the beginning of the last chapter reads: "From him to whom much is given, much is expected."

That idea applies to David Stockman in a variety of ways. Clearly, much has been "given" to Stockman, in the sense of intellect and drive. And that singular diligence has certainly paid off. Today he is a managing director of Salomon Brothers, in New York City, earning a reported million dollars a year. He and his wife and small daughter now live in posh Greenwich, Connecticut. His wife is no longer working for IBM, but runs a new consulting firm known as Stockman and Associates, which one knowledgeable Washington reporter with long-time access to both Stockmans says is a very legal repository for the money he has made in advance payments on his book. (As for that book, *The Wall Street Journal* reported on January 31, 1986, "Stockman's book leaves friends agog. A draft version that the former budget director has shown associates treats the president gently but skewers Regan, Weinberger, Meese, Kemp and several others in Congress. Some friends of Stockman counsel that he ease up on its belittling tone." And conservative reporter Donald Lambro writes, in the March 1986 issue of *Penthouse:* "The book . . . has created waves even before its appearance. Last fall, White House Chief of Staff Donald Regan reportedly warned Stockman not to tell too much. Indeed, politicians all over Washington are looking for cover in anticipation of Stockman's sizzling exposure of their self-serving backroom dealings in dividing up Uncle Sam's trillion dollars' worth of spoils. But Stockman is expected to spare no one.")

He leaves Washington with the high respect of most journalists, in part because he was almost always a good—off the record—source, and in part because many of them came to view him as the closest thing they could find to a closet liberal in the Reagan Administration. (There are not too many ardent supply-siders in the

Washington press corps.) Edward Cowan of *The New York Times*'s Washington Bureau, now the editor of a team of economic reporters, but for years before that a prolific reporter on economics, business, and government, says, "Stockman was the most able budget director we've ever had. And his staff at OMB liked working for him because he knew the numbers, and he had intuitive ideas and gave them imaginative problems and tasks."

William Greider, the journalist who almost inadvertently shot Stockman down in flames, remains a friend (Stockman showed him an early draft of the beginning of his book). Says Greider, "Whatever Washington thinks of David Stockman, his stock is through the roof in financial circles."

Another *New York Times* reporter with a perspective on David Stockman is John Herbers, but his view is quite different from that of many other Washington reporters, his colleague Ed Cowan included. Herbers has written books on the civil rights movement and covering the White House (which he did during the Nixon Administration), and is the author of the forthcoming *The New American Heartland.*[10] Says Herbers, "The real story on David Stockman and Ronald Reagan is in the way they operate: if you want to do something, don't do it with an honest and straightforward approach—lower taxes, raise the debt, which leaves only one area of the budget ripe for cuts, the domestic side. Why David Stockman is so admired here is because it's not 'Whaddya do?' but, 'What's your style?'

"Stockman wanted to cut waste in government, but he also wanted to cut back in keeping with Ronald Reagan's plan. They always claimed that people who needed help the most weren't hurt, but studies have showed that the working poor *were* most hurt, as were black children in Mississippi—in other words, the most deserving."

Herbers, who has seen the results of the Reagan–Stockman policies in action in his travels across the country as the *Times*'s national correspondent, points out, "Another way of looking at it is that federal aid to state and local governments has been reduced,

10. John Naisbitt called Herbers "one of the only three or four great American journalists. Herbers has the ability to place his individual news stories within the context of changing social, economic, and political realities, thereby offering the reader not just the facts but an interpretation of the way those facts relate to the rest of what is going on."

and that too has had a negative impact on the poor. And there have been lots of cuts in Medicaid, which functions as insurance for the poor, and hospitals no longer take as many indigent patients because they aren't on private plans. A direct result of the David Stockman–Ronald Reagan tax cuts has been to segregate the poor from the rest of us in regard to health care, and to make them different."

Herbers also has a clear impression of Stockman the person. "It used to be that young people normally wanted to help people, but David Stockman is typical of the young-old men in the Reagan Administration. A few years ago, nobody would have talked to him because of his ideas, but now people like him, they say he is 'the wave of change,' that he is a new type of conservative and a nice guy because he doesn't come on like one of those old conservatives. Nice guy? What he is is insidious."

Another journalist with strong views about Stockman, this one on the opposite side of the political aisle from the *Times*'s John Herbers, is the syndicated columnist Robert Novak (who was kind enough to give the authors of this book extensive interviews in 1983 and 1985). Novak has known Stockman well for more than six years. At one point they were even close.

"I got to know Stockman in about '79. I had been hearing stuff about him from the young turks in the House, and I had run into him on the Hill a couple of times. Then we spoke to the same group in Cleveland one time, and I had a long plane ride back with him. I found him to be a very fascinating guy.

"We started talking about presidential politics, and I had always associated him with the Kemp group in the House of Representatives, and I was kind of shocked [to learn] that he was for [John] Connally. We went on about that for a while, and he wasn't very convincing to me. But I found him to be a very, very bright sort of new Republican, non-orthodox supply-side Republican that interested me, that I thought was a hope for the party getting out of their austerity mode. I felt from the start that he was a little too heavy on the smashing-the-welfare-state-and-cutting-expenditures for my taste, but he seemed very good on the need to cut taxes, and on the general free market model. And he was very, very intelligent, very personable. After the election, I was some place on the road and [got] a couple of tips that Stockman had a really good chance of getting the OMB job. I called Stockman and he said he was interested in OMB. So, I think the first we wrote about him was that he was going to get the OMB job."

But, of the important national press figures who backed Stockman, Robert Novak was one of the first to become disillusioned with him.

"The first concerns I had were very early in '81. I used to see a lot of him at that time. I was having breakfast with him and he told me that it was very important to delay, that he had decided to push for a delay in the effective date of the tax bill, from January 1, 1981, to July 1, 1981. And I told him that, because of the size of the deficit, I thought that was nonsensical; I thought they had misunderstood the model. He became very apologetic, and he began to say that there was a sort of a cosmetic thing. That was the first real concern I had with him.

"But through all of '81, it became more and more obvious that he was more and more suspicious of the supply side, that he was moving toward an austerity model. I spent a couple of days traveling with him around Labor Day of '81, and I really had a lot of mixed emotions about him at that point. He was throwing in a lot of stuff, some of it for my benefit—he was talking about gold [Novak favors a return to the gold standard] and things of that sort. But there was a lot of austerity in there about the need to punch, the need to cut.

"We spent a lot of time together all through '81, and I was getting more suspicious and more suspicious. Was he really interested in this, or was he playing a double game? But he was always singing a very, very good tune with me."

Just as Novak neared the height of his suspicions, the Greider article appeared. "I was doing a piece for *Reader's Digest* on Jack Kemp, and I went up to Jamestown, New York, with Kemp, who was giving a speech. As we came back that same night, we were told about the *Atlantic* article. It was Stockman's birthday that night, and I hadn't seen Stockman in about a month, which was very unusual at that time because I did spend a lot of time with him, and these quotes were read to me by somebody and I just couldn't believe them."

That was also the first time Jack Kemp had heard of the *Atlantic* article.

"He called Stockman," said Novak of Kemp, "to wish him a happy birthday, and Kemp's the kind of person who never wants to believe anything bad about people. He's a very positive person. So he said to me, 'Do you want to say hello to Dave and wish him a happy birthday?' I picked it up and [Stockman] said, 'We got to get together and explain these things.' "

Was Stockman saying, in effect, I'm not a Judas?

"Yes," says Robert Novak. "And we never did [get together]. We've had conversations since, but we never had a meeting subsequent to that. I could never get in to see him, couldn't even get him [as a guest] on a television program."

Asked if he agreed with the anonymous former Reagan Cabinet member who said that the reason Stockman was in the press so little, comparatively speaking, after the second budget and the publication of the article in the *Atlantic* was because "That's when the Administration died," Novak quickly said, "I don't believe that. That's all based on the theory that the purpose of the administration was to cut spending. It's part of the orthodox Republicanism. What happened is that Stockman has had many, many lives, political lives and ideological lives—and I may say that there is no reason to think that he's finished; Stockman is still a relatively young man, and [one with] really very few ideological roots. I don't think he would settle down in one place. The change that occurred in the midst of the Reagan Administration is that he switched from a radical supply-side Republican to a conservative orthodox Republican in his economic views; he always had vestiges of the latter, but it became the dominant issue, so that instead of being a tax cutter who also felt that you had to have radical spending cuts, he became somebody who not only felt that the radical spending cuts were impossible, but you had to have tax increases. And so there was a major change in his outlook."

Might Stockman just as well have been, as some have charged, a *Democrat?* Novak won't go that far: "He was not interested in preserving the social welfare. He couldn't really cut 'em because of reality, but he wasn't interested in preserving them. I don't think he really was any less active in the administration. I think he was just less public about it."

Was he in the woodshed all that time?

"No. It was a very tolerant situation. Stockman was one of the smartest people, and he never stopped being smart. He was behind the scenes. He worked very closely with Richard Darman on a lot of issues. They were very good friends. Stockman was a major factor in the 1984 tax bill; he was a major factor in the down payment plan in

1985. From his first day to his last day, he was in there pushing at all times, winning some, losing some, but at all times after 1981, and in fact starting with the so-called 'Fall Offensive' in '81, his whole model was deficit reduction, with a major element of tax, of revenue, increases."

That, of course, put him very obviously outside the supply-side camp.

"Oh, yes," says Novak without any hesitation.

But was Stockman *ever* a real, hard, true believer in supply-side economics, or was it only a position, a stance that helped him get where he wanted to go?

"I think," said Robert Novak, "what's that old song? 'When I'm Not Near the One I Love, I Love the One I'm Near'? I think he is a man who is able to change his views and his ideological mien to match his coat. But I think he's very *staunch* on those views at the time. I think he was a supply-sider. I always felt that there were elements of his supply-side philosophy which were more or less austerity-conscious than others, but I don't think it was any kind of a guise. I will say this, though: if he had not espoused those views, he would not have had the patronage for the job that he had."

By the time Stockman had defected from supply-side, he had turned on an awful lot of people. There were several well-known and influential mentors with whom he no longer had good relations. Did Novak see this as part of a pattern?

"That's the story of his life. Of turning on people. John Block [former Secretary of Agriculture] really believes that Stockman has an emotional, passionate dislike of farmers. And there is a sort of hatred of the places he's been and the coats he's worn—most recently supply-side, but going all the way back to farming, the Anderson era being one of the most interesting periods. That was described to me, and described to other reporters, by David as a period where he was really *saving* Anderson from those liberal ideas, that he was really the anchor to the right in the Anderson camp. I had talked to a couple of Anderson aides, though I never wrote about it, who said he was the most liberal guy in that operation, [that] he was a long way from being an anchor to the right, [that] he was a real bomb thrower.

"He's a guy who does change his view on things. It might be opportunism and it might not, but he holds with great passion the views he holds at that time."

To shift the terms of the debate somewhat, does Novak see Stockman as a compassionate man?

"No."

That taken care of, Novak continues: "I saw a lot of him in the early part of the Reagan Administration, and since he was very busy, the most convenient time for me to see him was Saturday morning at the Hay–Adams. And one Saturday morning we had just finished breakfast and Bill Greider comes in, and I was a little puzzled. He had a tape recorder, and I assumed he was doing a piece for the *Post*. I later learned that there was a little mix-up—usually they were alternating Saturdays, between Greider and me, and he was telling me exactly the opposite of what he was telling Greider. With me, Stockman was the true believer.

"Stockman kept telling me he was going to attack corporate welfare and middle-class welfare. He was going to give me a list. I kept bugging him for that list, but he never gave it to me. Later he said there never was a list, but he *told* me there was a list."

Isn't that picture of Stockman inconsistent with Novak's overall view of the man? Or, at least, inconsistent with that of people in the media?

"I'm not saying he wasn't duplicitous," responds Novak. "I don't think those are mutually exclusive, that he can't believe in these things and still be duplicitous."

Finally, what about the question of arrogance?

"Well, I never worried much about that. I guess he is an arrogant person, but that doesn't bother me. He is very, very good company, very pleasant to spend an evening with. He was a lot of fun."

Has Novak ever seen anybody quite like him in Washington?

"I've never seen anybody quite like him *out* of Washington. In my whole life, I've never seen anybody quite like him."

Why then, given Robert Novak's hardly concealed opinion of David Stockman, do so many Washington journalists still speak so highly of the former budget director? Again, there is no hesitation before Novak answers.

"I'll tell you why—because he confirms the liberals' worst views of the Reagan Administration: that, number one, the tax cut was a disaster; number two, the deficit is leading us to catastrophe; number three, we are spending too much on defense; and, number four, you're really not going to get any more cuts in domestic spending.

"He wraps this up in rhetoric which makes him a hero to certain conservatives, but really this stuff titillates and satisfies the liberals. When I said I think he's got at least one more turn yet to make, I wouldn't be a bit surprised to see David emerge in later life as a *liberal*. I wouldn't be a bit surprised."

A Stockman-watcher of even longer standing is former Common Cause president David Cohen, who has been observing Stockman for over a decade, and in that time has seen what he feels to be a pattern in the behavior of the former budget director. Underlying Cohen's negative impressions of Stockman is a certain amount of what sounds like regret, a sense of loss perhaps over the way things turned out:

"I first ran across David Stockman when he was a staff member working with John Anderson, and he was incredibly sharp. Anderson, as the chairman of the Republican Conference, was the third ranking Republican leader, and was, as a member of the House Rules Committee, beginning to exert increasing independence, to think about things. Stockman was the principal staff member in relation to his being part of the House Republican Conference. And everybody put a lot of promise on David Stockman because he was interested in policy, he was unorthodox, he was clearly different from what could be viewed as a kind of a *Main Street* Republican, many of whom had bit the dust in 1964, but there were a lot still there. These other guys, the older mainstream Republicans, really were out of Gopher Prairie, but Stockman was different and exhibited the kind of issue entrepreneurialism that was beginning to emerge with John Anderson. So it was no accident that the first comprehensive campaign finance reform bill of the seventies, 1970 or so, was an Anderson–Udall kind of thing. They were reflecting. in both directions, the younger, policy-oriented, process-related kinds of people, and Stockman was a staff person feeding all that.

"Now, it was also clear to me that he was a person with a lot of his own energies and ambitions, and I watched him and another guy, who came to Washington then, by the name of Michael Harrington. Harrington was a very liberal congressman, and one of his first AAs [administrative assistants] was Barney Frank; there reached a point where Barney said, 'Well, you know, I don't want to do this, I want to run myself, I want to be a legislator.' And you could see this in Stockman, too.

"Ed [Hutchinson] did an inept job in the impeachment period and then just sort of survived that first '74 round. He was gonna be dead political meat in '76, so he retired. Stockman was prepared to challenge him in the primary if Hutchinson hadn't quit. So Stockman came to the House with an advantage of knowing a lot about how the system worked; he just wasn't an ordinary freshman congressman and you could see it. I remember once visiting him and his showing me all the equipment that he had on how you could use the versions of robo-type typewriters they had then and program the responses, so if you got a request from a farmer you could program it that way and if you got the same request from a teacher you could program it the other way. He was very, very technologically astute about organizing the office, organizing it for maximum efficiency, and how to make use of his incumbency, all the built-in advantages that an incumbent has. He was very sharp on that."

Had Stockman's politics changed by this point?

"Not yet. He went on the House Administration Committee, and we thought that would enable him to be a voice for campaign reform, but it was on the campaign finance issue that you began to see that his politics changed. His politics were influenced by audiences. And the audiences that he was tuned in to were really the Republicans in the House. What had happened was that Barber Conable, who was, as you know, a mainstream conservative Republican, ranking member on the House Ways and Means Committee, had really gotten fed up with the campaign finance system and was supporting the form of public financing, matching grants. Stockman originally co-sponsored the bill, but he was not very helpful inside the House Administration Committee. Now it was mainly a Democratic problem anyway, and the Democrats were not great either, and they were playing their own games, but I thought that the thing about Stockman was watching him *withdraw* from the issue. Here's a guy with lots of legislative talents, lots of smarts in a tremendous position to be a bridge-builder, and quite the reverse actually, [he] basically withdrew from the issue. This was in the period of '77 and '78, it was his first term, and he was capable of playing an active role.

"I remember at one point there was a major meeting in Barber Conable's office, and Stockman came to that, a little bit late, and it involved some discussion about the rule. Now the rule that the

Democrats were going through was not a rule that any Republican could in good conscience support, so we weren't pushing them to support that particular rule. But we were looking for a way *around*, a way to try and promote some method of getting around the opposition to the rule; we had supported the Republicans in the effort against trying to restrict parties from being able to compete in campaign financing. The main point that hit me at that meeting was that Stockman could have played an active role at trying to be part of the team that would deal with things, to overcome the difficulties, but instead, there was a withdrawal. Withdrawal was really a form of having it both ways: being a technical co-sponsor in public financing, but doing nothing to be constructive at a critical moment. Now, in no way am I saying that all this might have made the difference; it might not have, he might not have, but there was an absence of trying. *There were all the elements of taking a dive.*"

Cohen had never seen this behavior in David Stockman before.

"When I say 'take a dive,' I don't mean somebody came up to him and said, 'don't do anything.' I think this is the same David Stockman that would calculate how you would organize an office to get technological advantage to reinforce yourself to your constituents, but here the audience were the House Republicans. . . . Of course, he was able to rationalize it, but operationally, he stood by when he could have contributed to *making the difference in changing the campaign finance system.*

"That was the beginning of my understanding that Stockman was not really part of the Anderson wing, the Anderson legacy, the Anderson contributions. Or the Conable contributions. What Anderson and Conable had in common was that they really cared about the institution, and that was part of what was driving them about campaign finance. And Stockman could go with that in 1971 and 1972 and 1973 when the issue was on the upscale; even '74. Maybe especially '74. But when there were a different set of audiences coming through, a different set of criticisms, different set of comments, there he was maintaining the status quo, even though from a formal view he was a supporter of public financing."

This brings Cohen to his fundamental disappointment concerning David Stockman.

"You can say he had larger ambitions and that he should have his own ambitions, that he certainly was not Anderson's guy, or Conable's guy, or anything like that. *But what you had there was no effort at trying to square the present with the past*. It was a kind of going with the wind, being an other-directed guy, *no inner core of restraint*. That's the thing that hit me about Stockman in those meetings, and I have to say I developed a very strong mistrust, dislike, skepticism, about what he was really about. I thought he was highly overrated, even though he was as bright as could be, which is why he could write something as brilliant as he did when he wrote about the social pork barrel. That was a seminal article, and that was early. So the brightness never was lost, but where he was coming from was lost.

"What he reminded me of, in lots of ways, is two categories that I'm very low on. One are people who were in politics in the thirties, usually left-wing politics, who were great *rationalizers*. They were damn good writers; they could put together an argument. Often these same people, with an absence of principle in the thirties, then [later] would be the ones who could rationalize why you have to support the Vietnam War, or why blacks shouldn't get an equal opportunity because affirmative action was really a quota system, and things of that sort. The kind of people that he was associated with were neoconservatives. Irving Kristol is a good example of that. The other thing I'm low on is the Walt Rostow syndrome, which I call brief writers. These are people who are very articulate verbally. . . . They can make a seemingly persuasive case for anything—and that's what he was, and that's what he was becoming, in the absence of any inner core, the absence of inner restraint, the absence of a guiding principle. That lack is what leads to the grab on Gramm–Latta, or the use of technical know-how to rechange the direction of things without any kind of adequate discussion; it's the absence of inner core which to me he really demonstrated in the *Atlantic* article in the interview with Bill Greider, which I think did Stockman in."

On the question of Stockman's relationship with John Anderson, Cohen makes an intriguing comparison.

"It reminded me a lot of the Paul Douglas–Eugene McCarthy relationship. Though McCarthy never worked for Douglas, they came out of the same kind of progressive, liberal legacy. McCarthy was a superstar as a House member by everyone's account who knew something about it [but these same people] were very disappointed [by] his Senate career. Douglas, who of course had a strong stoical and puritanical streak in him, and was a Yankee reformer, and who had very high standards, was always disappointed in McCarthy's role on the Finance Committee. The reason I compare it is that it [was] a younger man with an older man, and the older man had some sort of a legacy, a set of values. There was a bit of a mentor relationship, maybe even protégé, in the Stockman–Anderson relationship; and there was a deep disappointment, the disappointment of the public person. . . .

"I think Stockman, while a House member, very shrewdly used the Commerce Committee as a vehicle, sort of attacking notions of regulation, of wounding, with a lot of political skill, the framework of regulatory mechanisms. But he was an effective prosecutor [against] the cost containment stuff."

Could it be that Stockman is really much better at tearing something down than he is at building something up? The former head of Common Cause says, "Yes, that's right, which is evidenced by his inability to try and put something together on campaign finance. He didn't try. There is a cynicism about not trying, and in that situation the reason I say, 'take a dive,' it's like the ballplayer who hits a grounder and doesn't run it out and then, by God, the shortstop bobbles it and he doesn't get to first base. And, it's that kind of always protecting yourself [by claiming] you are dealing with principle.

"The analytical side of David Stockman is far stronger than his ability to synthesize, his ability to articulate what his core values are. Here's a guy who was in Divinity School during the Vietnam War, opposed the Vietnam War and all that, [but] not once in anything that I'm familiar with, do you see a discussion of the concept of national service, or volunteer service, or 'What is it that I can give back?' or 'What is it that we should ask young people to give back to their community?' He cannot take a major idea and build on that, which is the reason that Bob Eckhardt's line is so *sharp*. We have some strong traditions in this country. One is the republican tradition, form of citizen participation, governance. Another is the civic virtue tradition; you want to do something about a problem, you roll up your sleeves and you participate and go to the town meeting, or whatever. The third is a cooperative tradition: help to build the barn; people help one another; and the 'neighborhood watch.' But he doesn't evidence any knowledge of it. He certainly evidences no feeling about it. The fourth is the biblical tradition, which deals with the covenantal relationship that this country was founded on—the 'city on the hill'—and responsibility for one another, instead of what Stockman did, with his analytic abilities, and his verbal abilities, which was to try to lay the groundwork for a theory of modern-day social Darwinism."

As to the question of compassion, Cohen says simply, "Where's the evidence? Where is the evidence?"

Cohen has a good deal more to say on the legacy of David Stockman. "Clearly there has been a shift in direction in the government, there is a shrinkage, but I think what we don't know yet is whether there will be some sort of adjustments to take place that draw more on the legacy of the New Deal than we realize. For example, if you have the kind of sorting out of functions, you may end up having much more federal responsibility for the so-called safety net that gets way beyond just Social Security and organized constituencies; it's *conceivable*. I think Stockman was the apparatchik who showed the principals how you can change the direction of the government. That will be his legacy. He was not able, in any way, to move the administration or the President on the things that the President didn't think were important. He didn't change any of Reagan's sacred cows. But Stockman didn't *do* anything. He didn't *do* anything to make it possible either to recoup the revenues. Look at all this stuff about revenue recoupment; compare that to the memo on the 'Economic Dunkirk.' It's another sharp shift.

"The other thing about Stockman, and this is what I feel in the Anderson situation, and this is what I felt when I read the *Atlantic* article, is that there is an absence, an absence of inner core which is not only about his own values and beliefs but about *loyalty*. Loyalty doesn't mean you follow the other guy blindly all the time, but it means you recognize that you are part of a team. And what he did in the Greider interview was engage in *teenage bragging*; [it] was a form of saying 'I scored.' John Anderson has never said anything to me about it, but that's my sense of what Anderson felt. I know that's what Douglas felt—in the Douglas–McCarthy relationship—and so not knowing what you are about also makes you not loyal and even makes you disloyal. Is there any set of things in which Stockman would have resigned on principle on? By these measures, never."

Another Democrat with a long memory is Californian Henry Waxman, who served in the House with David Stockman. By his own admission, he knew Stockman "very well," having been the chairman of a subcommittee (Energy and Commerce) on which

Stockman served. Henry Waxman's opinion of David Stockman and his legacy, while phrased somewhat more gently, is quite similar to that of David Cohen's.

"I think he was a very hardworking congressman and very tenacious, but he was not particularly skillful at pulling together coalitions. When he was successful, it was usually because he had very powerful interest groups behind him. The thing that comes to my mind is when he fought against hospital cost containment in the seventies with the backing of the American Medical Association and hospital groups. When the opposing groups gave way, hospital costs went beyond anybody's imagination. [That] was not a moderate Republican position; it wasn't a thoughtful position. It was an interesting position for him to take, in light of the later positions that he took when he was trying to hold down some of the increases in health care costs. While in office, he argued as a conservative economist that we shouldn't put a ceiling on, or control on, any sector of the economy, such as the hospital interest groups; yet when he became head of the Office of Management and Budget, he [wanted to] be architect of price controls on doctors' fees so that the federal government could be saved the increase in money that they would have to pay if they allowed doctors' fees to increase. He put a freeze on doctors' fees and a freeze on what they could collect in their pensions, which is antithetical to what you would think a conservative economist would want and what he argued when we were given the hospital control issue."

How genuine was Stockman's original belief in supply-side economics?

"I take him at face value. It turned out that he was not a genuine supply-sider, that the whole notion of supply-side economic theory was only a Trojan horse to accomplish the other objectives, primarily to give tax breaks to the wealthy individuals and corporations in this country at the same time that they were going to decimate the domestic programs designed to help ordinary people. I think he saw [supply-side] as a very attractive way to package an unpalatable position."

Congressman Waxman was "amazed" by the "revelations" in the *Atlantic* article, particularly the "candor of someone in the administration who actually was doing the opposite of what they were claiming. I was surprised he gave that interview and said those revealing things about what they were in fact up to. I recall thinking he had enough intellectual integrity to [recognize] that what they were proposing in 1981 under the cloak of supply-side economics was the old trickle-down theory of helping the rich.

"I think he lost power and influence in the administration, I suppose, partly because of that, partly because he came to the understanding that supply-side economics was not going to reduce the deficit, but increase it, and when he wanted to do some policies that would lessen the deficit, he was thwarted, by Weinberger and others."

What does Waxman see as Stockman's legacy?

"His legacy along with the Reagan Administration's legacy are incredible budget deficits. Yet, he was honest to admit, even before he left office, that supply-side economics theory was really a sham, had not worked, and has put six generations in this country in debt."

Waxman makes a point that has not been made often enough: "If he had the sincere qualms that he claimed that he did later about the policies that he pursued in 1981, the honorable thing for him to have done was to resign. He didn't resign; instead, he tried to carry out his activities as part of the Reagan team, while at the same time looking to undercut and publicly disassociate himself from it."

In an interesting comparison, Waxman calls this "Henry Kissingerism . . . I recall Stockman was a vigorous opponent of the Chrysler aid, which wasn't a bad policy; it turned out to be a fairly decent result. . . . But he did that because he had economic theories that you don't help anybody out, you let the market take the harsh realities that result from it whatever the consequences may be. I think he has a certain integrity about him, in terms of an adherence to a view of the world in economic terms when payments are cut, or to people in a city that have to breathe additional pollution, and because he doesn't want to require any government spending to help the mother out of government regulations and stop the poisoning of people. But that integrity caused him to be a little bit more candid than you would think someone in his position should have been when he gave that interview for the *Atlantic*. And his integrity was limited because an honorable person would have resigned if he had a serious disagreement on economic principles as Stockman claimed that he had with the Reagan Administration."

Reminded that Stockman left Washington with a lot of respect from journalists, Waxman noted, "So did Kissinger. All you have to do is be in an administration pursuing one policy, and tell the press that you really didn't believe it, and they love you."

Is David Stockman a man of compassion?

"Absolutely not," says Henry Waxman. "He was able to be dispassionate about the human consequences of the policies that he pursued and supported, *and* about those he supported but wasn't able to pursue. My impression of him is that while he was quite zealous and very bright, he was very single-minded and tied to a political philosophy that allowed him to be absolutely insensitive to the pain that would be inflicted upon people—plus other consequences—if [the Congress] followed and carried out his blueprint." For a variety of reasons, almost all of the former Reagan Administration Cabinet members who were asked, declined to be interviewed about David Stockman. One who agreed was Ronald Reagan's first Secretary of Transportation, Drew Lewis. Mr. Lewis, who recently served, at the President's request, as special envoy for the United States in a nine-month joint study with Canada of the problem of acid rain, left the cabinet in 1983, "having kept my promise to serve for two years." He returned to the private sector as the head of Warner-Amex, the cable television giant, and left that company early in 1986 to become chairman and chief executive officer of Union Pacific Railroad.

Drew Lewis prefaced his remarks about David Stockman with a strong statement of support for Stockman and the job he did for the Reagan Administration, "especially in the first two years." During that period, says Lewis, "Stockman did more for the president and his programs than any of us."

In the early cabinet meetings, as Lewis recalls them, Stockman would come in armed with long knives and sheathsful of data that purportedly justified the cuts he was seeking.

"The thing that was very clear [in the first cabinet meetings] was that the people who had been there [in Washington] were up to speed much quicker than the rest of us who were coming in from out of town. When we first started, David Stockman knew much more about the Transportation budget, obviously, than I did. The one thing I learned from my predecessor, Neil Goldschmidt, was the value of getting staffed up early, because if you don't, the people who are around town who know more about your department than you do will start running your department. The other advice I got from Neil Goldschmidt had to do with getting staff who are loyal to you, and he also told me, 'Never empty your In box, because if you spend your time doing that all day, you'll never get anything else done.'

"The thing that I found when I got there was that Stockman was in charge, was pretty much dominating all the budget decisions that would be made by my department. Fortunately, we got staffed up fairly early, and I found that a lot of the things that were coming out of his shop sounded good on paper—and he could throw out a few items here and there to make you look somewhat ridiculous—but on balance, after you're there and you're looking at things day by day, it's clear you could know much more about the budget than he did.

"I think, on balance, Stockman did a very good job overall. I think he was very political and very devious. In what sense do I mean devious? Well, for example, it was clear to me and others in the cabinet that our deficits were going to be considerably larger than he was reporting. You didn't have to be a whiz-bang economist to figure that out. And he kept reporting figures that I knew were not accurate, and finally I called him on it at a cabinet meeting; I forget what the exact figures were, but we were talking about having a twenty- or thirty- or forty-billion-dollar deficit, and I said, 'Mr. President, anybody that can add figures up and can understand economics *knows* the figures coming out of OMB are inaccurate— Ask Dave Stockman.'

"So what Stockman did, he sort of served his own purpose [in order to] accomplish what he wanted to accomplish. Nonetheless, I think he did more than any one single cabinet officer to drive down the cost of government and force us to cut our budgets."

That said, Lewis recalled something that apparently had always bothered him while serving in the same cabinet with Stockman, in addition to the budget director's having been something less than forthright and forthcoming with his budget data.

"The other thing that of course aggravated me was that he would keep dropping stuff to the press as he saw fit [that would] undermine whatever you wanted to do, if he didn't like the programs. He did that to me with *The Wall Street Journal*, with Evans and Novak, and with others when we were trying to get the voluntary restraints on Japanese automotive imports. . . .

"I can see both the good side to him and the bad side. There's no question that he manipulated whatever he was doing to serve his own purpose at the time. On the other hand, I think that the pressure that he put on all of us to cut our budgets was very effective."

After mentioning that Stockman "roughed up" several of Lewis's fellow cabinet members, the former Transportation Secretary made a point that echoes one made by Anne Burford when she recounted her appeal of Stockman's refusal to rescind his cuts in the EPA budget for 1982.

"One thing that's great about President Reagan, the guy has a knack for coming out on top and doing the right thing. He's got incredibly sound judgment, and his judgment never varies. Ronald Reagan has the ability to come down on the right side of issues. So you always had that going for you, going into a fight with Stockman.

"For example, Cap [Weinberger] caught on to Stockman and learned how to make a budget presentation. Stockman always came in with slides and examples and outrageous kinds of statements, and Cap caught on to it. He said, 'Now, if we have my kind of budget, the Army's going to look like this . . .' and he had a big strong tank with a lot of big soldiers on it, 'But if it's going to be Stockman's budget,' and then he had a Volkswagen with a little guy sitting there with a bow and arrow. That may be an exaggeration, but the point is, Cap just totally rolled him. Cap out-Stockmanned Stockman.

"What you'd find with Stockman [in these budget presentations] was that he would have put together about two-thirds of the facts, and he would make a very convincing argument, but you'd never hear the other third."

Drew Lewis nonetheless remains consistent in his praise for what Stockman accomplished. "I think we would never have had the success we had in the initial stages of the Reagan Administration in terms of cutting spending without David Stockman. He would tell me things about my department to look into as possible areas to cut, and I'd look into them, and he was almost always right."

That doesn't mean Stockman wasn't above, as Lewis (and others) suggested earlier, "cooking the numbers" to give his side of the argument a little edge.

"He also had a very strong feeling on the things that he wanted to win, and if he wanted to win something, he was clever enough with statistics that they could usually come out the way he wanted them

242 • The Stockman Legacy

to come out, and you wouldn't know until the last minute, so you couldn't refute him and do something to contravene him, and all of a sudden you're shot down. So, in the cabinet meetings, whenever I'd have a confrontation with Stockman, I'd bring three or four of my bright people and say, 'Okay, now what's Stockman going to do on this?' After you got used to him, he was not too difficult to counteract because he did the same thing every time."

If this was dirty pool, or unfair play, Drew Lewis doesn't recall looking at it that way, nor did he ever really blow up over Stockman's use of such tactics. "I never had a confrontation with Stockman in the sense that I don't like him personally, but you knew he had his ax to grind, and he had his job to do, and he did it very well. I don't object to him doing what he tried to do to me. I think he manipulated the statistics to the extent that he used the ones that proved his point, and he never got to the ones that proved the opposite point. Now, if you were smart enough to figure out the argument against the statistics he offered—which I wasn't, but I had enough people around me who were—then you were in a position where you could handle it."

Drew Lewis does believe, however, that Stockman could have served the President better "if he had been more straightforward."

According to Lewis, while Stockman was not arrogant in the normal sense of the word, there was a certain element of arrogance in his very deviousness. "When you'd catch him in something that was obviously misleading or a falsehood or whatever you want to call it, he would [react] with great indignation until you'd fully documented that you'd caught him, and then he'd say, 'Fine.' I never thought he was particularly arrogant. Take, for example, acid rain. He was not too pleased when I got that assignment as special envoy. His explanation on acid rain had always been, 'Just keep the prevailing winds blowing as they are, and we won't have to worry about it.' "

Stockman's use of the press is probably Lewis's biggest complaint about him, and was mentioned several times during our interview. On one reiteration he added, "He would use the press, particularly the conservative press, to try to make those of us who probably have a greater conservative philosophy than he does look like we're some kind of wild-haired liberals."

But Drew Lewis kept returning to his theme of Stockman's value to the first Reagan Administration. "On balance, if I had to give him a grade—Would I rather have had him there or not have had him there?—it would be a clear plus." And Lewis adds, "Despite the aggravation of dealing with him, despite the negatives that I saw in Dave, I think he was a great addition to the administration. I think in the first two years he contributed more than any of us."

Roughly speaking, the appearance of the Greider article in the *Atlantic* marked the end of those first two years. Does Drew Lewis think what Stockman said in that article could be termed an act of disloyalty to Ronald Reagan?

"It depends on how you grade disloyalty. I think you can serve the President and serve him well without having to agree with him on everything. I think, clearly, Stockman should not have done that, and I wouldn't have done that. I think he felt his intellectual integrity was grabbing him . . . and he was trying to document that he really was a straight guy, he was trying to say that the expediency of what he was doing was caused by a greater purpose."

This observation is in keeping with Lewis's overall evaluation that Stockman "was always devious—no question he was devious, manipulative, and he tried to steer things the way he wanted to steer them to satisfy his own ends. On the other hand, once you know a guy's like that, you have to figure out how you handle him."

But isn't this like saying "He's a son of a bitch, but he's *our* son of a bitch?"

"Right," says Drew Lewis. "In my department, he probably gave me more ideas on where to cut things than anyone, except for the Grace Commission."

Given what Stockman said in the *Atlantic* article, shouldn't the President have given him his walking papers? Drew Lewis thinks so.

"I find it inexcusable, what he did. And if I had been the President, I would have fired him. But the President didn't."

Why then did Stockman leave when he did? Lewis feels that he read the prevailing winds, especially the economic ones, and knew it was the right time to go, even though "Stockman enjoyed serving in government. I think Stockman got to the point where he saw he could make a million dollars a year with Salomon Brothers, and write a book, and cash in. I guess he figured that he had better cash in while the cashing in was still good, because if things went South, he would not be quite the hero he was."

*   *   *

Another Stockman-watcher with an intriguing vantage point is Wendell Belew, Jr., the lawyer who recently formed his own consulting firm after having spent ten years on the House Budget Committee, the last nine as its chief counsel. He went to work for the Budget Committee in January 1976, about the same time Stockman was seriously plotting his strategy for taking over Ed Hutchinson's Fourth District seat. Having worked with a variety of chairmen, and enjoying an intimate relationship with the budget process, Belew had an interesting window through which to view the rise of David Stockman.

"I was very active in the first reconciliation bill in 1980, the first time that Congress tried to use that approach to try to lower the 'outrageous' budget deficit of $16 billion which President Carter submitted in 1980, and which drove the stock markets mad. I was somewhat involved in 1981 [when] obviously, the House Democrats were defeated, both in the budget resolution and in their reconciliation bills, so my involvement was somewhat indirect, but certainly fairly substantial on the conference level, and obviously I was very familiar with what Stockman and others did in 1981 and thereafter."

Prior to that, Belew had known Stockman only slightly, and says, "One didn't think of Stockman as someone who was a budget person. One thought of Stockman as an Energy and Commerce [Committee] person. Perhaps that's where he got to know Phil Gramm. Their relationship runs throughout this whole period. They are very close. In that period, 1978 to 1980, Stockman and Gramm co-authored a budget plan. It was not widely noted, it was one of a couple of alternatives that were posed on the floor, it didn't pass, it wasn't debated extensively. But that was the first point that I recall Stockman and Gramm working together, or, in fact, recall David Stockman's name in connection with any kind of budget initiative. He was regarded as a hybrid of the New Right Republican and a kind of John Anderson Republican. He had worked for Anderson, and he had something of a moderate image, but he was perhaps a lot more a part of the more ideological Conservative Opportunity Society wing of the Republican Party—it hadn't been named that at the time, but it was identifiable, I think. One thought of Stockman as being closer to a Jack Kemp sort of Republican."

Belew admits that he was "surprised" when Stockman was named budget director. Part of his feeling stemmed from the fact that he was not all that impressed with the budget resolution that Stockman and Gramm had offered a few years earlier.

"It was very much of an across-the-board approach. We have seen a shift in the budget process from an attempt to identify specific policy decisions that are made in putting the budget together, and, on the other hand, a formula approach—'cut everything across the board' or 'freeze everything at last year's level.' And the House Budget Committee traditionally had opposed a formula approach on the basis that, one, it tends to be unrealistic, there are some programs that you can't cut across the board (interest on the public debt is the most obvious example, but there are others); and, two, it abdicates any kind of policy-making; it implies that all programs are equally good, and it abdicates any kind of choice. However, in the last few years, even the House Budget Committee, and certainly the Senate Budget Committee, has gotten more toward that formula approach, for a variety of reasons.

"This Stockman–Gramm budget was very much a formula budget. I also recall that there appeared to us to be assumptions in that budget which were simply not realistic. And it was the kind of formula budget that avoided making hard choices, such as, 'We're going to cut Social Security,' and balanced itself on economic and technical assumptions—'Let's take it all out of waste, fraud, and abuse, and assume that the economy will grow lickety-split'—and it wasn't taken seriously. [But] it was proposed seriously.

"Gramm was then still a Democrat, and it was an attempt, I think, then to be a bipartisan budget approach, and one that was not the traditional bipartisan conservative approach. It was an attempt to forge a kind of a new coalition, and it did share this *macro* approach at the budget. They were very, very careful, as I recall, not to say, 'We think these programs need to be reformed,' but rather to say, 'We're going to freeze spending, and no growth, and we'll balance the budget,' and appeal to the politics rather than to the substance."

Wendell Belew is a polite man. Rather than point the finger at people, he simply explains what should be obvious to everyone.

"In the budget area, one can be very successful, politically—at least on the short term—appealing to the public's preconception of how the budget works, and how the budget process works: 'Well, if we can just eliminate all the waste, we can balance the budget.' In fact, in the present situation, you can eliminate everything in the budget other than defense interests, Social Security, and Medicare, and still probably have a deficit. People don't understand how the system works, nor, necessarily, should they, because it is very complicated and arcane in some respects. I've been on the Committee for ten years and there are still some things that baffle me. But the public does have strong misconceptions."

Belew looked carefully at the Reagan budget positions as they were put forward in the 1980 campaign and found them to be: "Nonsense. I agreed with John Anderson. You can't increase defense spending, cut taxes, and balance the budget. It didn't make any sense to me at all."

According to Belew, Stockman initially made it look as if he and Budget Committee Chairman Jim Jones could work together. But it wasn't long before it became clear that they would work around the House leadership, by concentrating on the Republicans and the conservative Democrats. "Eventually," says Wendell Belew, "there was almost no communication between the Reagan White House and Stockman's OMB and the Budget Committee people on the Democratic side. It was almost funny. Normally the budget documents are delivered to the Hill a few days early, as soon as they're ready, so that the Budget Committee and the Appropriations Committee can read them. The leadership of the committees is expected to read it, and be able to answer questions, so as a courtesy the budget documents are made available. But we had a long series of mishaps: a truck got lost one year and couldn't find the Budget Committee; then there was a problem with the dog chewing it, or something like that; each year they'd have a story as to why the documents hadn't arrived as promised. Even something as straightforward as that, delivery of the basic budget documents, wasn't really shared."

In addition, the budget documents were, as Belew puts it, "very short on detail," yet "President Reagan was not held responsible at all for what turned out to be *gross* misstatements" regarding his policies. Belew feels, and says reporters have since verified his feeling, that there was a consensus that the press had become "too picky, too critical of presidential policies, and there was a sense of guilt about having picked too hard on Jimmy Carter."

Wendell Belew sheds some light on the question of how David Stockman was able to dominate congressional budget hearings so completely. He points out that while Stockman just plain "knew more than anyone else," he was helped by the fact that House members' terms on the Budget Committee are limited. "A *vet* on the Budget Committee is one who has been on for three years!" Also, "by policy and tradition, Budget Committee staff is not allowed to ask questions" of witnesses, which means Stockman could not be grilled by the people (like Wendell Belew) whose knowledge of budget details was closest to his own.

Perhaps this helps to explain why OMB's own budget figures increased so dramatically during Stockman's tenure. In FY 1982 he requested a $40.1 million, and actually spent $36.7 million; five fiscal years later, the respective figures were $41.4 million and $41.2 million.

Because he didn't have to face critics like Belew, Stockman was relatively unflappable. "You could take on [Don] Regan, and he'd lose his cool, but you couldn't get to Stockman. You could never beat him."

Finally, what, in his opinion, will be the legacy of David Stockman? Belew says, almost dispassionately, "David Stockman created the budget deficits. But in a sense he will get away with it, from the standpoint of history, because [in the *Atlantic* article] he confessed before the crime was committed."

Wendell Belew, like a select few among the hundreds of people interviewed for this book, compared David Stockman to Henry Kissinger in the sense that they both have a special standing within the Republican Party in particular and American politics in general. One might add that they both have had some problems with veracity, where Congress and the people are concerned, and also that both men, while having served in the innermost governmental circles, now seem almost professional outsiders.

Robert Walker, one-time aide to John Anderson and co-worker of David Stockman's, has an intriguing theory about the young man he used to view as a fellow liberal. Walker says that Stockman, who wanted so badly to get ahead, wanted the OMB job so desperately that he "struck a Faustian bargain. Stockman never subscribed to those wild-eyed theories of Laffer and Wanniski. He knew full well that their policy would lead to massive deficits, yet he came down and convinced Congress, as only Dave Stockman can do, and was disingenuous. The theory that Stockman suddenly 'got educated' during his first few months in office is *all wrong*.

"I am almost dead positive," says Walker heatedly, "that Dave Stockman *knew* this wouldn't work, but he went, anyway, to Jack Kemp and to others like him so they could provide the intellectual justification—just like Robert McNamara, who created an intellectual justification so he could believe that LBJ's Vietnam policies would work—and then he went and simply pulled the numbers out of thin air.

"David Stockman has presided over one of the worst cases of fiscal mismanagement in the history of this country."

In April of 1985, Robert Walker, on reading a *Washington Post* editorial that called Stockman "the best budget direct ever," responded with a short but stinging letter. It read:

"Fiscal Sin"

I read with interest Joseph Kraft's recent homage to David Stockman. (*Op Ed*, April 9). With all due respect to his considerable talents, Mr. Stockman hardly merits a claim as the "foremost budget director in our history." If he is to be remembered, he should be remembered as the chief architect of a budget policy that has led to a doubling of the national debt in less than five years.

His recent "personal triumph with the budget compromise," while perhaps "striking," is but a small atonement for a much larger fiscal sin. The canonization of Dave Stockman will have to wait.

Robert J. Walker
Alexandria

This echoed a letter to the *Post* by Ralph Nader:

The *Post*'s praise of David Stockman . . . invites incredulity. The editorial says that he "has been one of the important truth-tellers in this administration," even though he admitted that he testified several times before Congress using numbers and projects he did not believe. Does a civil servant need only to confide the truth privately, while saying the opposite publicly, to earn the *Post*'s commendation?

Second, Stockman seemed to display his budget-cutting muscle most vigorously against unorganized or defenseless people. His moves to eliminate legal services for the poor and to cut sharply infant nutrition programs are cases in point. But the really big dollars in the corporate entitlements and military contracting areas rarely received such clenched-teeth opposition from the budget director.

I read with interest Josepf Kraft's recent homage to David Stockman. . . . With all due respect to his considerable talents, Mr. Stockman hardly merits acclaim as the "foremost budget director in our history." If he is to be remembered, he should be remembered as the chief architect of a budget policy that has led to the doubling of the national debt in less than five years. . . .

Third, Stockman regularly interfered with the rule-making procedures of federal agencies invested by law with protecting the public's health and safety. Whether in the area of infant formula standards, auto safety rules, acid rain control proposals or simply providing citizens with health and safety information, Stockman and his band of OMB zealots blocked, overrode, bullied or delayed dozens of existing or proposed life-saving, disease-preventing and consumer-cost reducing measures. They did this both with ideologically driven ignorance and the power OMB wielded over these agencies generally. They also did this with many admitted *ex parte*, undocketed contacts that OMB personnel had with company lobbyists.

I consider Stockman's record at OMB quite distant from the "intellectual and moral integrity" that the *Post* ascribed to him.

Then there was the December 9, 1985, column in *The New York Times* written by Tom Wicker:

So the public demand for deficit reduction is questionable at best. No such ambiguity exists about the causes of the massive federal deficit. They are primarily the product of the Reagan tax cuts of 1981, greatly reducing federal revenues, coupled with the huge military expenditures he embarked upon in the same year. And as he doubled the national debt in a single term in office, enormous interest costs added billions to the annual deficit.

In fact, substantial evidence exists that the Reagan Administration planned in that way, on the shrewd political theory that only at a time of huge federal deficits might Congress be persuaded to kill off Democratic social programs of the last half-century. . . . [italics added]

If that is true, and it is the same charge made by Senator Daniel Patrick Moynihan in July of 1985—a serious charge that David Stockman flippantly evaded—then the record left behind by the real David Stockman is not a well-intentioned but tragically futile attempt to balance the federal budget, but rather a cynical attack on social programs that has resulted in millions more poor people— especially among the oldest and the youngest—millions more people who are inadequately fed, indecently housed, and improperly protected against illness, millions upon millions of people now and into the future to whom "the American Dream" is but a hollow reminder of better times past. If Senator Moynihan's unanswered accusation is correct, then that indeed is the true and terrible legacy of David Stockman.

Epilogue

ON FEBRUARY 4, 1986, the day Ronald Reagan gave his fifth State of the Union Address (delayed one week by the tragedy of the space shuttle *Challenger*), the message board outside the Holiday Inn in St. Joseph, Michigan, David Stockman's hometown, read: ELIZABETH IS 91 TODAY.

St. Joe is said to be a pleasant, even pretty town in the summer, but on a winter day with mounds of snow underfoot and a chilly, constant rain falling, it seems decidedly dreary. The restaurants within walking distance of the Holiday Inn are doing a slow business. In the Inn itself, the lunch crowd is brisk, and there is a function in the Coho Room (the Walleye Room is dark). The menu in the less-crowded bar is the same as that for the restaurant, but states at the bottom, with admirable honesty, that "prices in the bar are approximately 25% less than in the restaurant."

The people in the district office of Mark Siljander (R-MI) are friendly, but the man in charge happens to be in Washington, so no one is available to talk to the writer (from Washington!) about David Stockman. Mrs. Carol Stockman, Berrien County Treasurer, and mother of David Stockman, is less friendly. When told the caller is writing a book about her son David, she says, in a voice that is both hard-edged and weary, "What, another one? I just met for three hours with one of you people last week, and I don't think I have anything more I want to say." Asked if she had seen the article about David in the March issue of *Penthouse* magazine, the one in which he goes after *Republican* members of the House and Senate for resisting his budget-cutting efforts, she says, "No, but he's said that before." And when informed that the article is hyped on the cover as "David Stockman['s] Bitter Denunciation of the Reagan Regime," she says, "Well, that's journalism, isn't it?" She declines to be interviewed.

That morning the visitor from Washington had been picked up and driven into town by Bonnie Benner, the energetic executive director of the Fourth Congressional District and chief lieutenant to Democratic Committee Chairman Larry Nielsen. Benner, formerly a police officer in nearby Shore Haven, now races around the Fourth District rallying the outnumbered Democratic troops and getting out the vote. She is bullish on the Democrats. "When I started this job four years ago, I would tell people I was a Democrat, and then I'd duck. That's changed now, and I get a polite reception. I'm on the go in my car [a Fibber McGee's closet on wheels] from seven in the morning until midnight almost every day, and I get the strong feeling that the Democrats have begun to turn things around here in the Fourth District."

Bonnie Benner suggests the bar in the Holiday Inn as the best spot in town to watch the President on television that evening. "It's the only place in town that could be called a yuppie hangout."

The modernistic horseshoe-shaped bar is on a raised platform, below which are stuffed chairs and small glass-topped tables. Beyond the tables is a small wooden dance floor backed by hanging mirrored slats that catch the colored spotlights reflecting off a large swirling globe. To the right and above is a huge color television set, which at 8:02 is still showing an Eddie Murphy video.

A young man and woman sit closest to the set. She is blond and very attractive. He has a neat full beard and wears a dark blue suit, with red tie and matching pocket handkerchief. He has two bourbons for every one of her Tabs, and neither one pays any attention whatsoever to the State of the Union Address. Two other tables are occupied by men, one pair in their late twenties and the other probably mid-to-late thirties, and they all drink draft beer. A few minutes after the speech begins, two well-dressed, heavy-set businessmen arrive, take a table near the television set, and order vodka drinks. One sends the waitress for cigarettes. Suddenly Eddie Murphy disappears and we see the President walking into the House chamber.

"I'd vote for him," says a dark-complexioned man at a table, and his companion adds, "He's doing a good job," but there's a hint of sarcasm in his voice.

The President is in top form and the phrases roll out magnificently: "Private values must be at the heart of public policy. . . . Tonight freedom is on the march. . . ." But when he says that we must keep the country on that march "by breaking free of failed policies," the man who had said the President was doing a good job laughs quietly, his sarcasm becoming more obvious.

When the audience in the House chamber breaks into applause, the crowd in the bar at the Holiday Inn does not. Throughout the whole address, their mood is one of polite, if slightly bored, attention (except for the man and woman nearest the television set, who never glance up at it). One of the young beer drinkers says, "I saw the greatest TV ad I ever saw the other day. It was something about Ronald Reagan could be the greatest man in the world, but he's never tasted a Bud Light." His friend gives him a puzzled look.

The President is attacking welfare and quoting Teddy Roosevelt; across the bridge from St. Joe, over in Benton Harbor, the official unemployment rate is 31.5 percent, the unofficial rate about 65 percent.

When the President introduces one of his surprise guests, a young boy named Trevor from Philadelphia who covered the homeless poor with blankets, one of the young cocktail waitresses says it was "Reagan's policies that drove the people into the streets." Another waitress and the bartender tell her to be quiet.

And then, at 8:34, it is all over. No one applauds. A waitress cracks a side door to let some of the smoke out, or, perhaps symbolically, some fresh air in.

"What did you think," says the dark-complected man, "pretty good, eh?"

His friend, who has already made several sarcastic cracks, takes a moment to respond. Then he says, "Talk about politicians. He said every good thing anybody could say, and it all sounds terrific. But when you get down to the details, down to the actual problems and how you deal with them, you see it's all just a bunch of *shit*."

George Will is followed by the Democrats' canned response, which has hardly begun when three casually dressed young men come in. They sit down and order beers. "Let's party," says one of them. After a few minutes they ask, politely, if anyone in the room minds if the channel is changed.

No one minds, but it takes five minutes for the bartender to figure out how to get the music video channel back. When he does, it's showing John Cougar Mellencamp's "Small Town," the scenes of

which look distinctly better than St. Joe and light-years away from
Benton Harbor.

Larry Nielsen has lived in St. Joseph for almost all of his thirty-four
years ("I moved here when I was seven, and some people still kid me
about being a newcomer") and says he would never leave. "I've
become addicted to it." His decision pleases most Democrats, but
others wish he would set his sights on Washington. At present,
though, he says he is perfectly happy in his elected position as
supervisor of Benton Charter Township.

At eight o'clock in the morning on the day after the State of
Union Address, he met the Washington visitor for breakfast, after
which he gave him a thorough tour, with running socio-political
commentary, of both St. Joseph and Benton Harbor. His sincerity is
almost palpable.

"How has the Fourth District changed since Stockman was first
elected to Congress in '76? Well, we had a lot of the factory, the
manufacturing types of industry in the area, and we have suffered
along from that. We've had a lot of jobs move away, a lot of
industries move away or close their doors altogether. As a result, we
have a high number of unemployed former manufacturing workers,
basically unskilled labor, who now do not fit in anywhere, certainly
not at the rates of pay they had in the past.

"There have been no policies that have come out to assist them,
at least not in this area. The federal policies have all been to the
Southwest and the Western United States, and Stockman went
along with that, because, I guess, that's where Reagan's new
constituency was, compared to the big cities."

As Nielsen recalls, when David Stockman was in Congress, "He
had good constituent services, but I don't remember any big
programs [to help with problems such as high unemployment]. He
had the computer programs that would try to match businesses' and
municipalities' and groups' needs with grants that were available so
that he could always identify the sources for them and tell them to
go and apply—of course he never told them he was voting against
all those programs. That was one of the things that we in the
opposition were able to know, but nobody else would believe it."

Nielsen faults the local newspaper, *The Herald-Palladium*, for its blind support of Stockman through the years. "The paper, which is the largest daily and probably the only daily with a large readership in the district, was blatantly supportive of him. It didn't matter what he did, they were going to make him out to be God."

How is David Stockman viewed in his old home town these days? According to Larry Nielsen, "I think he has certainly lost a lot of credibility and stock in the area. I think they see him as continuing to betray the ideals that they *thought* he stood for. And I think that's accurate. He has betrayed those; he's presented one image and then done other things. And now, is the *real* Stockman coming forward, or is this some other new ploy?

"If he came back and ran for the congressional seat again, I doubt if he'd win. The congressman now representing us [Mark Siljander] has built a strong coalition based on his Moral Majority, extreme right-wing support that is prepared for any primary battle, even against Stockman."

Nielsen sees other important changes that have come to the Fourth District of Michigan in the troubled years since Ronald Reagan first became President.

"Mostly what we're finding now in the schools is that the kids who get educations move, and those that have the skills move to other areas of work. Very few are finding the cream jobs in this area because the offerings aren't what they were—and that's a *real* change—as Whirlpool moves more jobs away, as Clark Equipment moves more jobs away, as a lot of the other factory and foundry types of positions move away. Even though they had large numbers of unskilled laborers, they still employed a sizable number of management personnel. Now those [jobs] aren't here.

"If you look at, certainly, black students who come out of the Benton Harbor school system with the technical backgrounds or the qualifications to get into college, they go and do that and they come back and look for jobs, and there are none. So they all move away, and what's left in the community are those who fooled around in school and don't have the desire or talents to get good jobs."

Larry Nielsen seems the kind of man who would be slow to anger, but even though he speaks quietly and with control, when the subject turns to David Stockman, it is not hard to detect undertones of strong feeling marked by an obvious sincerity of disagreement and even disappointment.

"I guess you could use Benton Harbor as an example. What has

Stockman, or his policies, or the policies of the Reagan Administration that he advocated, ever done for the city of Benton Harbor? Nothing. Not a thing. To my knowledge, Stockman never said anything about Benton Harbor or its problems. He ignored it. And, in doing that, I think he expressed a lot of hidden resentment toward the city of Benton Harbor, an area that was able to get or attract entitlement grants from the federal government. People around here said it was their tax dollars going to help 'those folks,' with 'those folks' being of course somebody who were minorities and not just like them. And the people who would say that were the ones who became David Stockman's real constituency, who elected him and kept him in office."

Nielsen does not see Stockman as an opportunist. At least not *technically* speaking. "While he might have mapped out his career early in life, opportunities have come to him. He had an opportunity to leave Michigan State to go to the Harvard Divinity School; now if the motivation was to avoid the draft, that was a good opportunity. But while he was there, John Anderson came to him. Anderson brought him into the House Republican Conference. Ed Hutchinson screwed up on the Watergate impeachment hearings, and the Republicans in this area got Dave to be their congressman. And from there Reagan gets him to debate in the practice debate as Carter's stand-in on budget issues, and he impresses the hell out of Reagan, so then they grabbed him to be the head of OMB.

"Let's put it this way: maybe he isn't an opportunist, but he certainly has taken advantage of the opportunities that existed."

Finally, Larry Nielsen thinks Stockman has had a good bit of luck. "I have to say that I always thought David Stockman was overrated. He may have learned a lot about the budget and such things by studying and cramming, but where's the evidence that he ever mastered a deep understanding of anything? I used to say that in the real world Dave Stockman couldn't get hired as a controller at a third-rate mobile home company. I still believe that.

"He may be good with words, but he is not necessarily good with details. And, clearly, he is not much good with real people and their real problems."

APPENDIX A

"Avoiding a GOP Economic Dunkirk"

by David Stockman
December 1980

I THE GATHERING STORM

The momentum of short-run economic, financial, and budget forces is creating the conditions for an economic Dunkirk during the first twenty-four months of the Reagan Administration. These major factors threaten:

1. A Second 1980 Credit Crunch

By year-end bank rates are likely to hit the 15–17 percent range, causing further deterioration in long-term capital markets for bonds and equities, a renewed consumer spending slowdown, and intensified uncertainty throughout financial markets.

There are a number of potential contributory forces. The most important is the fact that the Fed [Federal Reserve Board] has been substantially overshooting its 1980 money supply growth goals ever since mid-summer. Were Volcker to attempt to use the interregnum to impose the severe constraint necessary to get back on track, MI-B, for example, would have to be held to essentially a *zero growth rate* for the remainder of the year to fall within the 6.5 percent upper target for 1980.

In addition, the Treasury will impose massive financing requirements on the market through January 1, including about $100 billion in refinancing and potentially $25–28 billion in new cash requirements at current budget operating levels (fourth quarter). While private credit requirements are likely to soften in response to the emerging slowdown in housing, durables, and other real sectors, year-end seasonal borrowing requirements are still likely to be heavy.

In all, President Reagan will inherit thoroughly disordered credit and capital markets, punishingly high interest rates, and a hair-trigger market psychology poised to respond strongly to early economic policy signals in either favorable or unfavorable ways.

The preeminent danger is that an initial economic policy package that includes the tax cuts but does not contain *decisive, credible elements* on matters of outlay control, future budget authority reduction, and a believable plan for curtailing the federal government's massive direct and indirect credit absorption will generate pervasive expectations of a continuing *"Reagan inflation."* Such a development would almost ensure that high interest rates would hang over the economy well into the first year, deadening housing and durables markets and thwarting the industrial capital spending boom required to propel sustained economic growth. Thus, Thatcherization can only be avoided if the initial economic policy package simultaneously spurs the output side of the economy and also elicits a swift downward revision of inflationary expectations in the financial markets.

2. A Double-Dip Recession in Early 1981

This is now at least a 50 percent possibility given emerging conditions in the financial markets and gathering evidence from the output side of the economy. Stagnant or declining real GNP [Gross National Product] growth in the first two quarters would generate staggering political and policy challenges. These include a further worsening of an already dismal budget posture (see below) and a profusion of "quick fix" remedies for various "wounded" sectors of the economy. The latter would include intense pressure for formal or informal auto import restraints, activation of Brooke–Cranston or similar costly housing bail-outs, maintenance of current excessive CETA employment levels, accelerated draw-down of various lending and grant aids under SBA, EDA, and FmHA, a further thirteen-week extension of federal unemployment benefits, etc. Obviously, the intense political pressures for many of these quick fix aids will distract from the Reagan program on the economic fundamentals (supply-side tax-cuts, regulatory reform, and firm long-term fiscal discipline) and threaten to lock in budget costs and policy initiatives that are out of step with the basic policy thrust.

There is a further danger; the federal budget has now become an automatic *"coast-to-coast soup line"* that dispenses remedial aid with almost reckless abandon, converting the traditional notion of automatic stabilizers into multitudinous outlay spasms throughout the budget. For instance, the estimates for FY 81 [Fiscal Year 1981, ending October 1, 1981] trade adjustment assistance have exploded from $400 million in the spring to $2.5 billion as of November, and the summer drought will cause

SBA emergency farm loan aid to surge by $1.1 billion above planned levels.

For these reasons, the first hard look at the unvarnished FY 81 and 82 budget posture by our own OMB people is likely to elicit coronary contractions among some, and produce an intense polarization between supply-side tax-cutters and the more fiscally orthodox. An internecine struggle over deferral or temporary abandonment of the tax program could ensue. The result would be a severe demoralization and fractionalization of GOP ranks and an erosion of our capacity to govern successfully and revive the economy before November 1982.

3. Federal Budget and Credit Hemorrhage

The latest estimates place FY 81 outlays at nearly $650 billion. That represents a *$20 billion* outlay growth since the August estimates; a *$36 billion* growth since the First Budget Resolution passed in June; an outlay level *$73 billion* above FY 80; and a *$157 billion growth* since the books closed on FY 79 just thirteen months ago.

The table below illustrates the full dimension of the coast-to-coast soup line problem mentioned above and the manner in which it drives outlay aggregates upward at mind-numbing speed. A worsening of the informal "misery index" (i.e., higher inflation and interest rates, or lower output growth and employment rates) drives hard on entitlements, indexing, debt servicing, budget authority spend-down rates, and loan facilities spread throughout the federal government, resulting in a surge of incremental outlays.

Between June and November, for example, federal outlay estimates have risen from $613 billion to $649 billion. Of the $36 billion growth in outlay estimates, fully *$26 billion* or 72 *percent* is due to automatic budget responses to the mechanisms listed above.

The $3.2 billion increment for interest outlays represents a revision of the 1981 average T-bill rate from 9.6 *in June* to 11.0 in the latest estimate. Similarly, the $9.2 billion increment for trade adjustment assistance, food stamps, cash assistance, and unemployment benefits represents a revised assumption about the expected *duration* of high unemployment during calendar 1981. The continuing disintermediation crisis in the thrift sector will cause nearly a billion dollar draw-down from the savings and loan insurance fund. Category (4) presents still another example of the soup line dynamic: when private sector orders soften, federal defense and "brick and mortar" contractors tend to speed up delivery on contract work, increasing the spend-out rate against obligated authority in the pipeline—in this case by about $5 billion.

These illustrations drive home a fundamental point: achieving fiscal control over outlays and Treasury borrowing *cannot be conducted as an accounting exercise or exclusively through legislated spending cuts in the orthodox sense.* Only a comprehensive economic package that spurs output and employment rates has any hope of stopping the present hemorrhage.

The deficit and total federal credit activity figures are even more alarming. When the off-budget deficit is included, which it must be since most of these categories represent Treasury advances to the Federal Financing Bank (which in turn are financed in the government market for bonds and T-bills), the pre-tax cut deficit for FY 81 ranges between $50–60 billion.[11] This follows a closing level of nearly $80 billion for FY 80 (including off-budget).

The vigorous tax-cut package required to spur the supply side of the economy could raise the total static FY 81 deficit to the *$60–80 billion* range, depending upon the timing of tax-cut implementation and real GNP, employment, and inflation levels during the remaining nine months of the fiscal year. These parameters make clear that unless the tax-cut program is accompanied by a credible and severe program to curtail FY 81–82 outlays, future spending authority, and overall federal credit absorption, financial market worries about a "Reagan inflation" will be solidly confirmed by the budget posture.

An alternative indication of the fiscal management crisis is given by the figures for new loan and loan guarantee activities during FY 81 by federal agencies. These are now estimated at *$150 billion*, with only $44 billion of this amount included in the *official on-budget accounts*. Thus, federal credit absorption parameters are generating market expectations of a chronic and severe Reagan inflation: market participants simply will not accept the Federal Reserve's money growth and anti-inflation goals in light of this massive governmental domination of credit markets.

4. Commodity Shocks and the Final Destruction
of Volcker Monetary Policy

The U.S. economy is likely to face two serious commodity price run-ups during the next five-to-fifteen months. First, if the Iran-Iraq war is not soon terminated, today's excess worldwide crude and product inventories will be largely depleted by February or March. Under those conditions, heavy spot market buying, inventory accumulation, and eventually panic bidding on world markets will once again emerge. Indeed, unless the war combatants exhaust themselves at an early date and move quickly back into at least limited production, this outcome is almost certain by spring. Under these circumstances, OPEC contract rates will rise toward spot market levels in the $40–50 per barrel range during the first and second quarters of 1981, with a consequent price shock to the U.S. economy.

11. This assumes current estimate revenues of $615 billion, outlays of $649 billion, an on-budget deficit of $35 billion, and an off-budget deficit of $20 billion.

Even a $10 per barrel increase in average U.S. refiner acquisition cost would add $50–60 billion annually to aggregate national petroleum expenditures (assuming full decontrol).

Similarly, the present rapid draw-down of worldwide feed grain and protein oil reserves could turn into a rout by the fall of 1981, if the Soviets have another "Communist" (i.e. poor) harvest, and production is average-to-below-average elsewhere in the world. Under an adverse, but not improbable, 1981 harvest scenario, $4–5 corn, $6–7 wheat, and $10–11 soybeans are a distinct possibility.

The problem here is that demand for these basic commodities is highly inelastic in the very short run; and this generates strong credit demands from both the business and household sectors to finance existing consumption levels without cutting back on other expenditures. If the Federal Reserve chooses to accommodate these commodity price/credit demand shocks, as it has in the past, then in the context of the massive federal credit demand and financial market disorders described above, only one result is certain: the *already tattered credibility of the post-October 1979 Volcker monetary policy will be destroyed*. The Federal Reserve will subsequently succumb to enormous internal strife and external pressure, and the conditions for full-scale financial panic and unprecedented global monetary turbulence will be present. The January economic package, therefore, must be formulated with these probable 1981 commodity shocks and resulting financial market pressures clearly in mind.

5. Ticking Regulatory Time Bomb

Unless swift, comprehensive and far-reaching regulatory policy corrections are undertaken immediately, an unprecedented, quantum scale-up of the much discussed "regulatory burden" will occur during the next eighteen-to-forty months. Without going into exhaustive detail, the basic dynamic is this: during the early- and mid-1970s, Congress approved more than a dozen sweeping environmental, energy, and safety enabling authorities, which for all practical purposes are devoid of policy standards and criteria for cost-benefit, cost-effectiveness, and comparative risk analysis. Subsequently, McGovernite no-growth activists assumed control of most of the relevant sub-Cabinet policy posts during the Carter Administration. They have spent the past four years "tooling up" for implementation through a mind-boggling outpouring of rule-makings, interpretative guidelines, and major litigation—all heavily biased toward maximization of regulatory scope and burden. Thus, this decade-long process of regulatory evolution is just now reaching the stage at which it will sweep through the industrial economy with near gale force, preempting multi-billions in investment capital, driving up operating costs, and siphoning off management and technical personnel in an incredible morass of new controls and compliance procedures.

In the auto manufacturing sector, for example, new, if substantially tougher, regulations in the following areas will impact the industry during 1981–84: passive restraint standard (airbags); 1981 passenger tailpipe standard (including an unnecessary 3.4 gram/mile CO limit); unproven five mph bumper standards; final heavy duty engine emission standards; vast new audit, enforcement, and compliance procedures, and a new performance warranty system; light duty diesel particulate and NO_x standards; heavy duty truck noise standards; model year 1983–85 light duty truck emission standards; MY 83–84 light duty truck fuel econo standards; bus noise standards; ad infinitum. These measures alone will generate $10-20 billion in capital and operating costs while yielding modest to nonexistent social benefits.

Similarly, a cradle-to-grave hazardous waste control system under RCRA will take effect in 1981 at an annual cost of up to $2 billion. While prudent national waste disposal standards are clearly needed, the RCRA system is a *monument to mindless excess:* it treats degreasing fluids and PCBs in the same manner; and the proposed standards and controls for generators, transporters, and disposers, along with relevant explanations and definitions, encompass more than 500 pages of the Federal Register.

Multi-billion dollar overkill has also bloomed in the regulatory embellishment of the Toxic Substances Control Act, which threatens to emulate FDA "regulatory lag" on new chemical introductions. The proposed OSHA [Occupational Safety and Health Administration] generic carcinogen standard and the technology based BACT, RACT, LAER and NSPS standards under the Clean Air Act also represent staggering excess built upon dubious scientific and economic premises. Three thousand pages of appliance efficiency standards scheduled for implementation in thirteen categories of home appliances in 1981 also threaten to create multi-billion dollar havoc in the appliance industry.

There are also literally dozens of recently completed or still pending rule-makings targeted to specific sectors of the industrial economy as follows: proposed NSPS [New Source Performance Standards] for small industrial boilers (10–250 million BTU per hour) are estimated at $1–2 billion over 1980–85; proposed utility sector standards for bottom ash, fly ash, and cooling water control could cost $3.3 billion; pending OSHA hearing conservation standards, $500 million; abrasive blasting standards, $130 million; and asbestos control standards, up to $600 million. New industrial waste water pretreatment standards . . . EPS's proposed fluoro-carbon-refrigerant control program . . . the CAA stage II vapor recovery and fugitive hydrocarbon control program . . . the vehicle inspection and maintenance program . . . all have price tags in excess of $1 billion.

Moreover, most of the country will fail to meet the 1982 compliance deadline for one or more regulated air pollutants, thereby facing a potential absolute shut-down on the permitting of new or modified industrial sources. All told, there are easily in excess of $100 *billion in new environmental safety and energy compliance costs* scheduled for the early 1980s.

II THE THREAT OF POLITICAL DISSOLUTION

This review of the multiple challenges and threats lying in ambush contains an inescapable warning things could go very badly during the first year, resulting in incalculable erosion of GOP momentum, unity, and public confidence. If bold policies are not swiftly, deftly, and courageously implemented in the first six months, Washington will quickly become engulfed in political disorder commensurate with the surrounding economic disarray. A golden opportunity for permanent conservative policy revision and political realignment could be thoroughly dissipated before the Reagan Administration is even up to speed.

The specific danger is this: if President Reagan does not lead a creatively orchestrated high-profile policy offensive based on revision of the fundamentals—supply-side tax-cuts and regulatory relief, stern outlay control and federal fiscal retrenchment, and monetary reform and dollar stabilization—the thin Senate Republican majority and the de facto conservative majority in the House will fragment and succumb to parochial "firefighting as usual" in response to specific conditions of constituency distress.

For example, unless the whole remaining system of crude oil price controls, refiner entitlements, gasoline allocations, and product price controls is administratively terminated "cold turkey" by February 1, there is a high probability of gasoline lines and general petroleum market disorder by early spring. These conditions would predictably elicit a desultory new round of Capitol Hill initiated energy policy tinkering reminiscent of the mindless exercises of Summer 1979. Intense political struggles would develop over implementation of the stand-by conservation programs, extension of EPA controls and allocations, and funding levels for various pie-in-the-sky solar, conservation, synfuels, and renewables programs. The administration would lose the energy policy initiative and become engulfed in defensive battles, and frenetic energy legislating would preempt Hill attention from more important budget control, entitlement reform, and regulatory revision efforts. In short, if gas lines are permitted to erupt due to equivocation on revocation of controls, debilitating legislative and political distractions will be created.

Similarly, failure to spur early economic expansion and alter financial market inflation expectations will result in a plethora of Capitol Hill initiatives to "fix up" the housing, auto and steel sectors, hype up exports, subsidize capital formation, provide municipal fiscal relief, etc. Again, the Administration would be thrown on the defensive. Finally, persistence of "misery index"-driven budget deficits, high interest and inflation rates, and continued monetary policy vacillation at the Fed would quickly destroy the present GOP consensus on economic policy, pitting tax-cutters against budget-cutters and capital formation boosters against Kemp–Roth supporters.

To prevent early dissolution of the incipient Republican majority, only one remedy is available: an initial Administration economic program that is so bold, sweeping and sustained that it—

—totally dominates the Washington agenda during 1981;

—holds promise of propelling the economy into vigorous expansion and the financial markets into a bullish psychology;

—preempts the kind of debilitating distractions outlined above.

The major components and tenor of such an orchestrated policy offensive are described below.

III EMERGENCY ECONOMIC STABILIZATION AND RECOVERY PROGRAM

In order to dominate, shape, and control the Washington agenda, President Reagan should declare a national economic emergency soon after inauguration. He should tell the Congress and the nation that the economic, financial, budget, energy, and regulatory conditions he inherited are far worse than anyone had imagined. He should request that Congress organize quickly and clear the decks for *exclusive* action during the next hundred days on an *Emergency Economic Stabilization and Recovery Program* he would soon announce. The administration should spend the next two to three weeks in fevered consultation with Hill congressional leaders and interested private parties on the details of the package.

Five major principles should govern the formulation of the package:

1. A static "waste-cutting" approach to the FY 81 outlay component of the fiscal hemorrhage will hardly make a dent in the true fiscal problem. Persisting high "misery index" conditions in the economy will drive the soup line mechanisms of the budget faster than short-run, line-item cuts can be made on Capitol Hill. Fiscal stabilization

(i.e. elimination of deficits and excessive rates of spending growth) can only be achieved by sharp improvement in the economic indicators over the next twenty-four months. This means that the policy initiatives designed to spur output growth and to lower inflation expectations and interest rates must carry a large share of the fiscal stabilization burden. Improvement in the "outside" economic forces driving the budget is just as important as success in the "inside" efforts to effect legislative and administrative accounting reductions.

2. For this reason, dilution of the tax-cut program in order to limit short-run static revenue losses during the remainder of FY 81 and FY 82 would be counter-productive. Weak real GNP and employment growth over calendar years 1981 and 1982 will generate soup line expenditures equal to or greater than any static revenue gains from trimming the tax program.

3. The needed rebound of real GNP growth and especially vigorous expansion in the capital spending sector of the economy cannot be accomplished by tax cuts alone. A dramatic, substantial *recision* of the regulatory burden is needed both for the short-term cash flow relief it will provide to business firms and the long-term signal it will provide to corporate investment planners. A major "regulatory ventilation" will do as much to boost business confidence as tax and fiscal measures.

4. High, permanent inflation expectations have killed the long-term bond and equity markets that are required to fuel a capital spending boom and regeneration of robust economic growth. Moreover, this has caused a compression of the financial liability structure of business into the short-term market for bank loans and commercial paper, and has caused a flight of savings into tangible assets like precious metals, land, etc. The result of this credit market dislocation and inversion is that super-heated markets for short-term credits keep interest rates high and volatile and make monetary policy almost impossible to conduct.

The Reagan financial stabilization plan must seek to restore credit and capital market order and equilibrium by supporting monetary policy reform and removing the primary cause of long-term inflation pessimism: the explosive growth of out-year federal liabilities, spending authority, and credit absorption.

This points to the real leverage and locus for budget control: *severe recession of entitlement* and *new obligational authority* in the federal spending pipeline, which creates outlay streams and borrowing requirements in FY 82, FY 83, and beyond. The critical nature of *future spending authority* is dramatically illustrated by the experience during FY 1980: new budget authority increased from $556 billion (FY-79) to nearly $660 billion in FY 80, an increase of more than $100 billion, or 18 percent. Much of this authority will create outlay streams and Treasury cash borrowing requirements in FY 81 and beyond.

The fiscal stabilization package adopted during the hundred-day session, therefore, *must be at minimum equally weighted between out-year spending and entitlement authority reductions* and cash outlay savings for the remainder of FY 81. Indeed, the latter possibilities are apparently being exaggerated and over-emphasized. Of the current $649 billion FY 81 outlay estimate, $187 billion stems from prior year obligations or authority and cannot be stopped legally; $97 billion represents defense-spending from current obligations and should not be stopped; another $260 billion represents permanent authority primarily for Social Security and interest. The latter can only be reduced by "outside" economic improvements, and the former would be a political disaster to tinker with in the first round. This leaves $159 billion in controllable outlays, half of which will be spent or obligated before Congress acts in February–April. In short, $13 billion (2 percent) in waste-cutting type FY 81 cash outlay savings must be gotten from an $80 billion slice of the budget. Achieving this 16 percent holddown will be tough and necessary, but if it is the primary or exclusive focus of the initial fiscal package, the ball game will be lost.

Again, the primary aim of the fiscal control component must be to shift long-term inflation expectations downward and restore bond and equity markets. Severe reductions in out-year authority and federal credit absorption can accomplish this. In turn, robust long-term capital markets would lessen the traffic jam in short-term credit markets by permitting corporate portfolio restructuring and by drawing savings out of unproductive tangible assets. The conditions for reestablishing monetary policy credibility would be achieved and short-term interest rates, demand for money and inflation expectations would adjust accordingly.

5. Certain preemptive steps must be taken early on to keep control of the agenda and to maintain Capitol Hill focus on the Stabilization and Recovery Program. Foremost, all remaining petroleum product controls and allocations should be cancelled on day one. This will prevent a "gasoline line crisis," but will permit retail prices to run up rapidly if the world market tightens sharply as expected. This prospective price run-up can be readily converted into an asset: it can provide the political motor force for a legislative and administrative program to set up U.S. energy program production (see below).

In addition, some informal agreement should be sought with Chairman Hatch, Garn, and others to defer the labor policy agenda (minimum wage, Davis–Bacon, etc.) until the fall of 1981. Both committees will have a substantial role in the stabilization program, and there is no point in antagonizing organized labor during this critical period. Similarly, the Moral Majority agenda should also be deferred. Pursuit of these issues during the hundred-day period would only unleash cross-cutting controversy and political pressures which would undermine the fundamental administration and congressional GOP economic task.

The following includes a brief itemization of the major components of the Stabilization and Recovery Program:

(a) Supply Side Tax Components

The calendar year 1981 and 1982 installments of Kemp–Roth, reduction of the top income tax rate on unearned income to 50 percent, further reduction in capital gains, and a substantial reform along 10–5–3 lines of corporate depreciation.

(b) Fiscal Stabilization Component

This would consist of two parts. First, the cash outlay savings measures for the remainder of FY 81 would be aimed at holding outlays to the $635 billion range. A hiring freeze and a severe cutback in agency travel, equipment procurement, and outside contracting would be the major areas for savings.

The second part would be oriented toward entitlement revisions and budget authority reductions in FY 82 and beyond. Some of this could be accomplished through budget authority recisions included in the remainder of the FY 81 appropriations bill. This would have to be enacted before the expected December–March continuing resolution expires. Expiration of the continuing resolution would provide strong leverage. Another part could be accomplished through the revised FY 82 budget and scaled-back requests for new budget authority. The remainder would require the legislative committees to address a carefully tailored package of initial entitlement revisions.

Expressed in functional program and spending areas the out-year authority reduction package should address the following items, with a view to reducing federal domestic program levels by $30–50 billion per annum in the FY 82–83 period:

1. *Public sector capital investment deferrals.* We are now spending about $25 billion per year for highways, mass transit, sewer treatment

facilities, public works, national parks, and airport facilities. These are all necessary and productive federal investments, but their benefit stream will accrue over the next twenty-to-forty years. In light of the current financial crisis, a modest deferral and stretch-out of activity rates (a 10–20 percent reduction) in these areas should be considered.

2. *Non-Social Security entitlements.* Current expenditures for food stamps, cash assistance, Medicaid, disability, heating assistance, housing assistance, WIC, school lunches, and unemployment compensation amount to $100 billion. A carefully tailored package to reduce eligibility, overlap, and abuse should be developed for these areas—with potential savings of $10–20 billion.

3. *Low priority program cut-backs.* Total FY 81 expenditures for NASA, CETA, UDAG, the Community Development Program, EDA, urban parks, impact air, Action, Department of Energy commercialization and information programs, arts and humanities, and the Consumer Cooperative Bank amount to $25 billion. Most of these programs are ineffective or of low priority and could be cut by at least one third or $8 billion.

4. *Federal credit, lending, and guarantee reform.* As was indicated previously, concessional direct lending and loan guarantee activities by on-budget, off-budget, and government-sponsored enterprises is now running rampant, absorbing ever bigger shares of available credit market funds. These programs are buried in HUD, SBA, FmHA, EDA, USDA, Commerce and HHS, as well as in the traditional housing credit and farm credit agencies. Controlling SBA direct grant activities, for instance, will accomplish little if program activity is simply shifted to concessional loan authorities, with the resultant outlays laundered through the FFB.

(c) Regulatory Ventilation
This component also has two segments. The first and most urgent is a well-planned and orchestrated series of unilateral administrative actions to defer, revise, or rescind existing and pending regulations where clear legal authority exists. The potential here is really staggering, as this hastily compiled list of specific actions indicates. The important thing is that the workup on these initiatives must occur during the transition and very early after the inauguration. Again, the aim would be to firmly jolt business confidence and market psychology in a favorable direction.

These are suggestive illustrations with rough savings parameters from among literally dozens of potential unilateral administrative actions of this sort. A centralized Transition Task Force charged with identification of targets for early action and determination of required legal and rule-making procedures to commence after inauguration could help speed this initiative.

On a second front, both temporary and permanent statutory revisions will be needed. There are literally dozens of rule-making and compliance deadlines on the statute books for the next twenty months that cannot be prudently met. An omnibus "suspense bill" might be necessary during the hundred-day session to defer these deadlines and to implement the one-year moratorium on new rule-makings proposed by Murray Wiedenbaum.

Finally, a fundamental legislative policy reform package to be considered after the hundred-day period will have to be developed. This would primarily involve the insertion of mandatory cost-benefit, cost-effectiveness, and comparative risk analyses into the basic enabling acts—Clean Air and Water, Safe Drinking Water, TOSCA, RCRA, OSHA, etc. Without these statutory changes, administrative rule-making revisions in many cases will be subject to successful court challenge.

(d) Contingency Energy Package

The probable 1981 "oil shock" could entail serious political and economic disruption. Therefore, the preemptive step of dismantling controls before the crisis really hits is imperative. Incidentally, the combination of immediate decontrol and a $10 rise in the world price would increase windfall profits tax revenue by $20-25 billion during calendar 1981, thereby adding substantially to short-run budget posture improvement, if not to long-run energy production prospects.

But beyond this, a planning team should be readying a package of emergency steps to increase short-run domestic energy production and utilization. This should be implemented if the world market pinch becomes severe. The primary areas for short-run gains would be: accelerated licensing of a half-dozen completed nuclear plants; removal of all end-use restrictions on natural gas; changes in NGPA to permit accelerated infill drilling and near-term production gains; elimination of stripper, marginal and EOR oil properties from the windfall tax; emergency variances from SO_2 standards for industrial and utility coal boilers; and power wheeling from coal-nuclear to oil-based utility systems.

If the crisis is severe enough, rapid statutory revision of the natural gas decontrol program and modification of the windfall tax might be considered as part of the hundred-day agenda.

(e) A Monetary Accord

The markets have now almost completely lost confidence in Volcker and the new monetary policy. Only an extraordinary gesture can restore the credibility that will be required during the next two years. President Reagan should meet with Volcker or the entire Federal Reserve Board at an early date and issue them a new informal "charter"—namely, to eschew all consideration of extraneous economic variables like short-term interest rates, housing market conditions, business cycle fluctuations, etc., and to concentrate instead on one exclusive task: bringing the growth of Federal Reserve credit and bank reserves to a prudent rate and stabilization of the international and domestic purchasing power of the dollar.

The President and Congress would jointly take responsibility for ameliorating credit and capital market conditions through implementation of the Stabilization and Recovery Program and would stoutly defend the Fed from all political attacks. Insulation of the Fed from extraneous economic and financial preoccupations, political pressures, recalibration of its monetary objective, and restoration of its tattered credibility is the critical lynchpin in the whole program.

Appendix B

Introduction to *Retreat From Safety* by Joan Claybrook[12]

One hundred thousand US workers are exposed at their jobs to significant doses of ethylene dibromide (EDB), an insidious chemical fumigant used to protect fresh fruits and grains. Thousands of food products are exposed to EDB on their way to market, and recent investigation has found significant residues on food products. EDB can cause birth defects and is highly carcinogenic. It can also cause acute symptoms, often leading to death, as in the case of Robert Harris and James Harris, whose exposure on the job to EDB caused dizziness, numbness, and death in less than seventy-two hours. While the dangers of EDB are well known, President Reagan's Occupational Safety and Health Administration (OSHA) and Environmental Protection Agency (EPA) delayed even proposing EDP exposure limits for workers or residue limits for food products until they were publicly criticized by Congress and the press, and pressured by manufacturers—whose food products started being removed from supermarket shelves by concerned state officials in winter 1983 and 1984.

12. New York: Pantheon Books, 1984. Reprinted by permission.

Commercially made infant formula contains many ingredients that are essential to the health and development of newborn babies. Without vitamin B-6, for example, infants suffer convulsions; without chloride, learning disabilities result; without thiamine, brain damage can occur. Some vitamin deficiencies can be fatal. Mrs. Robert Bishop's son was fed Neo-Mull Soy formula for the first fifteen months of his life. Because of a vitamin deficiency in the formula, the child started to have difficulty running and within six months was almost completely paralyzed. To prevent tragedies like this, Congress passed a law and ordered the Food and Drug Administration (FDA) to issue quality-control regulations for infant formula. While the Reagan White House delayed eighteen months debating whether to issue the regulations, three million cans of defective formula were sold to unsuspecting parents and consumed by thousands of infants.

Many Americans are trying to eat less salt because it is a major cause of high blood pressure and heart disease. But unbeknownst to most people, canned soups and vegetables and processed meats contain huge amounts of salt, or sodium. Despite the clear desire by consumers for sodium labeling on food, the FDA has refused to issue regulations that would help consumers make healthier choices at the supermarket.

In 1981, the FDA announced it was instituting a "fast-track" approval process for new drugs. One of the drugs approved under this process, in April 1982, was a new arthritis drug, Oraflex, which its manufacturer, Eli Lilly, heavily promoted with press coverage and through mailings. Shortly thereafter, ominous reports began to surface. A forty-seven-year-old American woman died with liver damage that her doctor believed was caused by Oraflex. She had been taking no other drugs and had no illness other than arthritis when she started taking the drug. In June 1982, Public Citizen discovered that Lilly's drug was associated with twelve deaths in England, where it had been on the market for two years. Even as the evidence mounted, the FDA refused to withdraw its approval for Oraflex. It remained on the market in the United States until more deaths were disclosed and the British decided to ban it. Only then did Lilly decide to take Oraflex off the market. The same month that the Oraflex scandal broke, Vice-President Bush said, "I do want to stress that no one wants to expose American drug consumers to increased risk. Safety standards will not be compromised. We wouldn't permit that."

Acid rain is formed from the emissions of coal-burning industries. It is carried by wind and later deposited on terrain hundreds of miles away, killing massive numbers of trees and plants and suffocating lakes. In the United States, emissions from the coal-burning plants in the Ohio Valley have destroyed millions of acres of trees and ruined hundreds of lakes from Wisconsin to Maine and Canada. William Ruckelshaus, President

Reagan's second EPA administrator, made control of acid rain a top environmental priority and pledged to formulate a plan for action by September 1983. The White House Office of Management and Budget overruled Ruckelshaus, and the program is now on the back burner.

Every day, the Reagan White House makes decisions of critical importance to the health and safety of the American public. These are but a few examples. They illustrate the failure of the Reagan government to diligently implement and enforce statutes enacted by Congress to address the documented hazards of our technological society—dangerous drugs, polluted air and water, toxic chemicals, unsafe car design and engineering, and countless other known, significant risks.

Rather than bolster the federal health and safety regulatory agencies in their work to protect the public, the Reagan administration, animated by profound ignorance and rigid ideology, has inflicted severe damage on these unique institutions of our society. The agencies no longer respond to the needs of unorganized victims of technological hazards. Instead, they service the business executives and stockholders who are responsible for the hazards—a radical shift that can be traced to January 20, 1981, the day Ronald Reagan assumed the presidency from Jimmy Carter. This book concerns the basic power struggle between different segments of society over property rights and human values, and the role the Reagan administration has played in influencing the outcome beginning with that day in 1981. It is about the government's failure to carry out its responsibility under the law to strike a humane balance between the economic right of a business to act in its own self-interest and the public's right to be protected against unnecessary harm.

Who should pay for cleaning up polluted air? What level of safety do we want for food and drugs? Who should bear the risk of exposure to dangerous chemicals? During the past fifteen years, Congress has heard the opposing points of view on these issues and decided to enact statutes to control the antisocial behavior of business enterprises and to preserve the quality of American life. Since 1966, four new regulatory agencies have been created to limit the complex hazards of our industrial society:

- the National Highway Traffic Safety Administration (1966);

- the Occupational Safety and Health Administration (1970);

- the Environmental Protection Agency (1970); and

- the Consumer Product Safety Commission (1972).

These agencies joined two existing agencies, the Food and Drug Administration and the US Department of Agriculture's Food Safety and Inspection Service (meat and poultry inspection), programs originally established in 1906. Finally, the Department of Energy, created in 1975, administers a variety of energy conservation and production programs of great importance to consumers.

Each of these regulatory agencies and their statutes was established after weeks and sometimes months of congressional hearings that documented corporate abuses which endangered the lives and health of Americans. The laws sought to remedy problems that consumers, acting individually through their marketplace decisions, could not influence in a meaningful way, Congress understood, too, that consumers were ill-equipped to protect themselves from enormously complex technologies whose risks are sometimes unclear even to their manufacturers. Moreover, many of the dangers, such as asbestos, toxic chemicals, food additives, or dirty air, are invisible and do not extract their penalties for a decade or more.

This "new" type of federal regulation, often known as "social regulation," differs from the traditional "economic" regulation of such industries as broadcasting, transportation (rates and routes), or financial investment. This economic, or "cartel," regulation that many businesses favor seeks to limit competition in the marketplace, regulate business access to the market and the rates charged, as well as perform other "referee" functions. The health, safety, and environmental agencies, however, were meant to act as *advocates* for consumer health and safety concerns whose importance to society cannot be measured in dollars. The chief goal of these agencies is not to stabilize markets but to *alter* market behavior, where necessary, to minimize its antisocial side effects.

Without government regulation, a manufacturer side regulates the quality, content, design, and performance of products to suit *its* needs— and discloses only that information which serves its private ends. When the federal government regulates on behalf of health and safety, however, a measure of public responsibility is established for all manufacturers. This societal standard essentially governs the behavior of companies—in designing and producing a product, managing workplace safety and health, or disposing of industrial waste and pollution. Contrary to the rhetoric of the Chamber of Commerce, the question is not whether there is too much regulation in the marketplace, but rather *who* is doing the regulating—the manufacturer or the government?

Manufacturing companies and trade associations have usually resisted these regulatory laws because they prefer their own private regulation of our lives—an invisible, indirect, less accountable regulation controlled only by crude and often ineffectual marketplace forces. Occasionally, victims of private regulation pursue an after-the-fact liability lawsuit to recover damages. But by that point most victories are too little, too late.

Despite its obvious benefits to consumers, government regulation has been tarred by business groups as inefficient, often unnecessary and inept, and always irritating. Industry claims government regulations add burdensome new costs to the other fixed costs of doing business. Of course, industry rarely counts the benefits of regulation, for these accrue to the customer or the community. Nor do regulated industries like to acknowledge how they have often become more streamlined, efficient, and innovative as a result of the process and product changes stimulated by regulation.

Scapegoating aside, regulation is not motivated by spite or for frivolous reasons. By enacting health and safety regulatory statutes, Congress declares that business enterprises, in the course of daily profit-making activities, have intruded upon citizens' property rights in a way that conflicts with our social and moral values. The laws are enacted to prevent innocent victims from suffering harm by reducing the imbalance of power between the perpetrators of technological harm and the consumers affected by it. Thus, it is now unacceptable for children's sleepwear to be flammable, for drugs to be unsafe, and for meat to be contaminated or adulterated. The very enactment of these laws is a rejection of the mythical "free market" model and a finding that business is incapable of regulating itself in these areas to protect the public health and safety. The public understands and accepts this governmental role. Public opinion polls show that most Americans continue to overwhelmingly endorse the actions of the health and safety regulatory agencies.

The Reagan administration, in servicing its "constituents" (as former EPA official Rita Lavelle called the regulated companies), has abolished existing health and safety standards in wholesale lots and has virtually halted the development of new standards. Reagan's deregulation has been a rampage that has brushed aside rational, scientific arguments and scorned due process and democratic participation. The three-year war against regulation, waged from the inner sanctums of the White House and its Office of Management and Budget, has seriously altered the quality of America's air and water; the crashworthiness of new cars, the cleanliness of foods; the cancer risks of workplaces; the development of safe, efficient energy alternatives; and more. Virtually every American is affected in major or minor ways by Reagan's deregulation.

The federal regulatory process is governed, under the Administration Procedures Act, by concepts of fairness and openness. Under the Act, an agency must publish in the *Federal Register* (a daily government publication widely available in public libraries) its proposal to issue, amend, or revoke a regulation. The notice must explain the proposed regulation in detail, describe the reasons for the proposal, and cite the legal authority under which it is being issued. The public must be given a meaningful opportunity to participate by submitting comments or testifying at public hearings. The agency's final decision must also be published in the *Federal*

Register and must be supported by the public record developed by the agency and public comments.

The Reagan administration has often ignored these fundamental principles. In some cases, the public has not been informed of agency decisions. In others, the agency has conducted secret proceedings before inviting public comment. In still others, the rule-making record does not support the final decision. And the White House has been deeply involved behind the scenes in subverting the process.

The farsighted checks and balances built into the US Constitution nearly two hundred years ago have helped stop some parts of the Reagan deregulatory agenda. The courts particularly have not been receptive or deferential to the politicalization of the regulatory process. The Supreme Court and the federal courts of appeal have struck down numerous regulatory actions of the Reagan administration. In April 1981, the Occupational Safety and Health Administration (OSHA) tried to withdraw a pending challenge to the cotton dust standard that is designed to protect textile workers from the crippling lung disease byssinosis on the pretext of preparing a cost/benefit analysis. But the move was rebuffed. The Court upheld the standard and refused to permit a cost/benefit analysis, indicating its implementation is "part of the cost of doing business." In June 1983, the Supreme Court overruled the rescission of the automatic restraint standard for cars (requiring air bags or automatic belts) as an "arbitrary and capricious" decision.

In 1983, a federal appeals court chastised OSHA for failing to protect hospital workers from a cancer-causing sterilant, ethylene oxide (the agency was ordered to issue a permanent standard within a year). To avoid a lawsuit challenging its failure to adequately control benzene, another carcinogen, OSHA promised to initiate an expedited rule-making. Federal appeals courts struck down the EPA's attempt to reduce pollution requirements in various regions of the country and prohibited EPA from suspending regulations controlling toxic discharges into municipal sewer systems. The federal appeals court also forced EPA to reimpose hazardous waste incinerator controls that the agency had arbitrarily suspended without the required public notice, and in 1981, a federal district court overturned the Treasury Department's repeal of requirements for labeling ingredients in alcoholic beverages. The court said the revocation was "ill-considered and superficially explained." Thus, although numerous decisions to deregulate or to not issue standards have not been challenged in the courts during the Reagan term, and some others have been upheld, it is clear that the courts have been skeptical of the ideological drive to eliminate or drastically weaken health and safety standards.

Congress, too, has restricted supporting the Reagan campaign against regulation. Despite considerable administration pressure, none of the health and safety laws have been significantly altered. In the environmental area, this is particularly important because the clean air and clean water statutes are written with great specificity and include deadlines that agencies must meet. A massive battle to amend the Clean Air Act in 1981 and 1982 failed to make any headway because of the raw determination of Rep. Henry Waxman (D-Calif.), the chairman of the Health Subcommittee in the House of Representatives, and Sen. Robert Stafford (R-Vt.), chairman of the Public Works Committee in the Senate. Vigorous attempts to cut back the pesticide laws have also failed. In fact, nine out of ten major environmental statutes currently up for renewal are awaiting action by Congress. Amendments to weaken the Delaney Clause, which bans cancer-causing additives in foods, have been stalled in Congress for two years. In short, it is unlikely that the administration will succeed in making wholesale revisions in health and safety laws, as business lobbyists had initially hoped.

If Congress and the courts disapproved of much of Reagan's deregulatory agenda, and could occasionally thwart its advance, there is much that the Reagan deregulators have accomplished on their own, administratively. This is indeed where they have focused their efforts. Their chief tools in this area have been budget cuts, staff reductions, and enormous enforcement cutbacks. While condemning crime in the streets and welfare cheaters, Reagan has drastically cut funds and activities to enforce the law against companies who violate health and safety standards or fail to recall defective products. Enforcement activities have been cut more than 50 percent in most of these agencies, and information about regular offenders, which used to be publicized, is no longer available. Rep. Albert Gore, Jr. (D-Tenn.), described the result: "They just decided not to enforce the law. This sets up a conflict between those who would obey the law and those who would violate it, and gives the advantage to the violators." The irony has apparently been lost on presidential counselor Edwin Meese, honored as "Crimefighter of the Year" by the Conservative Free Congress and Education Foundation, and on Attorney General William French Smith, who has called for tougher criminal laws and enforcement—for individuals, not corporations.

Several administration officials have been at the vanguard of the deregulatory campaigns. The most visible is Vice-President George Bush, who headed up the Task Force on Regulatory Relief that was formed in March 1981. Working closely with Bush and the task force have been Office of Management and Budget (OMB) director David Stockman; Christopher DeMuth, head of the OMB Office of Information and Regulatory Affairs; and James Tozzi, his assistant, who resigned in 1983 in order to represent private clients. The task force and OMB collaborated closely in identifying "burdensome" regulations, soliciting industry's views, and intimidating agencies to "suspend" or eliminate certain regulations.

Not long after the task force was formed, White House staff boasted about its role of servicing industry interests. C. Boyden Gray, who represented a number of America's large industries in private practice and now is legal counsel to Vice-President George Bush, told the members of the US Chamber of Commerce that his office welcomed the opportunity to intervene on their behalf:

> If you go to the agency first, don't be too pessimistic if they can't solve the problem there. If they don't, that's what the Task Force is for. Two weeks ago [a group] showed up and I asked if they had a problem. They said they did, and we made a couple of phone calls and straightened it out, alerted the top people at the agency that there was a little hanky-panky going on at the bottom of the agency, and it was cleared up very rapidly—so the system does work if you use it as a sort of an appeal. You can act as a double check on the agency that you might encounter problems with.

But the heady destruction of government programs during Reagan's first two years was slowed considerably by congressional investigations in late 1982 that revealed a series of scandals at the EPA. The revelations essentially marked the end of Reagan's most brazen regulatory rollbacks, and immediately cast suspicion on the decisions of other agencies. The press became more alert to the alarming scope and consequences of the deregulatory mayhem. The public became more sensitized as well, with daily headlines and lead stories on the evening television news about cover-ups and conflicts of interest. Reagan was forced to dismiss his appointees at EPA and persuaded William Ruckelshaus, with his reputation as Mr. Clean, to give EPA integrity again. Five months after Anne Burford had resigned as EPA administrator, the Bush task force quietly closed its doors. The vice-president did not even attend the final press conference. One high-level White House aide commented, "Deregulation doesn't have the same priority for us it used to have. The political dividends aren't very high."

As public opinion, Congress, and the courts caught up with Reagan's antigovernment cowboys, a period of normalization began. The dismissal of personnel stopped, the indiscriminate attacks on entire programs subsided, and a few relatively minor safety and environmental standards actually began to be issued by some agencies. But Reagan's top regulatory czars continued to pursue procedural, backdoor strategies to deregulate, keeping most of them away from the media spotlight. Rep. John Dingell (D-Mich.), the combative chairman of the House Energy and Commerce

Committee, described the president's attitude toward Congress: "You go ahead and write the substance [of a given federal program], and I'll write the procedure and I'll shaft you every time."

While many of the administration's deregulatory strategies, therefore, came to rest on procedure, their intent was highly substantive. The administration's plan has three primary components. First, all decisions about regulation are centralized in the White House and the OMB, which has based many of these decisions on political considerations. This has required a tight web of secrecy to shield OMB's questionable off-the-record contacts with regulated industries and its strong-arm pressures against agencies. Second, the scientific framework for regulatory decisions has been largely discarded and highly discretionary tools—chiefly cost/benefit analysis, weaker cancer guidelines, and "voluntary" regulation—have been substituted. In the guise of more rigorous analyses, the deregulators actually subverted the government's scientific and research capabilities and conducted slipshod regulatory analyses. Third, the Reagan deregulators systematically undercut public access to government information and to the regulatory process itself.

CENTRALIZING AND POLITICIZING REGULATION

This has been the centerpiece of the Reagan deregulatory battle plan. Without consulting Congress, Reagan made OMB the clearance center for all regulatory decisions, within three weeks of taking office, by issuing Executive Order 12291. The order sets up new procedures shifting authority over major regulations from cabinet secretaries to the OMB. The executive order also authorizes the OMB to require sweeping analyses of proposed regulations, to review existing programs, and to postpone and eliminate regulations. The significance of these changes was noted by Representative Gore, a vocal critic of the Reagan regulators: "The critical question is, who makes the decision on the substance of a regulation? Is it made in the agency where the procedural safeguards are present, or is it made in OMB, outside those procedural safeguards?"

The answer is now quite clear. By dint of its historical authority to set the president's budget agency by agency, and its responsibility to control paperwork and approve government requests for industry data, the OMB is now in total control—of agency budgets, agency information, and agency regulatory decisions. This enormous power has been harnessed by the Reagan OMB (Stockman, DeMuth, Tozzi) and the White House itself (Reagan, Bush). Empowered as no other White House office ever has been, Reagan's OMB set about working behind the scenes, in concert with regulated industries, to eliminate government safety and environmental standards, often with only passing regard for the agencies' statutory obligations.

It is revealing that most of the initial standards targeted by the administration for elimination or amendment came from lists supplied by the regulated industries. On April 6, 1981, for example, Vice-President Bush announced thirty-four "Actions to Help the US Auto Industry"—a list adapted from a longer shopping list prepared by Ford, General Motors, and Chrysler. The thirty-four "actions" dealt with existing standards and proposals of the National Highway Traffic Safety Administration (NHTSA) and the Environmental Protection Agency (EPA) to reduce auto deaths and injuries and to curb auto emissions. Consumer and environmental organizations were never consulted for their comments.

In June 1981, a legal specialist of the Congressional Research Service challenged the constitutionality and legality of Reagan's Executive Order 12291. In a major report, Morton Rosenberg argued that the executive order is illegal because it "totally displaces" the "discretionary authority of agency decision-makers," in violation of congressional statutes, and centralizes that authority in another agency, the OMB. To protect against legal challenges and enlarge OMB's legal authority, Reagan lobbyists pressed to enact a deceptively titled "regulatory reform" bill that would institutionalize the procedural changes included in the executive order. The bill centralizes power in the White House, excludes the public from the regulatory process, and bypasses the fairness requirements of the Administrative Procedures Act. The bill would also make the independent regulatory commissions, such as the Consumer Product Safety Commission and the Federal Trade Commission, conform to the political control of the OMB for the first time in history. Although the bill passed the Senate unanimously in 1981, it was stopped in the House by the opposition of a number of Democratic committee chairmen who oversee the various regulatory programs. It now has minimal chances for enactment by the end of Reagan's term.

The executive order not only provided the administration with the ostensible legal rationale for seizing power that formerly belonged to regulatory agencies, it ushered in a new era of regulatory subversion in which regulated industries and sympathetic government officials could broker deals and violate the law without any public record of the transactions. The examples abound:

- On behalf of the tire industry, the OMB pressed the National Highway Traffic Safety Administration (NHTSA) to eliminate a treadwear rating system of great value to consumers.

- EPA's former chief of staff, John E. Daniel, testified before Congress "that the OMB stalled, tried to reverse, or altered EPA regulations on water quality, uranium mill tailings, and air quality standards." OMB also leaked proposed regulations to the regulated industry so it could bring tremendous pressure on EPA.

- OMB blocked the Occupational Safety and Health Administration's proposed regulations for the labeling of chemicals in the workplace. After six months, OSHA administrator Thorne Auchter was so angry that he asked beer magnate Joseph Coors, a key Reagan political supporter, to intervene with the vice-president to allow issuance of the proposed regulation. Auchter wanted a weaker federal regulation to preempt tougher state labeling laws.

- In 1982, the FDA and HHS secretary Richard Schweicker wanted to require aspirin makers to label their product with warnings about Reye's syndrome, a disease causing convulsions and sometimes death in children who take aspirin when they have chicken pox or the flu. But OMB official James Tozzi intervened on behalf of aspirin manufacturers and stopped the FDA from informing the public.

- When EPA's Anne Burford issued a regulation for high-level radioactive wastes over the objections of OMB, EPA's chief of staff John Daniel testified that he received a call from an OMB official warning "There was a price to pay for doing what we had done and we hadn't begun to pay."

- On November 7, 1983, Christopher DeMuth sent EPA administrator Ruckelshaus a letter chastising him for interpreting the Toxic Substances Control Act too narrowly and for making "excessively conservative decisions" about potential risks of toxic substances. Several EPA proposals, including one on acid rain, had been stopped by OMB. DeMuth complained that the agency "can and should be more willing" to tolerate some risk in new chemicals "without imposing either controls or testing requirements. Presumably, some risks should be regarded as reasonable."

The pattern of OMB intervention was blasted by Representative Gore: "I think it was no accident that only thirty days after a secret meeting between OMB and the Chemical Manufacturers Association, the hazardous waste disposal regulations were ordered by OMB to be reviewed . . . that shortly after a secret meeting between Air Transport Association and the OMB, air carrier certification rules were designated for review by OMB . . . that shortly after a secret meeting between OMB and the American Mining Congress, the Interior Department's rule on extraction of coal was postponed indefinitely."

Few of the Reagan deregulatory initiatives could have been secured without a protective veil of secrecy to hide procedural improprieties. That is why, once OMB had established itself as the point of access for regulatory decisions, its top officials became extraordinarily secretive about its reviews of agency regulations. They refused to disclose to the public or press which regulations they were reviewing, which ones they insisted be changed, or to document their *ex parte* (private, off-the-record) contacts with regulated industries for inclusion in the agency dockets. "One is impressed with the total lack of supporting documentation," complained Representative Dingell in 1981, "evidencing the reasons why a particular regulation was found to be inconsistent with the executive order [i.e., why it should not be issued]."

All this violates the underlying premises of the Administrative Proce-dures Act of 1946, which requires public access to the regulatory process and disclosure of information. Thirty-five significant instances of disregard for the law's requirements were documented in October 1983 by Robert Nelson of the Democracy Project. Nelson concluded that "secret and preferential influence is now characteristic of Reagan's regulatory process."

SLIPSHOD SCIENCE AND ANALYTIC
HOAXES

The engine for much of the regulatory process is the scientific and economic research conducted by agencies. Research must identify and verify hazards, design test instruments for safety standards, justify new regulatory proposals, help industries determine how to comply with regulations, and design and adapt regulatory programs to be cost-effective. Yet the Reagan administration has undercut the scientific, technical resources of the regulatory agencies and has substituted such analytic hoaxes as cost/benefit analysis and "voluntarism." Currently being formu-lated are new cancer guidelines that would discount animal studies and require human epidemiological evidence—i.e., people actually killed, maimed, or diseased in significant numbers—before any action could be taken.

The anti-intellectual bias of the Reagan deregulators is most apparent in its budget and staffing cutbacks. Environmental research; energy conserva-tion research; cancer research; research at the Centers for Disease Control; research in auto safety, drug safety, toxic chemicals; and consumer product safety—all have been drastically cut. At the NHTSA, the experimental safety vehicle program and the fuel economy research program, both critical for setting future safety and fuel economy standards, were elimina-ted completely. At the time, they constituted more than one-quarter of the agency's motor vehicle safety research. The knowledge developed in these regulatory agency research programs is critical to making effective decisions. It is the intellectual bank account for the nation. Not conducting this research inhibits citizen participation in government, hinders press and congressional understanding of government activities and inactivity, quashes academic research, and discourages business innovation. To drastically cut government funding for health and safety research is to destroy the seed coin for informed policies that can anticipate emerging hazards and the technologies to control them.

Similarly, these health and safety agencies have lost highly skilled technical staff whose expertise is vital to the functioning of the regulatory programs. Most agencies have lost over 30 percent of both their budgets and staff. The vibrant, idealistic younger staff has been discarded through reductions-in-force while the experienced senior staff has been lost through early retirements, transfers, and resignations. Ethical scientists have quit rather than promote or sustain programs they believe to be scientifically incorrect. OSHA scientist Peter Infante was fired (and later reinstated under pressure) for asserting that there is strong evidence that formaldehyde can cause cancer in animals. The brain drain will continue as President Reagan implements his latest proposal to severely cut back on the number of middle-management personnel. And future agency administrators will find it even more difficult to attract capable staff and get them hired through the Civil Service maze. Even outside experts have been discounted. Rather than engage in open, spirited debate, President Reagan has stacked advisory committees with ideological clones and dismissed dissenters. An EPA research bill was vetoed because it required the advisory committee to have diverse representation.

Even the government's Merit Systems Protection Board, which protects the rights of federal employees, has protested. (Two of the three board members are Reagan appointees.) In a recent report, the board speculated whether the government could stand the strain of severe personnel cuts. "Does the merit system have a point of 'metal fatigue,' a point at which critical elements in the alloy of its human capital fail and the 'framework of continuity' collapses?"

Besides cutting budget and staff, the OMB has exploited its control of government paperwork to restrict the flow of industry data to regulators. In 1980, without the specific authorization of law, the OMB initiated a new Information Collection Budget to limit the amount of information that agencies can request from regulated industries. Fifteen months before an agency can send a request for information to companies it regulates, it must estimate how long it will take them to respond in succeeding fiscal years. But realistically, no agency can know that far in advance what requests it will need to make, how many questions will be asked, or how long a company might take to answer the questionnaires. This Orwellian scheme, intended to minimize the paperwork of regulated businesses, has the effect of greatly restricting the flow of information to federal decision makers.

The result of the concurrent reductions in research budgets, talented and experienced agency staff, and agency information gathering capability is that the government has far less information than the regulated industry with which to make key regulatory decisions. It also encourages companies commenting on detailed proposals to withhold critical data because if it is not submitted voluntarily, the information budget and research funding limitations might prevent the agency from ever getting it. This is hardly the way to address complex, highly technical issues such as controlling cotton dust in the workplace or diesel emissions from motor vehicles. What inevitably occurs then are decisions based on whim, simplistic preference and intuition, or simply raw, crude data supplied by regulated industries without any critical analysis by an independent-minded government. And in many cases, the absence of knowledge and information prevents any decision from being made at all.

The subtle hypocrisy of the Reagan deregulators is that while slashing research and information programs, they insist (through Executive Order 12291) that agencies perform complex cost/benefit analyses of proposed regulators. Also, before a regulation can be promulgated, the benefits must be shown to exceed the costs, and the lowest cost alternative must be selected, even if it is not among the most beneficial. Although cost/benefit analysis is officially enshrined as an objective, neutral tool for evaluating regulations, its actual use is highly selective and biased. For example, it is not used to evaluate the need for tax expenditures, Pentagon appropriations, business subsidies, or other programs *favored* by business; it applies primarily to health, safety, environmental, and a few other regulatory programs. Moreover, the OMB summary worksheets do not even have space for listing the benefits of regulatory programs. The focus of the OMB review is on the alleged cost savings to industry based on information supplied primarily by the beneficiary industry. While benefit data is admittedly hard to acquire, and even more resistant to quantification (how much is your life worth?), cost/benefit analysis degenerates into a crude hoax when the benefit side of the equation is ignored. Cost/benefit analysis is, as a 1981 House committee report noted, "simply too primitive a tool."

Despite its boasts about pioneering a more rigorous, analytic approach to regulation, the Reagan administration has in fact moved willy-nilly to deregulate without having the faintest idea of the actual cost to the public. The Reagan White House has promoted the thesis that voluntary action by industry works and that modifying the behavior of the general public—for example, asking them to voluntarily wear safety belts—will reduce death and trauma without new product designs or installation of engineering controls. But the administration has not published any evaluations demonstrating that the health and safety standards they attack either do not work or are less effective than nonregulatory approaches. The serious analyses that have been made outside the White House confirm the time-tested notion that preventive remedies are far cheaper than treatment after harm has already occurred. "The main prevention program of the Reagan administration," commented Dr. Sidney Wolfe, director of Public Citizen's Health Research Group, "is one designed to prevent industry from paying the cost of doing business."

What makes the OMB's claim to scientific rigor so ludicrous is its own technical inexperience. "OMB has no technical knowledge," said OSHA deputy director of safety standards Thomas Seymour. "They get their slant from contacts in industry." Although the OMB successfully established itself as the clearinghouse for most regulatory programs, its staff has virtually no scientific expertise to analyze complex decisions dealing with toxic wastes, food additives, air pollution, unsafe drugs, defective consumer products, or automotive design and engineering. The OMB staff is comprised chiefly of economists and budget analysts predisposed to quantify benefit information, even though the benefits of life and health and clean air cannot really be quantified. In 1982, the General Accounting Office, the investigatory arm of Congress, confirmed that the Reagan regulatory analyses are inconsistent and inadequately documented; in addition, OMB's comments are rarely in writing, making it impossible to determine what role OMB plays. It also noted that even when effective analyses are made they could be ignored because Reagan's OMB reserves the right to waive the requirement for a "regulatory impact" analysis.

The slipshod science and bogus analysis conducted by many OMB officials and regulatory agencies reaches its culmination in gross misstatements about the success of the deregulatory program. "In contrast to the charges we have heard," said Christopher DeMuth in October 1983, "the air and water is getting cleaner. Occupational accident rates have been dramatically down. The highway safety rate in the last three years has been dramatically improved." Claims such as these are highly suspect not only because data-collection systems are no longer as reliable, but because as has been documented in the case of workplace and automobile deaths, the Reagan recession has led to drastic reductions in employment and much less discretionary driving by vulnerable populations that in turn has led to the declines in death and injury.

It is this kind of dishonesty that helped catapult Murray Weidenbaum's famous calculation—that regulation is costing American business more than $100 billion a year—into the limelight. Weidenbaum, a St. Louis economist tapped by Reagan to head his Council of Economic Advisors in 1981, arrived at this figure by multiplying the budgets of regulatory agencies by a factor of twenty—a crude estimate of the ratio of the cost of industry compliance to the agencies' budgets, based on studies Weidenbaum made in the early 1970s. Weidenbaum has promoted the $100 billion figure, and it has been widely quoted, but, in fact, it is merely so much hot air.

In the name of improved scientific rigor, the Reagan regulators are cooperating with the White House Office of Science and Technology Policy to develop new scientific standards for deciding whether to regulate cancer-causing substances. The only trouble is, these new guidelines represent a retreat from the scientific principles that have traditionally governed cancer regulation. For example, scientists generally agree that laboratory tests on animals are useful in predicting human cancer risk, that it is scientifically valid and necessary to test high doses on animals, and that there is no safe level of exposure to carcinogens. Each of these principles, which logically demand a strict level of carcinogen regulation, is being challenged. If weaker cancer guidelines gain respectability, regulators could reject animal data and insist that human fatalities occur before taking action to protect against exposure to carcinogens. Of course, by the time cancers are discovered in humans, decades later, it is too late.

SUPPRESSING INFORMATION AND RESTRICTING CITIZEN ACCESS TO GOVERNMENT

The third major strategy used by the Reagan administration to cripple health and safety programs involves the suppression of information. The preceding section described how information gathering and collection has been crippled; the companion goal is to withhold government information that already exists. The federal government generates and distributes authoritative research, statistics, technical analyses, and consumer publications about the scores of technological hazards we face. The regulatory agencies are the fountainhead for reams of valuable information, commissioned in the public interest and funded by public taxes.

"A nation that is afraid to let its people judge truth and falsehood in an open market," said President John F. Kennedy, "is a nation that is afraid of its people." For the Reagan government, this seems to be the case. Mindful that some information can be embarrassing or explosive, or might undermine its policies, it has systematically tried to restrict public access to information about the government or supplied by the government. Consumer publications have been one of the first casualties. Overall, at least two thousand different publications are no longer available. These include "The Car Book," a comparative guide to car crashworthiness requested by more than 1.5 million consumers, and an OSHA publication on cotton dust for textile workers, which was later reprinted after its cover was changed and the text toned down.

When publications have survived the budget cutters, they remain available only at higher prices. USDA's "Dietary Guidelines," which had been distributed free to seven million Americans, is now sold for $2.25. Subscription rates for many periodicals have been drastically raised, including such basic documents as the *Federal Register*.

Despite its professed belief in "an informed marketplace," the Reagan administration has eliminated many consumer labeling proposals. New cars will not have crash ratings on their windshields, as once proposed; ten classes of prescription drugs will not be sold with "patient package inserts," leaflets that warn consumers about the risks and side effects of the drugs; companies making alcoholic beverages will not have to disclose the contents of their products on their labels; meat processors will not have to disclose whether their meat products contain a lower quality and potentially harmfully "mechanically deboned" meat; the Department of Energy has refused to require energy efficiency labels for appliances. The list goes on and on.

Still other consumer information programs, such as the USDA's Nutrition Education and Training program, which educated children and school food managers about food nutrition, have been slashed. OSHA's New Directions program, which helped educate workers about workplace dangers, has been severely cut back.

Many government facilities that dispense information—libraries, information catalogs, film collections, and more—have been restricted by budget and staff cutbacks. Spurred by the OMB, many agency libraries have been reduced in size, both physically and in the number of volumes. And many government libraries also have shorter working hours. At NHTSA, the administrator terminated a contract for outside photocopying services that made it possible for the public, and the automotive industry, to get overnight service on documents in the public file. Now it can take three to four weeks.

On the surface, the suppression of government information may seem to be a policy that is more obnoxious than truly damaging. But in fact it perpetuates the tremendous information imbalance in our society between those who can afford to gather it, study it, and use it, and those who cannot. Government-produced publications, labeling requirements, and other information play a significant role in correcting this imbalance and represent one of the most cost-effective ways to empower citizens.

Beyond the many specific publications and labeling proposals that have been eliminated, the most serious assault on the public's right to know has been the Reagan administration's attack on the Freedom of Information

Act (FOIA). This 1966 law, strengthened by amendments in 1974, is one of the most important bulwarks in ensuring that our government is kept accountable to the American people. Just as the Constitution sets up important checks and balances among the three branches of government, the FOIA constitutes an essential citizen "check and balance" on government policies and practices. The Act has proven invaluable to citizen groups in uncovering evidence of unsafe products and law violations, and in petitioning the government. Although the Constitution guarantees the people's right to petition the government for the redress of grievances, without adequate information that right can be meaningless.

But the Reagan administration has launched a lobbying campaign in Congress to make the FOIA more costly, cumbersome, and time-consuming to use. So far, defenders of the FOIA have been able to fend off major revisions in the law, but the pressure for weakening it remains strong.

Meanwhile, Attorney General William French Smith has sent a signal to government agencies implying that delays and resistance in carrying out the spirit of the present law *will* be tolerated. In 1982, he repealed a standard set by the Carter administration that agencies should release information unless it would be "demonstrably harmful." Under Smith's directive, however, the Justice Department stands ready to defend any federal agency against court challenges to their refusal to release information.

In January 1983, Attorney General Smith went even further by issuing new guidelines for waiving fees to obtain documents under the Freedom of Information Act. The most offensive aspect of the guidelines is the instruction to assess whether, in the agency's view, the public has any legitimate interest in the documents. The agency is also instructed to judge whether the requestor is sufficiently "qualified" to understand the information contained in the documents and to convey the "correct" meaning to the public. The FOIA makes no such distinctions. It presumes all Americans should have access to government information.

The Reagan administration's criticism of the Act usually focuses on arguments that it inhibits government performance and costs too much. According to a Justice Department estimate, the Act costs about $45 million a year to administer. That seems a very small price to pay to deter government waste and illegality. The Pentagon spends twice that amount annually on marching bands.

Given the enormous role we have asked the government to play in the relationship between business and consumers, there is a critical need for the citizenry to participate in shaping government decisions as effectively as business does. Beginning in the mid-1970s, funds were allocated by government agencies to assist citizens who otherwise could not afford to be represented in government regulatory decisions. These participation programs were just getting established when Reagan was elected. He eliminated every one. In mid-1982, Michael Horowitz, the general counsel of the Office of Management and Budget, developed legislation to drastically limit the payment of attorneys' fees under sixty statutes in cases brought by private citizens and public interest groups against state, local, and federal governments. Often these groups, who do not receive their fees unless they win their case, would not be able to challenge arbitrary government action if fees are not payable. In addition, Horowitz has attempted to issue an OMB regulation (Circular A-122) using the government's leverage over government contractors and grantees to stop their advocacy activities before government agencies and on Capitol Hill. This overreaching caused a firestorm, since it affected defense contractors as well as consumer and poverty groups, and delayed its implementation.

When the curtains of secrecy are thrown over government activities, when the government refuses to reach out and provide citizens with the information they need to exercise their rights, when citizens are de facto excluded from involvement in government decision-making, the control of special interests over our society grows stronger. Only the most powerful gain when government turns off the lights. That is the real waste and fraud in the Reagan administration's war against the production and availability of information.

In 1980, Reagan was elected on a platform of "getting the government off our backs" and "regulatory relief." But what is relief and freedom from government regulations for industry, is hazardous to the health of the public at large. The most controversial regulations, those most opposed by business organizations, are designed to enhance the freedom of the citizenry by protecting them from disease, from death, from injury, from polluted air and water, and from the destruction of the land to maintain our heritage. Do we have more freedom if we can turn on the tap water and drink it without fear or if we have to boil it to assure we don't catch some dreaded disease? Do we have more freedom if we bump into a nylon bag of air in a 35-mile-an-hour crash or if we crush our head without one? Do we have more freedom if our child is injured by a dangerous toy or if she never had it to play with? Ronald Reagan has neither addressed nor answered these questions.

While this administration faithfully represents its narrow ideological concerns of the moment, it is unconcerned about the government's broader mission. As columnist Goerge Will said several years ago, "Government exists not merely to serve individuals' immediate preferences, but to achieve collective purposes for an ongoing nation. Government, unlike the free market, has a duty to look far down the road and consider the interests of citizens yet unborn. The market has a remarkable ability to satisfy the desires of the day."

Indeed, his [Reagan's] policies are like Alice in Wonderland. For example, the interest payments on Reagan's budget deficits exceed all the savings from his heavy cuts in social welfare budgets for the years 1982 through 1985. In 1981, Reagan argued that his economic programs would spur the economy and balance the budget by 1985. To accomplish this, social welfare program budgets were cut by $110 billion for the next four years, while military expenditures were increased and taxes were cut. The result has been huge deficits. For 1984 and 1985, they exceed $180 billion. The Congressional Budget Office estimates that the increased spending on interest payments for Reagan's deficits will cost taxpayers $124 billion for 1982 through 1985, thus swallowing up the funds Reagan saved by drastically cutting the social welfare programs.

By 1984, the deficits were a political issue in the election, and an embarrassment. To promote a frugal image, Reagan premiered a report prepared by business executive Peter Grace and a select group of white, male business executives on reducing government costs and improving government management. The Grace Commission identified over $400 billion in "waste" it recommended be cut from federal budgets over three years. Consumer groups complained, however, that the numbers were grossly exaggerated, that programs providing nutrition and health care for the poor (and other social programs) are targeted, and regulatory changes with little budgetary impact are recommended. In addition, many of the commission members are compromised by conflicts of interest, as their companies would benefit from the commission recommendations.

Appendix C:

Stockman Is Still Cooking the Numbers—"Now he wants us to believe Reagan is fair."[13]

David Stockman is at it again.

After he confessed to rigging the computers in 1981 to make the prospective Reagan deficits shrink, one would have thought that the budget

---

13. Robert Greenstein, director of the Center on Budget and Policy Priorities. *The Washington Post*, Outlook Section, Sunday, June 19, 1983.

director had had his fill of numbers juggling. But it was not to be. This time, of all things, Stockman has been fiddling with figures in the hope of demonstrating how *fair* the Reagan administration really is in its treatment of rich and poor.

Stockman unveiled his latest statistical wizardry before the Congressional Joint Economic Committee last month. He came fully equipped with charts, each to illustrate a remarkable assertion.

Claim 1: The poor have been affected only marginally by Reagan administration budget cuts. Indeed, if all of its proposed cuts for fiscal 1984 were enacted, Stockman contended, low-income benefit programs (food stamps, Medicaid, low-income housing, child nutrition, Supplemental Security Income and Aid to Families with Dependent Children) would still be reduced only 5 percent below the levels sought by Jimmy Carter.

Claim 2: Large parts of programs for the needy weren't serving the poor anyway. Before the Reagan cuts, Stockman maintained, more than two-fifths of the benefits of low-income programs went to families with incomes exceeding 150 percent of the poverty line.

Claim 3: The wealthy really were not the big winners in the 1981 tax-cut act. In fact, he asserted, they had received less than 1 percent of the benefits.

It was an impressive performance, even if it was based on some peculiar evidence.

Start with Stockman's contention that actual spending for low-income benefit programs in fiscal 1982 and 1983—plus Reagan's proposed spending for fiscal 1984— is only 5 percent below the levels sought for these years in the last Carter budget.

Here Stockman has deftly made use of the high unemployment experienced under the Reagan administration in an effort to bolster his case. The costs of a number of these basic benefit programs vary with unemployment levels—when more people are out of work, the number of households qualifying for the programs multiplies and program costs rise. By one estimate, for example, food stamp costs rise about $600 million for every percentage-point increase in the jobless rate.

The Reagan budget numbers Stockman cited reflect the impact of 10 percent unemployment on the costs of these programs. By contrast, the Carter budget numbers used by Stockman were calculated back in 1981, based on projections that unemployment would average only about 7 percent in the 1982–84 period. The result: Stockman was able to use the additional costs in the Reagan budget stemming from higher unemployment to make Reagan's spending levels look closer to Carter's—thereby making the Reagan cuts appear smaller than they actually are.

Stockman was not content to stop his strange comparison there. Further manipulations occurred when he adjusted the Carter and Reagan budgets for inflation, converting both to "constant 1981 dollars."

To do this, Stockman adjusted downward both the actual Carter and the actual Reagan budget numbers for 1982, 1983, and 1984. He reduced the projected Carter spending levels for 1983 by 16 percent—since the Carter budget had projected that prices in 1983 would be 16 percent higher than in 1981. And he adjusted the Reagan numbers for 1983 downward by just 10 percent—the inflation level for 1981–1983 reflected in the Reagan budget. Since the Carter numbers were reduced by larger percentages than Reagan numbers, this made Carter spending levels appear smaller in relation to Reagan's.

To be sure, such adjustments are valid in most cases—but *not* for two of the major programs, Medicaid and subsidized housing.

Medicaid budgets are based on projections of inflation in health care costs rather than on projections of the *overall* inflation rate. When you do the proper inflation adjustment—using health care costs rather than overall inflation—you discover that the Reagan Medicaid cuts are about $2 billion deeper for the 1982–84 period—or more than double what Stockman indicated.

Equally egregious was Stockman's manipulation of the housing numbers. A substantial portion of federal outlays for subsidized housing consists of fixed costs under long-term contracts for construction or rehabilitation. These costs do not vary with inflation any more than a homeowner's fixed monthly mortgage payments do. Stockman adjusted these costs anyway, and reduced the fixed payments in the Carter housing budget by a greater percentage than he reduced the identical fixed payments in the Reagan budget.

This bit of legerdemain made it appear that Ronald Reagan—whose administration has cut billions from new appropriations for subsidized housing, raised rents for all 3.5 million families and elderly persons living in subsidized units, and reduced the number of new low-income housing units being constructed or rehabilitated by more than half—actually spent more on these programs over the past two years than Carter would have.

How significant are Stockman's manipulations? A new Congressional Budget Office analysis shows that as a result of the last two years of budget reductions, fiscal 1983 expenditures for the low-income benefits programs were cut $5.2 billion below what they would have been had no changes been made by Congress. Stockman's chart, however, showed a reduction of only $1.7 billion. In other words, Stockman made two-thirds of the Reagan cuts disappear.

The administration's reductions, of course, would have been far deeper had all of its proposed cuts in aid to the poor been enacted. Of $20 billion requested last year in further cuts in these programs for the 1983–1985 period, Congress agreed to less than $4 billion.

Among the reductions rejected outright were administration proposals that would have doubled rents over several years for some of the poorest families living in subsidized housing, ended or reduced food stamps for more than 90 percent of the elderly who receive them, and sliced 700,000 low-income pregnant women and children from a food supplement program that has been proved to reduce infant mortality.

So much for Stockman Claim 1.

Next, Claim 2: that large chunks of benefits have been going to persons far above the poverty line. Indeed, Stockman maintains that before Ronald Reagan came to the rescue, average workers were being taxed to bring welfare families up to virtually the same standard of living as themselves.

Specifically he contends that in 1981, 42 percent of all benefits in these programs went to families over 150 percent of the poverty line, and that 150 percent of the poverty line for a family of four that year was $13,390— or 92 percent of the median annual income for employed workers.

The misuse of statistics is particularly striking here. First, Stockman has compared 150 percent of the poverty line for a *family of four* ($13,390) to the median income for an *individual* worker. Sorry, but you can't do that. The real numbers go like this: The median income for a family of four in 1981 exceeded $26,000—not $13,390—and 150 percent of the poverty line is about half—not 92 percent—of the median income for a comparably sized family.

Then Stockman counted as part of the income of program beneficiaries the value of health insurance coverage provided by Medicaid and the benefits from living in subsidized housing—but he did not include in his median income figures for workers either the comparable fringe benefits for employer-paid health insurance or the tax subsidies for mortgage and medical payments that many middle-income families receive. This makes for a neat comparison of apples and oranges.

When you do these comparisons properly, you find that the income and benefits of those participating in the federal programs were far below the living standards of average American families—even before the Reagan budget cuts took effect.

Nor is Stockman's claim valid that 42 percent of low-income benefits went to families over 150 percent of the poverty line. While these figures are derived from Census data, Stockman misuses the evidence in ways that the Census Bureau itself warns against.

Drawing on the Census Bureau's work, Thomas C. Joe, a former Nixon administration welfare expert who now directs the Center for the Study of

Social Policy, has prepared a devastating critique that shreds Stockman's claims on this issue.

A number of Stockman's "high-income" families were actually unemployed and receiving federal benefits for just a few months in 1981. Once back to work, they stopped receiving aid. But Stockman's figures reflect families' incomes for *all* of 1981 (rather than just for the months they actually received benefits), which enables Stockman to count many of these families as "high income" beneficiaries. The Census Bureau explicitly warns about this problem in the data, but Stockman ignored the admonition.

Similarly, Stockman data distort income patterns when the composition of a household changes. The data attribute to households the income earned during the entire year by persons who were household members for only a small part of the year. Yet the absence of households members for part of the year (especially deserting fathers) may be the very reason that the remaining family members needed aid. The Census Bureau warns about this, too, stating that the data "may not always reflect the true economic status of the household during the year."

In short, the numbers Stockman uses have a major impact in exaggerating the number of high-income households receiving aid. When those distortions are removed, the picture is quite different. For example, Agriculture Department evidence that is free from these distortions shows that no more than three-tenths of 1 percent of food stamp benefits in 1981 went to families whose cash incomes exceeded 150 percent of the poverty line during the months they received food stamps.

While these manipulations are disturbing, Stockman's numbers-juggling reaches its zenith in his description of administration tax policies.

The wealthy, according to Stockman, received *all* of their tax cut when the top tax rate was lowered from 70 percent to 50 percent. Since this change constituted less than 1 percent, Stockman tells us, the wealthy ended up with less than 1 percent of the largesse and can hardly be described as the prime beneficiaries.

These startling conclusions contrast sharply with the findings of virtually every independent study of the 1981 tax cut. The Joint Congressional Committee on Taxation, for example, found that the wealthiest 5 percent of taxpayers would gain 35 percent of the benefits from the tax act. Congressional Budget Office studies have shown that in fiscal 1982 through 1985, the tax and budget changes enacted under the Reagan administration will take more than $20 billion in benefits away from households with incomes below $10,000 a year—while increasing the after-tax incomes of those making more than $80,000 a year by $64 billion.

How did Stockman get such different results?

First, his claim that lowering the top rate represented all of the tax cuts for the wealthy is nonsense. He simply ignores the plethora of new loopholes and expanded tax breaks incorporated into the 1981 act, such as the changes in estate taxes, IRAs and Keoghs, the All Savers Certificate and dividend reinvestment.

Second, Stockman carefully limited his definition of the wealthy (without informing his audience) to the top two-tenths of 1 percent of all taxpayers, those with incomes of more than $200,000 a year. This suited his purposes admirably: With so few taxpayers defined as wealthy, their aggregate tax benefits would not look so large. The sizable tax benefits going to the much larger number of taxpayers in the $50,000–$200,000 range were simply excluded from his calculations.

Moreover, Stockman omitted the fact that the elite group he did define as wealthy received, on average, a whopping $22,000 apiece just from the changes in tax rates—before even counting the new tax shelter opportunities. Ronald Reagan himself saved $90,000 on his taxes last year because of the 1981 act. His after-tax income went up almost as much as if his salary had doubled.

The final part of Stockman's tax presentation was an attempt to discredit independent studies showing that those with high incomes received very large tax breaks. The problem with the studies, Stockman declared, was that for the wealthy, tax gains or losses stem less from rate changes (which the studies focused on) than from changes in the extent to which income is diverted into tax-free investments (which most of the studies did not treat).

Stockman's implication was that by reducing the top rates, tax shelters were being made less attractive—and that declining use of shelters would reduce the gains for the wealthy below the levels cited in the studies.

While lowering the top rate may, by itself, reduce the use of shelters, Stockman again failed to disclose all of the facts: the 1981 act created so many new shelter opportunities that use of shelters has exploded despite the reduction in the top rate.

Use of syndicated shelters grew 12.5 percent in 1982, far more than the rate of inflation. Moreover, preliminary data indicate that for the first quarter of this year, syndicated shelter use is up 50 percent from the comparable period last year. The burgeoning use of shelters, which confer the preponderance of their benefits on the affluent, suggests that tax benefits for the wealthy from the 1981 act are likely to be larger—not smaller—than previous studies and analyses have indicated.

Finally, there is the question of purchasing power. A favorite Stockman (and White House) theme is that the average American's purchasing power has increased sharply during the Reagan presidency because inflation has come down so much. Purchasing power, however, is not determined solely by prices—but by the interaction of prices and wages.

What the administration has failed to say is that wages have come down about as much as prices, leaving the average American with virtually no gain in real purchasing power.

What is widely regarded as the best measure of purchasing power—the Commerce Department's index of real per capita personal disposable income—shows that purchasing power under Reagan has increased at an annual rate of only four-tenths of 1 percent. This is well below the average rate of increase under every other president for the past 30 years.

The growth in purchasing power that did take place in the Reagan years occurred primarily from January 1981 until August 1981—before the Reagan economic program took effect. Since August 1981, when the Reagan tax and budget program was enacted, real per capita personal disposal income has declined. The average American's standard of living has fallen since the Reagan administration's program was enacted.

Stockman's manipulation of the numbers makes rational debate on these spending issues more difficult. But perhaps most significant is the new dimension that Stockman has added to the much-discussed "fairness" issue.

For what can raise more basic questions about whether this administration is fair than when one of its principal officials—with access to data, staff, and resources that few others in this town possess—utilizes this power to rig the terms of the debate and misrepresent the nature of his administration's policies.

Index

300 • Index